MW01275701

Slightly Offshore

CASKIE STINNETT

Slightly Offshore

More reflections on contemporary life
from a small Maine island—by Down East
magazine's award-winning essayist.

DOWN EAST BOOKS

Individual essays copyright © 1984, 1985, 1986, 1987, 1988, 1989,
1990, 1991, 1992 by Down East Enterprise, Inc. Book introduction and
chapter introductions © 1992 by Caskie Stinnett. Illustrations © 1992
by Chris Van Dusen.

ISBN 0-89272-321-1
Library of Congress Catalog Card Number 92-74425
Illustrations by Chris Van Dusen
Design by Dawna Hilton

5 4 3 2 1

Printed at Book Press, Inc., Brattleboro, Vermont
Down East Books, Camden, Maine

For Joan B. Werblin

Books by Caskie Stinnett

Will Not Run Feb. 22nd
Out of the Red
Back to Abnormal
Grand and Private Pleasures
This Great Land (co-author)
One Man's Island

Contents

Preface

I have never known whether the essayist is whistling to keep other people's spirits up or whether he is trying to work his own way with some dignity through the darkness. Some essayists feel that the ideas currently being expressed are in a confused state and it is his or her destiny to sort them out. Others assume that we are all trapped on a ship of fools so let's have a little fun if we can. I belong to the latter group. If each day of our lives bore a specific number, and we saw the numbers racing toward a total, would we still pursue the monotonous lives that we live, see the same people each day, do the same boring job over and over? Such an existence brings us a shabby stability, but don't we want more than just getting by?

As the century ebbs to a close, we are all embracing nostalgia because the past looks more appealing than the future. Already the future looks a little frayed around the edges. Voltaire said that nature cures the disease while the doctor amuses the patient, and here's where the essayist comes in. If society is sick, or just lingering in a twilight of some vast political indiscretion, it may be the signal for the essayist to leap up on the stage and after a few grandoise bows do a turn that would send the audience home feeling better. All we should ask of the essayist is that he or she bring forth some arresting originality that will divert us. That's all that's hidden on the essayist's person and we shouldn't look for more.

Charles Lamb, the nineteenth-century essayist, warned against what I am now doing. He said essays "want no preface" since they are all preface. "A preface is nothing but a talk with the reader," he said, and that's what essays are. For myself, I can't remember any comparable instance of such sustained and uniform inaccuracy in English literature. I think a preface can give a reader some advance knowledge — some portent — of the kind of turn the essayist has in mind when he mounts the stage. If nothing else, this could save the reader a lot of time, a useless trip back to the library.

Houston Peterson, whose *Great Essays* includes work ranging from Arthur Schopenhauer to E.B. White, uses a preface to define what he considers an essay to be: "a short piece of writing, from up to twenty or thirty pages, dealing with almost any subject, but in a personal, informal and unpretentious way. It will have a kind of loose unity but will often be delightfully digressive." If the pieces in the volume you are now holding had any looser unity they would certainly fall apart, and they are digressive if I know the meaning of the word. That brings me to the word "delightfully," which intimidates me. I would like to think the serious reader of these essays may detect in them some truths, some gaiety, some unanswered questions, some enthusiasm, and a great deal of hope. But *delightfully* — that's crowding my luck.

—*Caskie Stinnett*

Author's Note

These essays of a man's experiences while living on a Maine island all appeared originally in *Down East* magazine. A former collection was published in a book called *One Man's Island* in 1984. This is a continuation of that journal, together with some new thoughts. I am not a general critic of the society which sustains me although I suppose I often appear to be. Actually, I'm just trying to get along, and I think an island offers me my best hope. Do not look for a chronological sequence in these pieces because it does not exist. They are arranged in a random sort of way, much the way we find life itself.

Island State of Mind

I Bought an Island

I would like to have a long, quiet talk with someone who is about to buy an island with the thought of living on it. I know a lot about island life, certainly not everything since I am constantly making new discoveries, but I know that island living isn't all poetry, or loon calling to loon over a stretch of water, or moonlight making a path of gold on the surface of the sea. For a large part of each year I make my home on an island a short distance off the coast of Maine and I am fully and completely in love with this place, but in the sixteen years that I have called this island home I have learned that life on an island is anything but simple and sometimes it can be almost unbearably complicated. The appeal of an island is to the psyche and not to the whole individual. One gets a psychological lift from the idea of insularity, otherwise island life can be just plain inconvenient.

Let's take a look at the setup I have here on Casco Bay, three acres heavily wooded, a frame house with four bedrooms renovated over a number of years to make it comfortable but not modern, a small sauna imported from Finland, a boathouse that leaks, and a small workroom in the forest that doesn't leak but which is so much a home to field mice that one of them once even got caught in the keyboard of my typewriter. Maine island property being what it is now, especially an island with deep water, I suppose the place has a fairly impressive market value, although I've never asked any knowledgeable person for an estimate and to tell the truth I'm not really very curious about it. What appeals to me about living here is not that it affords an idyllic life, since it is discernible to even a casual visitor that it doesn't offer that particular prize, but rather that I have found here a freedom unattainable on the mainland. One surrenders privacy too readily on the mainland; on an island intrusion is met with something very close to hostility. Since it's difficult for salesmen or errand boys or the aimless to get there, visitors almost invariably are invited guests or people coming with a specific purpose in mind. This is all to the good, especially for a writer. One's work is not interrupted by door-to-door salesmen, or people calling at the wrong address, or any of the other intrusions that mar urban life. Yet I know some people like these interruptions, like to chat with the mailman or the delivery boy, and I think they should keep away from islands because an island is not for a gregarious person. I have spent days on this island not seeing a soul and talking only to my dog and it did not seem a hardship, but I wouldn't want it to go on too long because I'm not a recluse by nature and quite soon I would want some weekend guests or someone to chat with over a few drinks on the sundeck. What I am saying is that one should examine closely his or her own nature before buying an island, because the likelihood of loneliness is always lurking somewhere around the place.

On this island I don't feel that I am hampered particularly by township regulations, and if I want to burn some leaves I haul them out to the mud flats at low tide and put a match to them, and say to hell with making a trip to town for a permit. I don't think island dwellers, as a rule, try to take the law into their own hands, but they certainly place a high value on seignorial rights, and where reasonable doubt exists I believe they usually go along with their own inclination. I had an old house on this island torn down a number of years ago and I imagine a demolition permit of some sort was in order, but I reasoned that if I didn't have it knocked down it would have fallen down, which would have been an act of God, and therefore I was engaged in the Lord's work. This is the way island dwellers think.

One of the first things an island owner learns is that anything that comes on an island sooner or later has to be taken off the island, and this knowledge governs his actions in a way that is of inestimable influence. It is bedrock philosophy. Bulky packages are unwrapped on the mainland wherever possible, so a return trip with the unwanted wrappings, is not required. I have a shack on the mainland which is a sort of halfway-house where objects are stored whose need or utility on the island has not yet been proven, and which remain in a sort of quarantine until their status clears up. Believe it or not, it's rare when an empty boat leaves the island; there are always a few wine bottles, a carton or two, some tool or appliance that has outlived its usefulness, or an accumulation of news-papers and magazines that need to be ferried across and dropped off at the recycling center. Mainland dwellers toss these things aside without giving them a second thought, but on a small island there's no place to toss them. I sometimes keep books in the shack for a couple of weeks while I'm mulling over their contents and trying to make up my mind whether or not I really want to read them. That's how acutely conscious an islander gets about that return trip; he doesn't just brood about it, he *frets* about it.

The most important thing about buying an island, of course, is making certain that even at low tide there is water deep enough to enable you to always get to your wharf. Maine tides being what they are, many islands look idyllic until the tide ebbs and exposes a mud flat that means the owner cannot leave until the tide changes or cannot get home if he happens to have tarried too long in the village. A friend of mine lived on such an island, and whenever I invited him to dinner he had to consult a tide chart — which he carried in his wallet, to see whether he could accept without jumping up after the soup course, throwing his napkin on the table, and racing to the wharf. Even so, he miscalculated a few times and had to spend an awkward four hours marooned in the mud smacking mosquitoes.

The owner of an island, without being aware of it, grows to accept the spare, and while this is a seemingly trivial thing it often is a complete reversal of his or her mainland character. Anything not a necessity on an island is very soon looked upon as an encumbrance. It gets in the way. There is no such thing as buying the vacant lot next door and expanding one's belongings. It's amazing how quickly, on an island, a superfluous thing becomes an ugly thing. I don't want anything more on my island than I have right now. In fact, I'm uneasy about the cordless telephone that sometimes works and sometimes doesn't, depending upon the weather. It is not a necessity — I got along fine without it for fourteen years — and now I'm beginning to see it as an encumbrance even if an invisible one. I know it is there, and I'm beginning to regard it as an intrusive irritant rather than a convenience. If I don't answer next summer after a few rings, just forget it; I've probably thrown the whole thing in the cove, base unit, receiver, antenna and all. It ties me to the mainland in a way that I don't want to be tied.

Island owners, I've found, react instinctively about costs of things, since the purchase price of something large or unwieldy is seldom the delivered price. Take a cord of firewood, for example. Delivered at my wharf on the mainland it is a reasonable purchase, but the price has doubled by the time I get a lobsterman to ferry it over to the island and toss it up on the rocks. I then must haul it in a wheelbarrow through the forest to where I stack it conveniently close to the house. By that time a single log has appreciated in value to the point that I must see my breath in the air before I feel justified in putting a light under it.

The free condition of island life, however, is perhaps its greatest prize; one is never concerned about what the neighbors will think since there aren't any. An island offers the privilege of almost unlimited freedom. I can walk around the place naked if I care to, and indeed I often walk back to the house unclothed after taking a sauna. The air drying my skin is a fine sensation, and I feel sorry for people who have never experienced it. One August night when there was a full moon and I couldn't sleep, I walked without clothes to a large rock at one end of the island and stood there entranced by the beauty of the landscape which I somehow felt completely a part of since both the night and I were exactly as we were created. It was a simple fact but it was an exciting one.

The belief that tranquillity can be found on an island depends upon the individual. I have found it. There are sunny days when the dog and I stretch out beside the bayberry bushes at the water's edge and, each of us locked in our own thoughts, feel only the weight of the sun. When we are alone there, the days slip by serenely; it is sunny or overcast or foggy or raining but whatever it is we are a part of it and we know we belong to the island and to the earth. We see the tides rise and fall, we hear the blue heron's mournful croak as it takes off from the mussel shoal, we gather driftwood, and in the evening we both slumber in front of the fire. I think that's tranquillity.

I doubt that there is any single foundation upon which the whole appeal of island life is built, but I believe it is necessary that one find a comradeship inherent in the peculiarities offered by islands. I have learned the contentment that comes from solitude, the high taste of adventure from starting a day knowing I can do what I want to do, the smell of balsam sweetening the air I breathe, a view of the horizon not blocked by buildings, the flash of lightning and the sound of thunder, the pleasure of repairing something with my own hands, and the glorious feeling of surrender when I am exhausted and slip into a warm bed and drop off to sleep listening to the greatest symphony ever composed — the sound of a gentle rain on the roof.

To me, these are the wonders of island life, and I think they are priceless.

Fog, Rain, Tide, Snow

If there has ever been just enough (but not too much) rain on this island, I've missed it. My cistern is either overflowing or drying up fast, I'm either doing a Navajo rain dance or I'm spending a large part of every day bailing out boats. It's not that I want to control the elements, it's just that I don't want to run out of water. Everywhere people are talking about great advances in science, but aside from some fumbling attempts to seed clouds from an airplane our progress in making rain is about where it was in the time of Pericles.

Urban dwellers can ignore the elements to an extent far beyond the reach of country people. They have sidewalks, taxicabs, and buses to get them from here to there, as well as snug little cafes and bars into which they can duck for something to cheer them up when their umbrellas drip and their feet get wet. On an island, a person gets out of bed and takes a look at the weather; if it is too bad he or she should get right back to bed again. Elements control almost every aspect of life on an island, especially the tides which determine the steepness of the ramp leading to the dock, and the wind which determines how long it will take to get to the mainland, and the temperature which can turn the journey into a numbing experience, and the rain which will ultimately find its way under the collar of the slicker.

It gets late earlier on an island than anywhere else, and that should be borne in mind. Man has a safe lead over the elements in most places, but he doesn't hold the rail position on an island. Here even a slow-drifting fog can cause a man to feel his lead is vanishing, that there is heat on his flanks. And yet, I've never known an island dweller who didn't disregard all of this, disdaining the elements and their power, to fully accept the fact that when the sun sets on an island it begins to shine someplace else.

Rain, Rain

As usual, it will be whispered that I'm behind times and out of touch with progress, but I must admit that I have a very low opinion of the science of meteorology and an even lower regard for the radio and television weather forecasters who radiate assurance and confidence while dealing in false and inaccurate predictions. In fairness, I must acknowledge that the latter merely read over the air what is handed to them, but they bear some responsibility for the cheerful exuberance and false legitimacy which they bring to the report, and this makes them, in my opinion, accomplices.

Scientists have built computers of such awesome capacity that few of us even recognize their capability, they have designed aircraft that stop short barely at the point of repealing the law of gravity, they have brought electronics to the point of incredibility, and for better or worse they have fractured the atom. But they don't know yet if it is going to rain tomorrow. The thoughts of scientists range widely and in unconventional ways, yet they are no more productive than a schoolboy's in predicting weather. I am familiar—aren't we all?—with the trappings of the TV weather forecaster: the impressive map, the arrows, the cloud shadows, the precipitation areas. We all speak knowledgeably about low pressure areas, Bermuda highs, tracking squalls by radar, and the meteorological rhetoric that has crept into the patois of the times from the television screen. Yet it is almost as much theater as the situation comedy which precedes it or follows it. Interesting, most certainly entertaining, but don't count on it.

Living on an island, as I do, weather becomes the dominant element in an individual's life. It determines not just the spiritual and emotional level of the island dweller's day, but it also governs all of his or her activities since even leaving the island in a wet boat in a steady rain is sufficiently distasteful to limit trips to the mainland to matters only of great urgency. If the island dweller's distrust of radio and TV weather predictions is greater than that of other people, it may be because he has been betrayed in a more personal and painful way, and these betrayals have left him with a distinctively sour taste.

I don't mean to imply that the radio or TV weatherman is compromising himself, that he is intentionally leading us down the unsettling path of falsity, but I'm disturbed by his failure to even acknowledge yesterday's disastrous miscalculations. Each day's exuberance and confidence, totally foreclosing recent inaccuracies, is exasperating to the listener. The week-long northeast storm in New England early this summer offered a splendid example. On a Wednesday it was raining hard, but there was the cheerful assurance that rain would end during the night and sun would shine in the morning. The next day saw an even heavier rainfall, but the forecasters—pointing to their maps—were confident it would clear by evening. Friday turned *really* ugly; the wind got behind the rain, lashing windows with sheets of water and turning low places into pools. A note of caution had crept into the forecasts by Friday evening; this thing was stubborn, no doubt about it, but it would all end before noon on Saturday. I recall Saturday as being the worst day of the entire northeaster; a heavy, dark day of unremitting rainfall. That night the forecasters, smiling apologetically, came somewhat to grips with their inaccuracies. The storm had tricked them, they said; it had headed out into the Atlantic and then, unaccountably, had turned and come back to the coast of New England. That's the way storms do, they explained; there was nothing defective about the forecasting system.

I knew on Friday the rain was not going to stop, but I didn't learn it from the radio and TV forecasters; I learned it from my neighbor on the mainland. He was patching lobster traps in the shed behind his house when I stopped by for a chat before heading back to the island. "Well," I said, "the rain is going to stop tonight, and it will fair by noon tomorrow. I just heard it on my car radio." He put down his hammer, removed a few nails from his mouth, and walked to the door and squinted up. He came back shaking his head. "It's going to do no such thing," he said, and there was the ring of authority in his voice. "Not until the wind shifts. It's going to be like this tomorrow. Count on it."

I find no evidence of my neighbor's sympathy with the problems of the meteorologists and forecasters; he scorns their language, their pretense, and their conclusions. "Now who in hell ever heard of a northeaster that lasts less than three days?" he asks angrily. "Anybody with the sense that God gave geese knows they don't come and go in one day." My neighbor thinks the basic weakness of the professional forecaster is his lack of a window; he deplores their dependence upon instruments. To draw an accurate bead on tomorrow's weather, my neighbor likes to see what it's doing now, likes to feel it, even smell it if all other indicators are inconclusive. It is a highly personal, total-immersion school of meteorology, but it has its limitation. He will tell you what it's going to do tomorrow, but he balks beyond that. He laughs out loud when I repeat to him the Weekend Roundup I have just heard on television. "Only the good Lord knows what it's going to do day after tomorrow," he says, "and sometimes even He hasn't made up his mind yet." There is a wisdom here that I recommend to the professionals.

Forty Percent Likelihood

The rain came sometime during the night, lodging in some subliminal level of my mind, and when I awoke I was not surprised to hear the steady drumming on the roof because I seemed to have known it all the time. I guess the dog knew too because, responding to some vestigial prompting she had brought with her from the caves of her forebears, she had abandoned her own bed during the night and sought warmth and companionship with me on the foot of my bed. Neither of us was in a hurry to get up; what we had at hand promised more comfort than the prospect we faced upon arising. As I burrowed deeper into the covers, it came to me that the meteorologists had been caught off-base again; they had predicted fair weather with the usual escape clause of increasing cloudiness in the late afternoon. An afternoon without cloudiness is rare; the forecast was as courageous as a prediction of dew on a July night. I wished my neighbor, the lobsterman, were still alive. He didn't consider a Bermuda High so much as he consulted his knee joints; he knew when it was going to rain and his predictions were not expressed in cowardly percentage points of likelihood. It was either going to rain or not rain, and to hell with that "forty percent likelihood" stuff.

I put on a robe and walked to the living room window. Cundys Harbor, two miles across Quahog Bay, was only a dark shadow on a gray and dripping landscape. It wasn't a gentle rain but one that meant business. It would leave the half-empty gasoline tanks floating in the boats; the gutters were alive and I could hear water gushing into the cistern. I went back to the bedroom and started to dress. The dog stretched, and looked at me with disapproval on her face. Humans didn't know how to gracefully accept the gifts of nature, she was thinking; their misplaced sense of responsibility constantly collided with the prizes of a providential charity.

The wind was blowing fresh, but it was not a strong wind and only the tops of the trees were moving, and there were no whitecaps in the cove. A lobsterboat, working its way around the southern tip of Pole Island, was encountering rougher water, burying its bow in the troughs of the channel as it headed toward Bailey Island and the open sea. On a shrouded day like this, an island seems more remote than it normally does and sometimes ceases to be real at all, as though it were cut off from the rest of the world entirely.

A moist chill pervaded the house, and I made a fire in the fireplace which sent a rosy glow dancing about the living room and chased the shadows from the corners. The crackling attracted the dog; I heard a dull thump as she left the bed and in a moment she stood in the doorway, her forelegs distended and her back arched in a luxurious stretch. This was more to her taste; the human race may seldom get its values straight but you can't fault a warm fire on a cold, rainy day.

All rains on a small island are harmless, since there is no danger of flooding. Small boats fill up, firewood gets soaked, and if a strong wind is blowing a little water may seep in under the doors, but a few hours of sunshine and everything is back to normal. Rain is inconvenient but never menacing. Fog is something different; opaque and relentless, it can strike terror in the hearts of coastal Mainers because there is no known way of dealing with it. My island is close in and even in the densest fog I can always get to the mainland and back, although one time I beached my boat on the island without recognizing where I was. I knew I had found land and had not passed through the cove entrance into Quahog Bay, but I didn't know I was home until I had tied up the boat and walked into the forest which suddenly struck me as familiar.

But in a heavy rain like this one I put off going outside until after breakfast, and then, seeing there was no lightening of the skies, I put on oilskins and went down to the wharf to check on the boats. The dog came along but her heart was not in it; she shook often, and glanced over her shoulder at the path she had just followed, as though to reassure herself that it would still be there when she had completed this fool's errand. On sunny mornings the boats bob on their lines, but today they lay heavily in the water. Coming back, I stopped in the forest and was suddenly aware of the stillness; on rainy days there are no bird songs, only the patter of heavy drops hitting the dead leaves. Even this is a muted sound.

Tides, wind, rain, fog, and snow make up a large part of the unworldly enchantment known as Maine, but we spend so much time dreaming, planning, yearning, postponing, and worrying that we seldom realize these things exist, yet they seem to exist here with a sharper edge of challenge than in most places. A man who makes his home in Maine, especially on a Maine island, knows he will win only partial victories over the sea and the weather; he will never master either of them. But there will also be golden days and nights that are soft and mysterious, and there will even be rainy mornings when awakening in a delicious trance one decides that maybe the dog knows best, and lids close again as the tattoo on the roof continues and drops beat against the window panes. When you're on a roll, ride with it.

Muy Peligroso

I don't think I could live very long in Nebraska or Missouri or Oklahoma, or any other state that far from the sea. I don't know the Great Lakes well enough to make a judgment about them, although I've walked several times along the shore of Lake Michigan without feeling any great sensations. Jan Morris, the Welsh writer, believes that the instinct that leads us all to the water's edge "offers a reassurance, perhaps, of nature's dignity" and reminds us that somewhere out there "beyond our credit-card conformities" some grand things are happening.

Miss Morris is content with any water, whether it is a lake, a river, a canal, a backwater, or even New York City, which she feels is a sea-city that has forgotten its origins, but I part with her at this point. I am overwhelmed by the majesty of her prose, but I am not moved into agreement with her. For me to get my money's worth out of water, I require the sea. I don't care if it comes thundering in with a roar as waves break and spray flies or whether it creeps in stealthily on a tidal flow that inches through the marshlands and silently fills the coves and reaches and tidal creeks, but it has to be salt water and it has to lead, ultimately, to Capetown and Sydney and Montevideo and Singapore. That, I believe, is the tantalizing magic of the sea kingdom, that it suggests to the romantic mind the thought of secret convoys, of offering escape from the necktie, jacket, and water cooler to a faraway land where tramp steamers lie at anchor in hot and crowded roadsteads, where palm trees lean out over blue water, where African towns end at the ocean's edge and naked children play in the shallows, where dhows sail from East African towns to islands in the Indian Ocean—to Zanzibar, to Lamu, to the Seychelles.

What I am saying now—although this isn't what I started out to say—is that the sea eases restraints on the imagination and permits it to soar unencumbered. I can't imagine that anyone wants to argue a point as palpable as that, so I'll move on. It doesn't take a feverishly romantic mind, however, to know that when one comes to the sea, one arrives at a frontier, that across that frontier lie not one but two alien worlds—the terrifying deep-ocean world and beyond that a land rising from the sea which may be beautiful or hideous, forest or desert, peaceful or violent, crowded and dirty, or remote and sparkling. They are all there somewhere. At Zihuatenejo, a small town on the Pacific coast of Mexico, I was cautioned one day not to go swimming and when I asked why, the lifeguard pointed to a small red flag flying in the breeze. "*Muy peligroso,*" he said. You don't have to speak Spanish fluently to recognize *peligroso* as dangerous. I went swimming anyway, partly because I am defiant by nature and partly because it didn't seem all that *peligroso* to me, no more than Reid State Park or Old Orchard Beach on any summer day. Nothing happened, but the swim was exciting and memorable because it was in a foreign place and I was dealing with an unknown danger (sharks? undertow? riptide?) in a watery and insubstantial civilization. This is the unspoken nature of the sea: it can charm, it can soothe, or it can kill. Step up and take a chance.

For those who came in late, let me say again that I live on an island in Casco Bay and a small island at that, so from no point on my domain am I out of sight of the sea. This would seem to indicate that I have either carried a fondness to the point where my emotional stability could be questioned or else I had stumbled upon a unique real estate bargain and couldn't resist such an appealing economic windfall. The latter explanation has to be ignored by anyone familiar with the price of Maine deepwater islands these days, and I'm not sure the other explanation tells the whole story either. The fact is that I love the sea, I think it has an ennobling effect upon mankind, and I believe that its gentleness and its violence stirs the heart and mind in a way that diminishes cruelty, greed, and deceit. I must shrug my shoulders when questioned about the dangers inherent in the sea. If you purify the pond, the water lilies die.

One day a couple of years ago, I had taken my open Whaler out into the sea a little farther than I normally go because I wanted to see the island where Edna St. Vincent Millay had lived. A summer squall blew up quickly from the west, and I hurriedly came about and headed back to my island. It was an uneven race and I was badly outclassed. The large drops began to fall before I was halfway home, and within a few minutes the wind came, carrying with it a sheet of water. In retrospect, writing these lines in a quiet study, I can't say that the situation was *muy peligroso* but it seemed so at the time and it most certainly was *muy* wet. The spray and driving rain soaked me within seconds, gusts now tugged at the little boat and built great troughs in the sea. Lightning flashed, followed by instantaneous thunder that rolled across the sky, booming and echoing until it faded away. But soon the strength of the storm weakened—I could feel it almost instantly—and the thunder moved farther and farther into the distance. The clouds hung low and scudded across the sea, but the violence was spent and only a gentle rain remained. When I reached my cove, a shaft of sunlight appeared, bathing the island in a strange yellow light. If my clothes clung to me, so did a feeling of grace. If the sea had not made this an odd journey of fulfillment, would I be writing about it two years after it had happened? The sea bestows strange prizes, and I feel sorry for the people in Nebraska who can't claim them.

False Spring

I think "winter sports" is an oxymoron, one of those odd figures of speech where one word cancels out the other as in "plastic glass" or "old news" or "studied indifference" or "down escalator." I can deal lyrically with spring and rapturously with summer but winter is a negative thing and mine is not the voice to speak up in its behalf. The warm day we had recently which brought more people out of doors than I have seen since September, restored the will to live so far as I'm concerned. In a way it reminded me of the Hollywood funeral of the late Harry Cohn, the cordially disliked president of Columbia Pictures, which attracted such an overflow crowd that one observer muttered, "It just goes to show that if you give the public what it wants to see, it will always turn out for it."

My honesty is the best known and most disagreeable of all my qualities and I have no hesitation in declaring that winter and I are enemies. I don't hear music when my tires are spinning in the snow (what I hear is earnest profanity and you can guess where it's coming from) and I don't see the majesty of a winter panorama when I look out the window (what I see is a neighbor with a shovel in his hand rapidly approaching cardiac arrest) and I don't yearn to curl up by the fire with a good book (even if I could find the book under a pile of disposable tissues, inhalators, and capsules all "for the temporary relief of headaches and congestion—Keep Out of the Reach of Children"). No, the nice warm day we had recently murmured something congenial and reassuring to me, and while I may be rushing things a bit I'm ready to put the screens back on the windows.

If I ever write another book—which is very unlikely since I have no interest in warfare in outer galaxies, see no need for another biography of Ronald Reagan whether or not he is described as possessing the tranquility of an unruffled mind, and I could never hope to equal Mrs. Krantz's or Miss Collins' turgid explorations into Hollywood adultery—it would be a pleasant book with a title such as *Our New Best Friend*—'The Greenhouse Effect.' I am uneasy about discussing the matter of winter (and how I wish that were the end of the sentence) because there are a lot of people around who profess to prefer it to the other seasons of the year and who respond unpleasantly to winter-bashing, which is what I'm doing right now. I haven't forgotten the hornet's nest I unthinkingly dislodged in this space a few years ago when I wrote glowingly of a pretty woman I had seen wearing a dress, of all things, at a shopping mall, and in the mail that came to me from the women's rights leaders nicer things have been said about Saddam Hussein. It blew over, but just last night my eye caught an item in the *New York Times* that told me how a woman at the Central Hospital in Bergen, Norway, had refused to accept a blood transfusion from a male donor because—her doctor said—"her feminist views made it impossible to accept a man's blood." The astute reader will notice that I am mentioning the item but enlarging it with no comment of my own. There was a time—we were all young once— when I would pick up a rock and look around for the nearest window, but this impulsive behavior cannot coexist with diplomacy which I have since embraced. A diplomat, someone said, is a person who can tell you to go to hell in such a way that you actually look forward to the trip.

I would like to plunge into new fields, but I am not through with winter yet. The worst of it is behind us now, except for that final treacherous backlash which we have all grown to respect, and which will send us feverishly covering bulbs and exposed sprouts with leaves and old tarps while the thermometer drops and snow clouds gather. In Maine, I would say that winter clearly holds the balance of power through most of April, and the unbearable lightness of spring is still out of reach. If my spirits and my words reflect the seamless grey of the skies, I can only say that I am a Scotch Calvinist by birth and by nature and that I know from experience that false spring is a snowed-on parade.

If I deal with winter as an object of scorn I feel I am not wholly without allies. As a very young man, E.B. White, the Maine philosopher, wrote, "I know enough about Nature not to call her Mother, for one thing." White was no coward, as I am. He once wrote an essay entitled "Getting Along With Women," a subject I wouldn't take on at gunpoint. I know which side of the bread my cholesterol-free margarine is on.

Spin Control

The geography of Maine, it seems to me, sets the mood of its people. It is a seafaring state, and the people of Maine are basically seafaring folk by nature. They recognize the capricious character of the sea, its beauty and its treachery; they are wary of its fury and they glory in its sunlit wonder. They know that sea winds are harsher and more persistent than land winds, and they know that those who are reckless where the sea is concerned die young. In the corridors of Washington these days there is a new art practiced called "spin control," which is making something appear to be quite different from what it actually is, a political device for misleading those whose opinions are hastily formed by the television sound bite. The sea tolerates no spin control; what is, is. Things are exactly what they seem to be, and because of this I believe the Mainer is less likely to accept deception than mountain people or plains people. The sea covers 71 percent of this planet, which I see as a splendid thing.

The seasons in the Maine corner of the nation have just changed, and on a sparkling day in early winter I am struck by the realization that coastal people are often in trouble but seldom over their depth. They believe in right and wrong, but they also know that, left alone, nature will correct its mistakes. I am still brooding over the past summer's pogie disaster, which turned my cove into a foul-smelling body of water that was covered, wall to wall, with brown, rotting menhaden, but I am not a born Mainer and do not possess that coastal man's ability to forget the stale smell of disaster and move on with zest to something new. When I mentioned the pogie matter this morning to my neighbor, the lobsterman, a quizzical expression swept across his face. "Oh!" he said quickly. "The pogies. You won't have to worry about them next summer. It'll be ten years, maybe twenty, before that happens again." He says this in a voice of calm resolution and I accept it as the truth. Mainers are extraordinarily superstitious and I could easily say that it was nothing more than superstition, an opinion based on symbols or some odd coincidence, but I know better than that. My neighbor knows the natural world and the laws of the sea better than I do, and while his opinion may lack scientific foundation it is based on experience, which in my mind is something better and more reliable. Experience seeks a man out and makes an impact; science offers a theory, but I have too weak a character to put much store in something as airy as that.

I received a bill today from a local chap who comes over to the island occasionally to do some work for me. The bill was clear and to the point: he listed the hours he worked and his hourly rate. Under the total he wrote: "If you have any ? about anything, phone me or right." I liked his precision and I liked his spare, forthright style. In fact, I think he should be a righter; unlike so many in the righting craft, he knows what to leave out. I think this is a Maine trait.

People say that the sea makes men silent, but nothing could be further from the truth. The most talkative people in the world are lobstermen. A group of them meets early every morning in a country store a few miles down the road from my landing where they have coffee and conversation before going out to their boats, and so far as I can judge not one of them listens to any of the others. The common thread, of course, is dissatisfaction and the decline of decency, and each of them seems to be competing for the distinction of being the least fortunate and the one that destiny has singled out for hard labor, poverty, poor health, and a tragically short life span. They all drive away in new trucks.

The change of the seasons is a miraculous and exciting thing, and I would consider life in the tropics to be a tiresome drama with no beginning and no end. But Mainers, I have noticed, pass from autumn to winter as casually as walking through a door. The days pass. E.B. White once wrote that spring came to Maine when the town clerk took the village records out of the Frigidaire and turned on the current. Winter was over, he said, with the breaking up of the skim of ice in the post-office inkwell.

A seasonal change involves a reawakening of interest in life, although I'm not at all sure why this is true. One buttons one's coat a little tighter at the neck these days before getting in a boat and the hand that is not on the tiller goes promptly into a pocket, but the eye is keener and sweeps the sea and the shore for signs of approaching winter. The flaming leaves of the sumac now lie on the ground, the cattails in the wetland are brown and brittle, and frost has seared the meadow grass. Afternoons wane quickly; we are told by the weather reports what time the sun sets, but I don't put much stock in those predictions. It starts getting dark long before they say it will. I have found that distances seem to shorten a little just before sunset, that I can see Cundy's Harbor a little clearer, and the thought has occurred to me that perhaps this sharpened visual acuity finds a parallel in a heightening of the spiritual well-being of the individual. I know that I'm looking around for answers that do not exist. Plants react violently to the change of seasons, geese fly hundreds of miles in response to some inner timing, salmon migrate, and bears crawl into caves to sleep off the summer's excesses. Is there any sensible reason why human beings should not react to some inner rhythm when autumn slips into winter?

Inhalators and Overshoes

There's something extraordinarily moving about a winter's day, and although most writers beat out a sort of *allegretto graziosa* rhythm about the other seasons, there seems no one around who wishes to speak up for winter. I would like to pass over handkerchiefs, inhalators, and overshoes long enough to write a brief eclogue celebrating winter. It has gotten a bum rap, and nothing measures the extent of this mistake until we come to grips with the realization that winter is nature's nighttime, the resting period when the land reclaims its richness, when wells fill and meadow brooks run clear from melted snow, and when man can get his feet up on a stool and read without wondering what's going on in the barn or the boathouse.

It's a cold, overcast day today and there is a sharp edge to the wind which somehow finds its way through the four layers of clothing I am wearing. Darkness will come early this evening, partly because the days are short anyway at this time of year and this, together with the heavy accumulation of clouds overhead, will bring night on quickly as the afternoon wanes. There will probably be more snow, but of all of nature's phenomena snow is the most difficult to predict accurately and since my neighbor, the lobsterman, passed away I must fall back on the radio or television weathermen who are pathetically inaccurate. My neighbor never failed. When I would stop by his house in the afternoon to inquire if snow was due, he would come outside, gaze at the sky, sniff several times, squint to where the sun should be, and then deliver his report. There was never any foolish talk of percentages: it was either going to snow or it wasn't. It never occurred to me that he could be wrong; if he said snow would fall during the night, my only curiosity would be how much.

If it snows tonight—and I have only Willard Scott's word for it, which doesn't mean a hell of a lot since he only reads the reports handed to him—I will take the boxer for a walk before breakfast because there is nothing more exhilarating than crossing a trackless field or seeing spruce trees loaded with soft snow or marveling at the strange silence that prevails in snow-covered forests. The spirits of the dog will soar, they always do when she runs in the snow. She buries her nose in it, snorts, shakes her head, and then strikes out across a field, kicking her feet high in the air out of sheer delight at the wonder of it all. I think children feel that way too about snow; it's only adults who are concerned about snow tires and drifted lanes. Yet early in the morning even these anxieties take a position in the dim recesses of the mind; one is impressed more by the splendor of the unblemished landscape, the glistening purity, the thin sunlight of early morning touching a snow-covered hill.

The early afternoon today is one of cold, wet mist, with a winter wind springing up, driving the gulls to shelter on the rocks and swaying the bare trees. There is a strange suspense in the air, as though nature is not yet sure what it has in mind and is warning the prudent to be prepared for anything. In the forest there are only occasional spots of old snow, and my steps make a rustling in the leaves that reassures the dog. She runs ahead of me, drunk on all of the odors of the forest, and it is only when I stop walking, and silence takes over the woodland, that she grows uneasy and comes racing back to where I am standing. One walks slowly in the woods; the leaves fill holes that can cause one to stumble, and everywhere there are broken branches, rotten logs, and fallen trees. There are almost no birds to be seen, although one can be heard occasionally from somewhere deep in the forest. A squirrel materializes from nowhere, leaping to a distant branch where it sways dangerously before moving on to another one, while the dog goes into a frenzy on the ground.

We come out of the woods to the rocks and the sea, and exposed here to the wind it is uncomfortably cold. The water is green and clear, and limpets cling to the rocks. They say that lobsters' eyes are very weak, and they would be unable to feed themselves but for their ability to feel and smell. This isn't true of most of the sea creatures in Maine waters; here in small tidal pools there is an unending cycle of eating and being eaten. Survival depends upon sensitivity to stimulation, a sudden ripple of the water, a shadow, an unusual sound. Here beside the sea I feel more alone than I do in the forest, and I wonder why this is true. Perhaps it has something to do with the cold; there is a dry cold to the forest and a moist cold on the rocks beside the sea.

The dog and I start back to the house, and it is cold enough now for us to take a shortcut. There is a small boat ride, and my fingers move stiffly as I tie a line to the cleat on the wharf. The walk to the house is brisk and rich in anticipation: there will be a fire in the fireplace, a stack of books, a Mozart tape on the stereo. I will make a drink and bring it back to the living room with me. The lights in the house will make the outside seem more dark than it really is, but another winter day has ended. As those in any other season of the year, it has been infinitely precious and worth remembering.

Spring Treachery

In spring, Maine deceives; she's not just a fickle lover, she is no lover at all. Spring's greatest deception comes when one trusts her the most, that period just before spring blends into early summer and the ground is soft and the weather is warm and the time for planting has come. One comes out, with seeds in hand, to discover the mosquitoes and black flies stacked up in a flight pattern, like planes over La Guardia, waiting to descend. A half-hour with your sleeves rolled up and you will be needing plasma.

I spent my youth in Virginia and in later years, fleeing the icy breath of Maine's winter, I have experienced springs in many other places where it is a genuine season, not the brief interlude—a casual token, really—that goes for springtime in Maine. On the whole I approve of Maine's other three seasons; it is only that tentative spring which I feel shortchanges me. A couple I know fled Vermont a few years ago because of the endless winter and the absence of spring, and settled in Georgia, from which outpost they send me glowing descriptions, beginning early in March, of how the dogwood is blooming, the peepers are heard at twilight, and the kid next door has a new fielder's glove. When they want me to taste the full extravagance of the situation, they start sending these missives in late February. I am still busy digging the snow out of the path to the woodpile, and it's fortunate that an icy wind takes the words I mutter in reply. It's a cruel test of friendship.

I know I've touched upon this subject before, the vagrancy and timidity of a Maine spring, but I can write a number of pieces about this and not be winded at all. Choler gives a writing man endurance. The late E.B. White, whose devotion to Maine was explicit in everything he wrote about the state, deplored the fact that his automobile license plate carried the word *Vacationland*, which he thought was the product of "a drab, untrustworthy mind." He came back to the subject frequently, having—since he wrote last about it—thought of some new objections to the state's misguided policy of turning a private vehicle into a public testimonial. "I can't even be sure that my state will not try to improve on its present form of advertisement," he wrote many years ago, and sure enough, he was right. In White's absence, I would like to point to the lobster which has taken its place above *Vacationland* to prove his accuracy as a prophet of ill tidings. Now that Maine is really in promotion, as the only state with not one but two advertising messages on its license plates, I think we may as well go all the way. In two corners of the license plate, I suggest a small sun representing summer and autumn, and in the other two corners there would be clouds emptying rain and snow to suggest spring and winter. While Maine winters are tough, they are straightforward and don't pretend to be what they aren't; it's spring that is filled with treachery and falseheartedness.

I recall from my boyhood in Virginia that spring there was a full and wonderful season, beginning the middle of March and melding into summer around the middle of June. In Maine, I would estimate the total span of springtime to be about two weeks. Fortunately, Mainers are not easily thrown off balance by meteorological reports coming from television personalities, who are particularly fond of reporting on weather tricks in the Ohio Valley, wherever that is. Most Maine people, especially on the coast where weather is of primary interest, predict weather with a fine-tuned accuracy. On those first warm days, when lilac and forsythia explode into bloom and the screens replace the storm windows, very few Mainers are lulled into a false sense of security. That first warm afternoon and evening doesn't mean a thing, and they know it. It may be O.K. to get the ladders out and extended, but don't start painting. It may rain during the night and there will be ice on the ladders tomorrow morning.

A man gets homesick for strange things sometimes, like a song he has carried in his mind for a half-century, or the scent given off by the husk of a black walnut, or the sight of certain cloud formations that remind him of a carefree childhood, but there is nothing in my memory bank quite so seductive and appealing as the arrival of true spring. It is a spiritual thing compounded of apple and wisteria blossoms, of the odor of fresh-turned earth, of paint not yet dried, of newly-arrived robins scratching around for worms to ease the hunger of the long trip north, of the feeling of the great vigor of the earth renewing itself. It is a magical thing and I am waiting for it right now.

Time Passes

Without trying to disinter the particularly malodorous subject of pogies, which the people in my part of Casco Bay felt completely erased the Summer of 1990 from the calendar, I've just had the encouraging report from my friend, the lobsterman, that he foresees no pogie problem whatever for the season now arriving. The lobsterman is correct in about half of his forecasts, which places him solidly ahead of the *Wall Street Journal*, the *New York Times*, and the President's Council of Economic Advisors, the latter of which drags in last and sometimes doesn't even make it to the ball park. I have to watch the lobsterman's premonition carefully, however, as he is inclined to wander once he moves into the world of portents and omens, and I can tell by the look in his eyes and the oracular tone of his voice that he has temporarily abandoned Harpswell, Maine, for the farther shore of shadow and prophecy. He is safe enough on the weather, hitting it eight times out of ten, but he's inclined to be too excitable where the lottery is concerned, and in politics he is apt to be noisy, optimistic, and consistently on the side of the losers. So far as pogies are concerned, I spent a large part of last summer locked in an unpleasant correspondence with my state government inquiring at what point the state would do something—anything—to help the situation (the fumes had already caused the paint on one lady's house to flake off). The government's attitude, of course, was one of wounded innocence, and they replied as though I had been writing hate mail to Mother Theresa.

Time passes. My attitude toward the pogie catastrophe is now more dispassionate, and with the assurance of my friend, the lobsterman, that the matter is behind us, I am willing to pass on to other things, even skipping the Gulf War entirely (though I have to acknowledge amusement at the British journalist who argued that there were Americans who would have asked Custer to give time for sanctions to work even as the Indians came riding into Little Big Horn). Right now I am more concerned with the springy texture of the soil and its promise to the new plants I am setting out, the number of lady-slippers that I have counted in my 1991 census, the smell of bayberry when I push my way through the waist-high thickets of it growing to the edge of the rocks, the arching of oak and spruce trees under the skies of cobalt blue. Early summer in Maine defines its own realm, offers its own prizes. The sun is in pursuit of brio; its glow strengthens daily.

The night noises of wind soften with the arrival of late spring, and a sunny day in early summer comes in on silent wings and bearing the moist scent of balsam and pine on its breath. I feel sorry for those who sleep late because they miss the truly fine things: the sparkle of dew in early sunlight, the pearly cobwebs sagging under the weight of captured dewdrops, the congregation of gulls all earnestly facing in the same direction as though waiting for one of the group to break the silence with instructions for the day's activities. They miss the small waves reaching higher and higher on the rocks as the tide flows, the blue heron standing patiently in the shallows waiting for an unwary shiner, all of the rituals of a new day that somehow seem spectacularly different from the day just past. A cormorant's head and neck rise suddenly from the water, its eyes glaring wildly like a lunatic, only to disappear a moment later as it swims off totally submerged in pursuit of a fish. Although cormorants spend much of their day underwater, they loathe being wet and one sees them in groups standing on rock ledges, their wings spread out like eagles on a dollar bill, hoping the sun and air will quickly dry their feathers. The most depressing aspect of the cormorant is that it likes fish but doesn't like getting wet catching them; man probably had the same dilemma until he discovered he could stand around in trout streams wearing hip boots.

I think the coming of summer is un-settling for all of nature and I think that this is particularly true for human beings. Personally, I reorganize in every department in late spring, and although the reorganization falls apart shortly after summer arrives, I always forget the failures and start out with the spirit of a man sailing uncharted seas. Cleaning out the boathouse has become for me the symbol of reorganization, although I know in my heart that I don't care one bit about whether the boathouse is clean or not. Actually, I like to come in and search around for a nut to fit a particular bolt or to find the right size paintbrush or a piece of rope just the right length so I don't have to cut anything, but I don't mind the self-deception involved in thinking I want the boathouse well-organized. By cleaning out a few things—parting with some old kerosene lamps, throwing out pesticides whose labels I can no longer read, agreeing to give up a rubber boot whose mate has disappeared—I am able to comfort myself with the knowledge that the warm, sweet airs of spring are helping me blow out the accumulation of waste from the boathouse and that my life will be richer as a result. It's a pleasing prospect that can be purchased cheaply.

My neighbor, the lobsterman, also says this will be a very hot summer. He knows this for a fact, he says, but he refuses to disclose the source of his knowledge. He wants me to persuade him to reveal it, which I refuse to do because wherever there is great creativeness there is also a little madness, and that is an atmosphere in which I don't care to loiter any longer than necessary.

An Oppressive Influence

You have to approach Maine's weather in easy stages, feeling it out slowly, sniffing its moisture and salt content, always expecting more rain and overcast tomorrow, and when you finally get the hang of it, you will find that a certain kind of indifference has set in. The weather hasn't changed any, but your outlook has.

The secret locked in the hearts of even those who love Maine the most is their knowledge that there is probably better weather in the Aleutian Islands than can be found on coastal Maine in spring or early summer. Not that other states and areas don't feel the classic New England huddle of systems coming in from the Great Plains in May and June and colliding with whatever witches' brew is being blown in from the North Atlantic, but Maine seems to be at the core of it all, holding on stubbornly to one edge of the storm mass as it disappears and seizing with an air of family comradeship the oncoming edge of the new system.

For some reason that mystifies me, weather is, or *seems* to be, more important in Maine than it does anywhere else I have been. When one crosses the Piscataqua River coming into Maine from the south, a door seems to close behind one as though a crossing has been made into some separate cosmos, and the visitor becomes tugged by different laws of nature. I am not suggesting that Maine is a continent of its own, but I am saying that certain adjustments and accommodations must be made in Maine and weather is one of them. One of the first, in fact.

One didn't rush headlong through May and June of this year; rather each sodden, gloomy day dragged by slowly as the conflict of systems fought for the upper hand, and a wan sun would break occasionally through the clouds to remind us of what it would be like when it was all over. Even so, it was not as intolerable as the early summer of three years ago when, as I recall, twenty-eight successive days of graceless weather—rain or heavy overcast—prevailed, pleasing no one but the mosquitoes who found it a paradise of unsurpassed richness. It was toward the end of that period that for the first time I seriously considered closing my island home and going to New Mexico or Arizona just to sense the penetrating warmth of intense sunshine again.

I believe something happens to the human spirit in lengthy periods of rain and gloom, as has been proven to occur in European countries subject to the debilitating winds known as *mistral, föhn, sirocco,* and *meltimi.* These oppressive winds blowing toward the center of low barometric pressure and the atmospheric turbulence surrounding them are said to be truly deranging, causing temporary disorientation, irritability, impatience, and hopelessness—even to the point where French law is said to take the prevalence of mistral into consideration where crimes of passion have been committed. Long periods of rain and gloom in Maine certainly lack the tumultuous character-altering effects of the European winds, but I think they possess some indefinably oppressive influence. Restlessness is not cured by resting; sleeping does not bring serenity.

For a long, rainy season, of course, one must be prepared. But how to prepare? Reading is said to be the work of an alert mind, but somewhere out there in that misty, gloomy world is a powerful little switch that derails thought and causes me to reread the same paragraph two or three times before I realize what an uphill job the writer has on his hands without knowing it. He or she is trying to tell me something, but the rain beating against the windows and drumming on the roof is speaking with a louder voice and the chain of intellect is broken so often that concentration on the written word becomes tiring. Besides, an extremely heavy rain possesses tremendous drawing power; I am always drawn to the window, putting the book aside, to look out at the sea, convinced that a drama of great importance is taking place there. It isn't, and I know damned well that it isn't, but I respond to the summons nevertheless. What I see are thousands, millions of ripples caused by raindrops on the surface of the sea, the rock ledges partially obscured by mist and rain, a lonesome lobsterboat beating its way to the cove, the geraniums on the sundeck, drooping and uneasy, their scarlet petals floating in small riverlets sweeping across the deck. As dampness penetrates the house, newspapers won't burn in the fireplace, and pine needles are tracked in and distributed with impartiality in every room of the house. Sooner or later one gets to the heart of the matter which is that Nature, as it always does, must take its course.

And then—the miracle occurs! One awakens to see the bright glare of sunlight on the wall, and the world has suddenly regained its primeval quality of simple joy. After a stormy period, Maine seems to glow with an awesome beauty as though it were atonement for an unkind act. The sky is bluer than it has ever been, the sea is calmer, there is a softness in the air that pledges this thing will never happen again. Battered flowers stand tall again, leaves on the trees no longer drip, the gulls reappear, and the world seems wise, undaunted, and filled with promise. What was a harsh landscape yesterday is a thing of magnificence today. Weather, like poetry, might be said to be emotion recollected in tranquility.

The Paradox of Tides

I'm thankful for small favors, and one of them is that I don't know very much about tides. Once you get involved with them, I'm told, your curiosity gets out of hand and the first thing you know you are crawling around in the mud looking for odd creatures, measuring high and low tides, charting moon effects on tidal flow, and becoming so preoccupied with the rise and fall of water that you lose all sense of the earth's other pleasant rhythms.

All I need to know is simple: is the tide coming in or going out? If the tide is going out, I have enough sense to wait until it turns before I go into town with a big shopping list because when I get back to the island I don't want the ramp leading from my float to the dock to have turned suddenly into a ladder. Maine folk will know what I mean by this, even if others find it an obscure reference. Normal tides rise and fall about thirteen feet around my island, and while there is something fascinating about the miracle of tide fall, the fascination disappears when I come home later than I had intended and have to wrestle a half-dozen heavy bags of groceries ahead of me up a ramp that has become nearly vertical. What adds an additional note of drama to these homecomings is the certainty that one or more of the bags will have gotten wet on the trip over from the mainland, and the dissolution of matter will occur about two feet from the top of the ramp. I know precisely where I can find two bottles of vodka, three bottles of California chardonnay, and a can of maple syrup any time I feel like diving off the float into fifteen feet of water.

I read recently that into the bay of Passamaquoddy, somewhat north of me but not too far, two billion tons of water are carried twice a day by tidal currents, but I can't say that this figure means much to me because I can't handle anything this size. When I deal with bodies of water I have a cut-off point at my bathtub where fourteen gallons brings me to the overflow drain. To me, two billion tons is merely a lot of water that I don't want to be involved with, and I don't think that's asking too much.

I have a friend who lives on an island lacking deep water, and two hours before low tide and two hours afterwards he is a prisoner because his boat is sitting in a sea of mud. When I invite him to dinner, he has to consult a tide chart to see what time he may have to throw his napkin down and race to the dock in order to get home before he runs out of water. He enjoys his after-dinner brandy as much as the next man, and on two occasions I have reversed the menu and served the brandy first, which is a blow against civilized living but one that solved his problem.

Tides present an odd paradox. The force that sets them in motion lies wholly outside the earth, and one would think it would perform impartially on all parts of the globe but this isn't the case. The character of the tide at any particular place is strictly a local matter and astonishing differences occur within a very short geographic distance. The Gulf of Maine from its southernmost point to the Bay of Fundy has a range of incredible variation, from a foot or two to a rise and fall of forty to fifty feet. The moon controls the tides, moreover, and as it waxes and wanes in its monthly cycle, the height of the tides varies. All of this, of course, is predictable for those who have the patience to figure things out, and my friend is one of these. With a cup of after-dinner coffee and a snifter of Courvoisier hanging in balance, he will bring out his pencil and work through a thicket of permutations on the back of an envelope and, with a chuckle of delight, will announce to me that he is safe until 10:07 P.M. if I can move dinner along promptly. Often I have seen him drum his fingers impatiently on the table if other guests lingered too long over the salad course.

The influence of the tides on small sea creatures is so great that their lives are dependent upon the sweep of it to bring them food, especially the sessile animals which are not free-moving. I am very fond of sessile animals, especially mussels, and there is a ledge a short distance from my island where mussels cling and where the water is clean and cold. If tides set an arbitrary limit to what I think of as my domain, I intend to make the most of it and if there is anything better than a mussel in clean, cold water it is a mussel in dry, white wine and a little olive oil and oregano.

At low tide there is an unexpected mussel bed in a passage between my island and a nearby ledge, and many years of miscalculations and minor disasters passed before I accurately judged when the tide was full enough for safe passage and when I had to lift up the motor. It was only a few days ago that a large boat came speeding through with a stranger at the helm, and I knew from his speed exactly what was going to happen. He was standing up at the rear of his boat with his hand lightly on the wheel, and since I dislike violence I closed my eyes. When I got to the edge of the water, he was struggling to his feet and the language coming from his lips was as coarse as anything I've ever heard. Good profanity depends upon cadence, originality, and force of thrust, and he scored very high on all three points. The incident only served to reinforce my theory that it's useless to try to fight tides; it's a battle that can't be won.

Wildlife

Encountering my friend, the lobsterman, on my wharf on the mainland one day shortly after I returned from a trip, I could tell by the gleam of urgency in his eyes that he had a riveting announcement to make. "You'll never guess what I saw on your island the other day," he said, "and when I tell you, you won't believe it." He was right, I didn't. He said going out of the cove in his lobster boat about five o'clock one morning, he had seen a moose on the island. The lobsterman likes to milk every situation of the last trace of any drama it contains, and I could see that he had no intention of just letting the unadorned statement lie there. "Yessir," he went on, "it was standing dead still under that big hackmatack tree by the boathouse, and it looked like this." The lobsterman also likes to act out the recon-struction of an event, and now he spread his legs apart, hunched his shoulders high, opened his eyes wide, and glared at me. The show at this point had acquired a slightly lunatic quality. "I hollered at it," he continued, "but it didn't move anything but its eyeballs, which rolled around a little." There was a slight pause. "Like this," he said, rolling his eyes. I decided to lower the curtain on the performance. "Did you ever see a moose over there before?" I asked calmly. He dropped the moose pose, and straightened up. "Never," he replied.

When I said I didn't believe the lobsterman it was more of an attempt to wipe the slate clean for a performance I knew was coming than to imply that my friend was being reckless with the truth. He is a truthful man, although his fondness for melodrama often causes him to set a rather gaudy stage and I've seen occasions when the script was more than just a bit overheated. I'm relieved that he saw a moose; he could have said he saw a yak.

The history of this island, certainly over the past twenty years when I have been here, is lamentably blank where animals are concerned. Porcupines, skunks, and raccoons come over fairly often, either by swimming or slogging through the mud flat at extreme low tides, and there has always been a number of chipmunk and field mice, but other than that the island is no ark. I've thought often of bringing over some rabbits and squirrels, but then I remember how one squirrel that was already here made my life a living hell for three years before I finally caught it in a Havahart trap and exiled it to a neighboring island that I will not name for fear of civil action.

I like animals and I would like to have more of them around, but the concessions can't be all unilateral as the squirrel demanded. I wonder what the lobsterman would say if he saw a llama over here.

Whose Island Is It, Anyway?

A short time ago, while reading the bulletin of The Nature Conservancy, my eye was struck by a reference to the "3,000 islands strewn along Maine's coast," and the fierce competition that existed on them for island resources. Everyone's disinterest is routed by the mention of some subject close to their hearts, a subject which like a flashing red light or an alarm bell going off immediately rivets one's concern, and my attention is gained by almost any reference to life on a Maine island since I live on one. The Nature Conservancy is concerned about the vulnerability of animal and plant life on islands since both are affected by anything that floats or flies by, and which by design or chance happens to land on island shores. I gather that the conflicts that arise among competing island users—people, animals, birds, fish, and plants—were the focus of a conference held early in the fall, and I'm sorry to have missed that conference. I would like to have said a few words about the vulnerability of human society on a small island, since this is a struggle I have been carrying on for nearly fifteen years now and with few measurable results.

I hope The Nature Conservancy doesn't think it detects in my comments the slightest sense of disagreement with its own goals, since I hold the highest admiration for what the organization is doing. But I am better acquainted with island life than most people and can recognize how easy it is to run into trouble when trying to balance the needs of one group with the wants of another. I will skip the matter of bees and ants, for the moment, since they are all Marxists anyway and preoccupied with their tedious Socialist theories, but I would like to discuss the matter of the chipmunks that live down at the end of the island near the boathouse. All summer long I took stale rolls and pastries down to them, placing these handouts under the juniper bushes where I learned they preferred me to place them, and I find it difficult to square this practice with the theory that the chipmunks have been thrown into fierce competition of any kind for island resources. If there is any competition here it is among the chipmunks themselves, although if a passing field mouse has not yet taken a venturesome nibble out of an old doughnut, the idea of doing so has at least entered the realm of the conceivable. No, the only competition the chipmunks face is with the owner of the island and his decisions as to when a roll or muffin is over the hill. In fact, since they have demonstrated a great fondness for doughnuts and sweet rolls, I would say their biggest problem is not competition, but cavities.

The other day I flipped over an old skiff, whose bottom had been exposed to the sun preparatory to a paint job, and found myself face-to-face with a couple of mice who were settling in for the winter. But what caught my eye, aside from the look of astonishment on the faces of both of the mice, was a small cache of smoked almonds that had been brought down one by one from the kitchen, some distance away. It had occurred to me before, that the drawdown, as economists like to say, on my smoked almonds had been unseasonably stable during the late fall, and this mystery was now solved. A few jellybeans, from the saucer on the mantelpiece, gleamed like miniature Easter eggs beneath a tuft of grass, evidence of a petty larceny that had interested me only insofar as I noticed that the mice, like me, avoided the licorice ones. In neither case was replevin considered.

To buttress my contention that human society is as vulnerable as anything else on an island, I would like to introduce the matter of my bird feeder, a gift from my daughter who thought that I would get pleasure from feeding the birds, which, in the language of The Nature Conservancy, by chance or by design happen to land on these shores. Awakened one night by a strange noise, I got my flashlight and went outside and in a moment I had brought the beam to focus on the disturbance. A large and irate raccoon, his eyes glowing fiercely in the reflected light, was systematically destroying the feeder and tossing remnants onto the ground. The feeder had been a small plastic house with a wooden roof, and the raccoon was taking it apart with all of the stoical pleasure of a small child reducing a Christmas tree to rubble. When only the floor of the feeder remained, the raccoon backed down from the tree, shot me a final glance of contempt, and disappeared into a clump of bayberry. I don't know how The Nature Conservancy would classify that episode, possibly as competition for living space, but I know better. I am fairly well-acquainted with raccoons and I know it was nothing more than an ill-tempered old raccoon out for an evening of hell-raising.

I have not finished with The Nature Conservancy people yet. Their conference, I learned by reading the program, touched on methods of "preserving preferred island landscapes," and where plant life on a Maine island is concerned, I'm afraid I must raise my hand again to speak as an expert. There is no plant life on my island that the good Lord didn't put there, and it isn't because I haven't tried to assist Him. It's just that nothing will thrive in that island soil but trees and bayberry and juniper and, at the edge of the sea, some salt heather. I put out a little basil every year, but I have to set the plants in a box filled with soil brought over from the mainland, and my geraniums were all potted in Boston and brought to the island as immigrants. They like it all right during the summer, but they grow apprehensive in the autumn and their relief is apparent when I put them in the boat for the first leg of the long journey back to Boston and urban life.

Crash Landings

The people guarding Maine's environmental purity have a great fondness, I notice, for such terms as "forest management strategies," "Biomass cogeneration," and "reclassification downgrading." I have no great dislike for shoptalk, since it flourishes in all lines of business, but I don't think the grandeur of the rhetoric should grow to the point of obscuring the meaning of what's being said. My neighbor, the lobsterman, sees eye to eye with me on this, and when I asked him over to the island to give me his opinion on the quality of my well water, he took a sip from the dipper, screwed his face up in a grimace, and let me have it straight. "There's better tasting water than that on the bottom of my boat," he said. To my mind, that's a straightforward environmental evaluation.

A man who owns and lives on an island comes to regard himself as the ultimate protector of the environment there, and he has no doubt that he could write a book about the peculiarities of that piece of land floating in the sea—a book that would be dead language to the uneducated visitor. On an island one deals constantly in practicalities; theory stays behind on the mainland. A few nights ago I read in the newspaper that salting Maine's highways was an economical snow removal practice but that it was proving to have some adverse environmental effects, including corrosion of automobiles and underground utility lines, damage to vegetation, and contamination of small streams and underground water supplies. This discovery strikes me as belated. I long ago learned that in winter I could not take my dog into town with me because the salt on the sidewalks was so caustic that it burned into her footpads and on the few occasions that I tried it I had to bring her back to the island quickly and soak her feet. A dog's feet are tough, but they aren't that tough, and it shouldn't require an environmental study to determine that if salt did that much damage to a dog's foot we should regard it with some skepticism. What I'm saying is that the good Lord put salt in the sea and that's all the salt I want around this island, and my advice to the state's environmental people is to forget salt and keep looking for something better.

Now that I've solved that problem for the environmental people, I would like to solicit their help in solving a worrisome one for me. A couple of years ago I had an all-glass dining room added to my house, and while it has brought me endless satisfaction and pleasure, it has created an environmental hazard which I never anticipated. Hardly a week goes by that I don't find a dead bird on the ground beside the dining room, a bird that failed to see the glass until it was too late to correct a navigational error. The environmental people will have to take my word when I say that I've brooded about this problem many an evening by the fire and although I'm an imaginative and resourceful man where most island problems are concerned, this one has me baffled. I even brought my neighbor, the lobsterman, over one afternoon to see what suggestions he could offer, and after accepting a beer and tramping around the outside of the room looking things over, he handed me the empty beer can and left. Walking down the path to the wharf, he said over his shoulder: "I told you not to build the damned thing out of glass but you wouldn't listen to me."

I didn't regard this as a helpful suggestion in any sense, and I hope the state environmental people will adopt a more positive attitude in the matter. I would like to write a dissenting opinion to the ruling that all people must like all birds, because I honestly can't bring myself to acknowledge any fondness whatever for blue jays, but this disaffection doesn't mean that I get any satisfaction at what's going on here now. Most of the casualties run to chickadees and sparrows, with an occasional robin or blue jay fatality, but once a heavy grackle collided with the wall with a thump so resounding that I heard it in the house. The grackle was only stunned, and was beating the leaves furiously with his wings when I reached him. He stopped struggling and glanced at me remorsefully when I picked him up and blew in his face. I sat him on a rock, where he swayed drunkenly for a few minutes before taking off in the direction of the mainland. I doubt that he's been back, but that's only an opinion.

Several possible solutions have occurred to me but they all possess drawbacks of one kind or another. Letting the glass stay dirty, so the birds can see it, is the most obvious course of action, but not to a Virgo who likes things to be neat. I've also discarded the notion of putting a diagonal strip of masking tape across the glass sheets; I don't want to give the impression that I'm momentarily expecting an armed invasion. Sometimes—when I've given the problem a lot of thought and no answers have swung within reach—I wonder if perhaps my neighbor isn't right. He wanders around with endless curiosity, sniffing the air and feeling the texture of things, and probably because he has a broader sense of natural history than most people, he is usually right. But if he isn't right, he lies to strengthen a weak position, and I find that unsettling. As I say, I've got a real problem here.

In Transit

A lone boatman held in the fearful grip of a heavy fog sees the enveloping shroud as a relentless enemy but from the shores of an island it is a whimsical thing that is more capricious than menacing. I studied fogs closely during the summer of 1986—a tantalizingly brief season that seemed to have arrived and departed the same week—because there was often nothing else to do. Fogs hovered over the island on a grand scale, often lingering for several days at a time, sometimes obscuring everything, other times opening up to reveal a lobsterboat working uneasily close to shore. Fogs and wind care nothing for each other, so foggy weather is invariably still weather with water dripping from the spruce trees as though a gentle rain were falling and with everything except life itself curiously suspended.

Only sounds come vibrantly alive in heavy fogs, sweeping across the water like something heavily amplified: the sound of automobile horns on the mainland, the raucous and shattering notes of a rock band coming from the radio of some lobsterboat, a fragment of laughter floating in the air, the lapping of water against the pilings of the wharf. But of all the sounds that fill my ears suddenly the most strident is the squawking of gulls, and for anyone eager to discover the mysteries of fog at first hand I suggest that there is something here worth kicking around a bit. In the first place, gulls cry constantly around boats, islands, rock ledges, and wherever they like to come gliding in, tilting their wings to apply the air brakes before settling down with a gentleness that Boeing has never been able to imitate. But on an island, the complaints of gulls are so constant as to be totally unnoticed; one grows accustomed to the sound and its persistence numbs the brain, as happens with the ticking of a clock or the sound of wind in the trees. One must deliberately make an adjustment in awareness to bring these sounds in, to fine-tune them back into existence. But on a foggy day, the squawking of gulls takes over center stage and fills the air with a dominance that commands attention. I must remind myself, when the noise becomes overpowering, that it is always there, that only the atmosphere has changed in a way that raises the sound level to a point that exceeds my normal tolerance setting. I know this yet I still grope around for a more scientific explanation. The truth seems too simple and I am looking for something more complicated.

Birds of all kinds, not just gulls, have recently entered my life and I am at a loss to account for this since I have never felt any friendship with birds in the highest and most intimate sense of the term. But this summer, if indeed there was such a thing, I noticed that very few birds paused on the Island and those that did show up didn't hang around long. I have always speared stale bread on low-hanging branches of trees, high enough to be out of the dog's reach, and noticed that it disappeared regularly, but aside from a few transient robins early in the season I've seen nothing but some quarrelsome grackles and I've fallen to wondering if birds have given this island a bad rating or whether birds find island life in general a little too dull for settling in on a permanent basis. I was heartened by the arrival of the robins and even brought out from town some supermarket bird food and spread it around, but after a few days they left, lured, I assume, by the promise of life in the fast lane on the mainland. The grackles fought over the rest of the supermarket grain, and discouraged by a lack of reciprocal response to my gesture of friendship, I have done nothing further to let birds know that I'm willing to meet them halfway if they decide to come over and settle down.

My record where birds are concerned is not spotless. A few years ago I wrote in this magazine a piece describing the blue jay as an ill-tempered and aggressive bird whose presence in the neighborhood brought me only uneasiness. Blue jays and I got off to a bad start some years ago when I was mugged by a blue jay in Central Park in New York; I was walking with my dog when the attack came, an attack that for its suddenness made Pearl Harbor look like an exchange of diplomatic notes. My skull was opened up by a dive-bomb assault, and above me I saw the enemy circling for another swoop. It's no wonder that two years ago when a pair of blue jays arrived and began scouting the island with residence in mind that I did not offer the hand of fellowship.

Nonetheless, I wish there were more birds around. The gulls and I get along splendidly; I throw old fruit and vegetables out on the rocks for them and in return they keep the rocks clean and well-policed. Our relationship is so even that often I forget about them entirely, except, of course, on foggy days when I am awakened early and don't get my shut-eye until late at night. The grackles are unsociable, and given to a great deal of quibbling and arguing among themselves, but they are about all I've got and I try to see them in their best light. What I'd really like are some robins and chickadees, the latter of which are the Maine state bird, who, for some reason or another, don't know that this island is part of Maine. I'd be willing to go back to the supermarket for some more bird food if the right birds showed up, but I wouldn't want them to come just to go on welfare. I'd use the supermarket grain to welcome them and to bridge them over the unsettling days of building new nests, and then I'd hope they would like it enough to stay. I did.

Air Bags for Birds

I think I must know what the French call a *homme a bonnes fortunes* because I know of no other way to explain the loyalty and the capacity to forgive which the readers of this column seem to possess. They grieve with me when I lose my dog, they correct me fondly—like a mother would a backward child—when I make a mistake, they gamely fight their way through rhetorical thickets to see what I'm trying to say on bad days when I shouldn't be writing at all, and they tolerate with bemused indifference my pronouncements of dazzling discoveries which they have known about all along. It is as though they have decided to join hands with me, for whatever reason, in some common despair and in a search for a gateway to something better.

A few months ago I set out on this page an account of a problem that had arisen on my island and my unsuccessful efforts to deal with it. The problem was that I had added on an all-glass dining room to my house, an annex that pleased me immensely but which possessed a somber side effect. Birds, it turns out, don't see the glass until they are too far along in flight to correct the error, and every week or so I have the unhappy task of tidying up after a head-on collision. So far, no glass has been broken, but a number of necks have been, and my guilt grows with each fatality. I explained the problem in my earlier article, and repeated what my neighbor, the lobsterman, had said after an inspection: "I told you not to build the damned thing out of glass but you wouldn't listen to me."

Things were shaky at best until the article appeared, and suddenly the sun came out and everything looked better. Reader after reader wrote in to say that I wasn't the first to face this problem—an announcement that I accepted with relish—and all of the letters contained suggestions for remedy. One man, it's true, offered only a reassuring verbal pat on the back along with the observation that "I think your neighbor is right," but that too helped to buttress sagging spirits. None of it was idle talk. "Take one or two pieces of bright red ribbon," suggested a fellow from Cape Elizabeth, "and hang them from the outside of the glass so the breeze sweeps them in motion. Let it fly." Obviously not too impressed with my ability to move outside the abstract world of writing, he obligingly enclosed a diagram. A lady from Easley, South Carolina, thought along similar lines. "My mother kept birds from roosting under her porch by using pie tins," she wrote, "but I reasoned that this would be an eyesore. Then the revelation struck me! Why not hang several metallic wind chimes around your dining room? The noise and the glittering from the wind chimes would cause the birds to reroute." In case I may be hesitant about asking advice from a woman, she added in a postscript: "My husband was pleased at this solution."

So it went. From Flemington, New Jersey, came the suggestion that I hang some lengths of fishnet outside the windows, and from St. Louis came a page from a catalog featuring a falcon silhouette decal to go on the glass. "I wonder if you or your guests will be comfortable dining in a room under the shadow of a soaring falcon or two," said a letter accompanying the catalog. "However, it may be an idea worth trying. The catalog says you can return the product for a full refund, although I confess I don't see how a used decal can be easily returned." A man from Cocoa Beach, Florida, thought that a solar film, such as those used on car windows, might darken the glass enough to make it visible to birds, while a man from Portland suggested that an old-fashioned rotating barber pole might do the job. ("Since you live on an island," he added hopefully, "you won't be bothered by people dropping in for a haircut.")

There were a number of variations of the streamer suggestion and quite a few improvisations on the decal theory, but my greatest gratitude must certainly go to Mrs. Cherie Mason, of Sunset, Maine, who bought and sent to me as a gift a handsome electrostatic vinyl owl, called "the proven bird deterrent," which is to go on the glass wall most directly in the flight pattern. Mrs. Mason concedes in her letter that the owl may not be 100 percent effective, "but it beats looking at aluminum foil streamers which we've also tried to no avail."

Acts of kindness, such as these, only make the hard job of the writer harder. It's much easier to criticize and scorn, to uncover rascality than to discover charity. The benevolence reflected here is all the more telling since it comes from many places and not just Maine, although I couldn't help but notice that there were no letters from New York City. This didn't surprise me because I lived in New York a number of years and I am convinced that New Yorkers don't care whether birds exist, either dead or alive, since they are far too preoccupied with the business of survival to notice anything so insignificant as Nature. Once, when I was working in Manhattan, I asked the chap in the office next to me, a native New Yorker, if he had seen the sunset the evening before. "No, I didn't," he replied, "but I heard about it. It went down somewhere over on the West Side, didn't it?"

A Lobster at Large

In every exclamation of appreciation for the tender clawmeat of a lobster lurks the guilt-ridden sense of how the lobster died, and this wincing thought takes me back to last year's highly publicized "Lobster Liberation." This occasion—for those who took their seats late—was a media circus which started out seriously enough when a pleasantly preposterous thing occurred in a New York restaurant where a small group of people were having lunch. Stricken by the sight of a crowded lobster tank, the patrons protested to the manager who agreed to dismantle the thing if he were given forty dollars for the remaining lobsters. The hat was passed, the money was paid, but the problem then arose as to how the lobsters could be returned to the cold water of Maine where they would survive. Well, as a far-sighted Greek chap named Euripides once observed, chance fights ever on the side of the determined, and in an afternoon devoted to what the sponsors considered a just and good cause, the rescue began to take shape. The $200 air fare of the lobsters from New York to

Portland (they flew coach) was easily raised, and an agreement was wrung from the Coast Guard at Portland to transport the lobsters fifteen miles out to sea on one of their regular training missions. All of this was considered fit to print in the *New York Times* which gave it two columns, the *Baltimore Sun* raised it to three, the *Portland Press Herald* stayed for three, and the *Wall Street Journal*, whose readers have a taste for the fine things of life, splashed it on the front page to show how far the soak-the-rich movement had progressed.

Once a good story starts there is no stopping it, and follow-ups appeared everywhere. One writer pointed out that lobsters have a long childhood and an awkward adolescence, which I didn't think contributed a great deal to the reservoir of knowledge on lobster behavior and character. Another explored the sex life of the lobster which starts out with flirtation and ends (haven't I heard this before?) with a pregnancy that lasts nine months. Some lobsters are right-handed and some are left-handed, I read in another story, and all are short-sighted. They like to walk (as opposed to flying, I presume), and in this respect I want you to know I see eye to eye with the lobster. A healthy lobster with a curiosity to see the world will amble over 100 miles a year, a lady writer asserted, although she neglected to say where she got this information. I suspect it came from an exit poll which seems to be the source of most information these days. Another news story revealed that the communications of lobsters "are direct and sophisticated" and when a male feels amorous he doesn't fool around but gets straight to the point. Frankly, I think this is carrying the new flair for investigative journalism a bit far, and I stopped reading the follow-up stories at that point. I felt we were getting close to some *National Inquirer* stuff.

Let's go back a little because I think I detect some basic mismanagement here. No one, or no one that I know of, has ever come up with a means of cooking lobsters without causing them to experience a very painful death, usually one resulting from being thrown alive into boiling water. An organization called CEASE (Citizens to End Animal Suffering and Exploitation) has examined the common substitutes for boiling—from tail-stroking to hypnosis to severing the brain from the spinal cord—and has reported it is very unlikely that any of the 20 million lobsters eaten every year in the United States die painlessly. Me, I accept that. I boiled my last lobster six years ago when I decided I didn't ever again want to hear that frantic sound of the lobsters trying to claw their way up the sides of the pot after the top was put on. Nonetheless, I hear a voice I consistently recognize as my own ordering lobster rolls in restaurants, which puts me in the same class as the caring lady who warms the water before she drowns the kittens. I am guilty of the worst kind of hypocrisy, and I wish there were some way out of this because only a cretin would deny that lobster is a very tasty dish. The misman-agement to which I referred in the early lines of this paragraph lies in the fact that the State of Maine provides lobstermen with all kinds of advice and help in growing lobsters but has done no research in how to kill them. In other words, Batteries Not Included.

It is hard to say what precisely is taking place these days where animal cruelty is concerned. There seems to be a sickening realization on the part of the civilized world that we have been treating our animals shamelessly and that Smokey Bear, for example, is born with certain rights even if they are not defined in law books as are yours and mine. There seems to be some improvement where animal cruelty is concerned, such as the Lobster Liberation, but the improvement is suspect because we can't trust the underpinning. A person who would not kill a horse would kill an ant, as though size is the determining factor in weighing the morality of a killing. I doubt that it is, or rather I doubt that it should be. And as for the religious, did the Sixth Commandment apply only to humans when it said thou shalt not kill because I don't think Moses was that explicit? The unanswered question, of course, is where do we draw the line of compassion? To the lobster this is the ultimate and unbearable question, and I suspect it would like each of us to face the answer before we melt the butter.

Boxers

It's true, there's no doubt about it; what's one man's meat is another man's undoing. I could depose endlessly here about the differences between Margaret, my boxer, and me, especially our attitudes towards what is known as the Key of Life. The normal monotony of life fills her with good cheer; what she did yesterday and the day before are ideal for repeating today. When we take our daily walk along a path well worn by these outings, a sort of inaudible singing rings in my ears. She is as pleased with the familiar as I am when we start out in a new direction looking for novelty. Man's fascination for the unknown, of course, has always gotten him in trouble, and the cards are stacked in Margaret's favor so far as peace of mind is concerned. She knows this in the curious way that animals accommodate certainties that man long ago forgot if indeed he ever knew them. Margaret has the edge right there, and she knows it. I've shared my life with a lot of boxers, and the one characteristic common to them all is stubbornness; in their minds there is a right and wrong way to do everything and the boxer way is the wisest, the most proven, the least threatening, and, when the chips are down, the most pleasant.

There is no question that Margaret is a matriarch and a stern one at that, and she possesses all of the arrogance of her own rightness. Sometimes that amuses me, as when her jaw sets and she locks eyes with me, well aware that I will blink first. If Margaret were human, I think she would function at her highest skill in Customer Service. "I'm sorry," I can hear her say, "the final date for the return of this merchandise was last Tuesday."

But the Devil often makes the best music, and I'm a sucker for innovation and temptation. I like to crowd my luck. This leads to frequent stalemates, which when all is said and done are nothing more than differences of opinion. Didn't Tolstoy proclaim Shakespeare's *King Lear* to be "beneath serious criticism?" Margaret thinks my opinions are largely irrational and I think hers are gnostic. Sometimes I wonder how this struggle for the upper hand started, how I fell into this way of life. The one thing I am sure of is that it will go on indefinitely. I will want to take the new path through the woods and she—possessing all of the calmness of rectitude—will tug me gently down the old trail. I sometimes think there has sprung up a deep understanding between us and nothing will break the spell under which we are now held. If she followed me blindly, I would feel strangely lost. When I follow her she glances up at me and I see all of springtime in her eyes. I do what I can do, but I'm only human.

Grief

Grief is better left to poets to describe; wingless writers of prose find it too difficult. Despite its searing pain, grief is without substance, an affliction of the spirit and soul but not the body. I do not need to look at all the crumpled pieces of paper on the floor around me now to realize how indescribable grief can be; the heart is mute and one suffers in solitude. I have lost my dog, an unusually sensitive little boxer who has stood at my side for ten years fully convinced that I could make lightning flash and thunder roar and that I could cure her of any sickness. But in the end I let her down where a brain tumor was concerned, and so did the doctors at the University of Pennsylvania where I took her in final desperation. I have just driven back from Philadelphia alone, making the long journey back to Maine as quickly as possible so that I might confront my grief at the place where we spent the most time together—at the island, where of all the places we have lived we both felt the most at home.

There is a painful ritual required of those who have suffered a loss and the sooner this is enacted the better. I knew I must walk around this island alone—without her—and visit the scenes of comic experiences and happier days, and not have these ambush me later when I did not expect it. I have now done this as carefully as I could, leaving only a place that was special for her and which I haven't yet summoned courage to face.

Dogs differ, and so do people, and the relationship one can have with a dog depends upon many things but, I think, mainly upon the kind of heart and mind the human possesses. This dog joined me at a strange and irresolute period in my life, when I had left the magazine world of New York and taken a small cottage deep in a Maine forest to live for a winter while I wrote a book. During that first winter we were never away from each other; we walked the fields together, we rode to the village together for the mail and groceries, we did evening chores together, and she slept at the foot of my bed at night. A closeness was forged that winter that pleased us both; we understood each other and in that understanding were the seeds of contentment.

We had disagreements, of course, and they were always over the same issue and that was whether or not I had the right to leave her, even for a short time. A writer has to travel, and although I always left her in the care of someone who loved her, she always greeted my return with all the symptoms of hurt betrayal. First, of course, was the great rush of affection and delight at seeing me, then she would remember what an unforgivable thing I had done and the chill would set in. But by morning the deep freeze would have thawed, and she was herself again. She liked other dogs, but she liked them in their place; I was the sun around which her world turned.

In her more mature years she began to develop traits that were palpably matriarchal. Secure in the knowledge of my devotion to her, she couldn't resist the temptation to take over some of the authority which I haphazardly left lying around. She would snort noisily when she wanted something—her evening meal, for example, or for someone to move over who may have taken a seat at the end of the couch which she considered hers—and her persistence was a startling thing to strangers. I had grown used to it and, in fact, was amused by it; others shook their heads in disbelief that a dog could be so pointedly outspoken. I never thought of her as being spoiled, although that is certainly another way of putting it. Nonetheless, I couldn't complain since she spoiled me in many ways. When I was depressed, she would amuse me with antics and games she had devised for those times, and when I was restless she would coax me out for a walk or a boat ride, and when I was tired, she would crawl up beside me and place her head in my lap and let me know bedtime was not far off. In retrospect, I feel she knew me much better than I knew her. I was often startled at her reactions and understanding, but she was never surprised at anything I did, and I came to feel I was often totally unpredictable.

Last night I got up for a drink of water, and when I walked by the sofa in the dark I unconsciously felt around for the afghan spread which I usually threw around her to ward off the chill of early morning. Boxers have short hair and they are susceptible to cold. There was a stab of pain when I realized there was no brown form at her end of the sofa, that it had departed that sofa and my life forever. Beside me now, as I write this, is the couch in my study where she joined me each morning when I came to write. After sleeping a while, she would jump down, stretch, and wander out to lie on the bayberry leaves in the sun. There is a small place where the coiled weight of her body caused a slight indentation in the cushion, and I should have smoothed it out before this. I will tomorrow. William James said, "Acceptance of what has happened is the first step in overcoming the consequences of a misfortune." So, I will do it tomorrow for certain.

Interregnum

I find it difficult to believe that there are a lot of people—perhaps even most people—to whom an animal is some inanimate thing like a plant or a shrub or a tree, and certainly not something that can feel pain, much less despair, loneliness, fear or heartache. I am well aware of the risks in stepping across the sophistication line that separates humans from animals because there are dangerous pitfalls in this area for writers; there is always the danger of slipping on the treacherous slope of coyness and cuteness in describing animal behavior. Many good writers come to grief here; readers will listen to facts but they tend to nod off when the going gets slushy.

Nevertheless, it is my belief that animals have individuality of their own—most certainly dogs possess what we call a specific personality— and that they respond to certain social situations according to their emotional outlook and in the way they feel they can best get across to humans their idea of what's right or wrong with the setup. Often humans have a sense of something being quite wrong when in the dog's view it is the beginning of something being right. I'm going to turn the volume up a little here because I want to make a point. The little boxer who shared my life on this island for eight years concluded very early in life that her best interests were served by being with me every minute of the day and night, and when I left her anxiety showed on her face. Sometimes the anxiety was so intense, and her unhappiness so plainly asserted, that I would make a last minute change of plans and take her with me. This, of course, suggests insecurity on my part; understanding the situation in a way she could not, I was still willing to alter plans to buy my way out of guilt. Thus we suffered through these separations together; she in her way and I in mine.

The big difference in our outlook was that I knew I was coming back to her, but she had no guarantees of this that she could accept; for me to leave was for me to empty her life and she did not possess, as humans do, the means of concealing her feelings. But in honesty must I not confess that this manifestation of her dependence on me was probably why I had a dog in the first place? Wasn't there something in me that required tl ˟ reassurance of her need? I guess we were meant for each other, my reactions carefully controlled, hers honestly reflecting the dark fear that resided in her soul.

I have gotten a little deeper into this topic than I intended to; actually I meant only to kick around a bit the subject of man's relationship with a dog because for some time now I have felt a new dog coming on. It's been almost a year since I lost the little boxer and I suppose I have held off trying to replace her, much as a widower feels a decent period of mourning should pass before remarrying. Bringing a new dog on the island is not going to be easy for either of us; my attachment for the boxer was extraordinary and it will not be easily replaced. The new dog will have to contend with that, which is an unfair burden for a puppy to bear. Despite her innocence, she will be compared with her predecessor, weighed constantly on scales she has no reason to trust, and will have to fight constantly to prove her invincibility over an invisible foe. She is not to be envied but neither am I. The first time she curls up beside me on the couch in my study for an afternoon nap will be a melancholy reminder of all the siestas the boxer and I enjoyed there. What I should feel as a precious new relationship will most likely be a sorrowful retrospection of an old one.

I first became interested in boxers many years ago when I read a long article by Louis Bromfield, the novelist, on a family of boxers he had raised on Malabar Farm, the famous nature conservancy experiment in Ohio. The boxers came to control his life, a rather far-fetched notion I thought when I read it but which I came to understand after I had acquired one. Each evening at sundown, Bromfield drove in a jeep to the crest of a hill to watch the sun go down, and invariably he took the boxers with him. His favorite, Prince, sat on the bucket seat beside him, with the others occupying the rear. After a period of silence on the hilltop, he drove back to the farmhouse in the gathering twilight. It was the part of the day that Bromfield cared about the most, a ritual of serenity and comfort, and one that neither weather nor guests nor urgency of business could cause him to forego.

On the day that Prince passed away, Bromfield drove to the hilltop with the seat beside him vacant. It was a painful occasion, but he felt that the crest of the hill was the proper place to confront his grief, that this is what Prince would have wanted. And then a strange thing happened. One of the puppies in the rear of the jeep leaped over the seat and settled himself in Prince's place, looking up at Bromfield with pleading eyes. For a moment the author hesitated, then placed his hand on the puppy's head. In that moment they both knew that the continuity of life had been asserted, that nature held the upper hand and that the consequences of misfortune are washed away when a proper chord is touched.

I am going to try to remember that story when the boat arrives at the island with the new boxer puppy.

First Night, New Dog

There is nothing half-hearted in the nature of those people who like dogs; there is a persistence there that never seems to be diminished by disaster or grief. I write the above remarks not as one who takes the stand of watchful neutrality, but as one who has always found the companionship of a dog a profoundly shaking experience. For the past few weeks I have been the owner—what a misleading description of a relationship with an animal possessed of such a free spirit!—of a small brindle boxer, and already she has taught me a great deal, although the manuals insist that it is I who should be teaching her. She has taught me to come when she barks at the other end of the island and I'm not sure whether she is in trouble or not, she has taught me to fetch things when I find the mate to a pair of shoes lying in the path in the forest, and she has taught me to be deeply suspicious of people who don't like a nice, warm puppy creeping into bed with them during those early hours of the morning when the cold settles in. Intuitively, I've always known that without a dog I am voluntarily cutting myself off from a love affair that will bring me an enormous amount of pleasure, as well as some anxiety, pain and grief. But grief resides in all relationships, human and animal, and the man who forgoes the pleasures of life because he is haunted by fear of grief is a man who has given up riding his luck and now is only taking up room on this planet.

It is a sunny autumn day as I am writing this, and my new boxer has just wandered away from my workroom on one of those jaunty little exploratory rambles that she seems to find endlessly interesting. Through the window I last saw her heading down toward the south end of the island, and I could tell by her gait that she was on the trail of something extremely important; she was in a half-trot, as though pressed for time. I could also see that she was preoccupied since she passed without hesitation the sole of a sneaker that had washed up on shore, one of those *objets du jour* that when not on some burning mission she would find irresistible.

A sane man would realize that this dog is an independent-minded individual and should be trained before she gets the upper hand, but I find her greatly amusing and as long as I laugh at her I am giving her enough rope to hang me with. Although less than a year old and still a puppy, she has an exaggerated sense of pride and dignity and insists on pretending that every blunder or stumble is actually a part of an overall plan that only she possesses the key to. Yesterday, while manipulating a stick, she managed to hit herself smartly over the head with it, and when I began to snicker she glared at me patronizingly as though regretful that I was not able to see down the road far enough to understand the whole picture. Whacking herself on the head, she wanted me to believe, was only a small fragment of an otherwise impressive mosaic.

Only last year I lost an extraordinary dog to whom I was greatly attached, and I was very hesitant about opening up my heart to another one and, indeed, not at all sure that I could. I think I did right in making certain that the new dog was as different from the old one as possible; I knew the foolhardiness of trying to bring to life the old dog in the body of another. The new puppy has a different manner, a different outlook on life, a completely different personality, and I am discovering this with relief. There was a touching moment when she entered my workroom for the first time and jumped up on the sofa where the old dog spent many hours, but she looked at me so appealingly that I could only pat her head and tell her to lie down. Dogs manage to work things out in a far more straightforward way than humans are capable of doing.

I think dogs know some important truths, and I suspect that any dog taken home with me is a dog that has hit the jackpot, that here is a man who will be an unendingly soft touch. The night that I brought this puppy home from the kennel, she waited on the living room sofa just long enough for me to turn out the lights and get settled in my own bed before she moved. There were a few moist licks around the neck, a few sniffs, and she curled up beside me and fell immediately into a sound sleep. For the first time in her short life she was away from her father and her mother and sisters and living in a strange house on an alien island, yet she put enough trust in this strange creature lying beside her to feel secure. Several times during the night I reached out and patted her, and in her sleepy way she snuggled closer, stretched and breathed deeply. I had enough sense to know that a chain was being forged that night, and I suspect she knew it before I did.

A Boxer's Favorite Breed

I can't imagine a dog living alone, as some humans choose to. The dogs that I have had, which have been mostly boxers, would last about twenty-minutes without companionship and while they would be content to play with dogs for a while, it is human companionship that they really want and to which they think they are entitled. My present dog, an extremely sociable little female, for the sake of congeniality will join me on the bed the moment I decide to take a nap, although up until that moment she had been quite content to sleep on the rug. And once settled on the bed she begins a series of artful maneuvers to reduce the space between us; first, there is the stretching, then nothing in particular, then some vague wriggling, all of which are executed to narrow the physical gap. If I move away, she takes up the slack without a second's delay; I have learned from experience I have nothing to gain by advancing toward the edge of the bed. In that direction lies only disaster. There have been times when, sufficiently motivated, I have gotten up and walked around the bed and entered it from the unoccupied side, but this is just buying time and very little time at that. She brightens a bit, her interest revived by changing circumstances, and then the inexorable inching towards me resumes. My only victory comes when I can drop off to sleep quickly.

As nearly as I can tell, this dog faces life with a single purpose in mind and that is to spend every minute, night and day, in my presence. She knows in her heart that there will be obstacles to this plan, but her intentions are clear and I must admit that I admire the cheerful manner in which she approaches these barriers. Aware that humans permit their lives to be cluttered beyond all reason, she goes her way in sympathy and understanding but obstinately refusing to be personally involved in what she knows to be nonsense. In her opinion, the sensible things in life are a nice long walk along hedgerow where an occasional rabbit can be flushed out for chasing, a cool drink of water from a brook that meanders through a meadow, plenty of shuteye on a rainy day, and a hearty dinner served at a reasonably early hour, with no stinting on the table scraps especially whatever gravy remains on the plates. If she could only teach humans to put these things first, she is convinced, everything would get back on the right track in a hurry.

It may be boxers are bossier than most dogs, and it is my personal belief that they are. They have that German sense of a burning mission to perform, a destiny to fulfill. A boxer doesn't walk away from an argument; it sticks around until it gets its way whether by charm, by deviousness, or by sheer endurance. Too often I've folded my hand and given in to my boxers simply because I didn't possess the patience to go the full route, and they did. My present dog is strong on personality; she radiates good cheer and lots of laughs but when the chips are down she is as immovable as if she were a cast-iron statue. There is a right and a wrong way to do things and it's useless to ask her to take the shortcut.

My last boxer succumbed to a brain tumor, and even in her final days when she was in considerable pain and often badly confused she carried herself with enormous dignity as she did the things she thought were expected of her and which she considered her responsibility. The last time I saw her she was walking down a hall in the University of Pennsylvania Small Animal Hospital on her way to another world, but she held her head high and she did not look back. More than any animal I have ever known, she demonstrated that nobility could be found as much outside the human race as within it.

As a puppy she lived with me during my last few months as a resident of New York City, and it was here that we got to know each other. I had decided to leave Manhattan and move to an island in Maine, and I thought I would be ahead of the game a little if I got the dog several months before departure so we would have time to work out our differences before we settled down permanently in the new place. It became clear quite early in our relationship that whatever changes were required in order for us to make a go of it were alterations in outlook and behavior on my part, not hers. Moreover, it spelled out for me, there wasn't going to be time for me to turn around in; I had to shape up fast.

One day we were coming out of the West Seventy-Second Street entrance to Central Park when a middle-aged lady wearing dark glasses, a suede jacket, and a gray flannel skirt stopped us. "May I see your dog a moment?" she asked. We paused and the lady bent to examine the dog critically. "When I lived in California a number of years ago my husband and I had boxers," she said. "I got to know them very well." She straightened up. "This is a very fine dog," she said. I introduced myself and said that I lived in the apartment on the corner. "My name is Lauren Bacall," the lady said, "and I live there." She pointed at the Dakota across the street. She patted the dog lightly on the head and started across the park. Standing there in the afternoon sunlight, I fell to wondering who in that family had held the upper hand. Those who knew Humphrey Bogart said he could be an inflexible and difficult man, but my money is on the boxers.

Constant Excitement

One heavily overcast day last summer, a day of suspicious warmth and moist air from the east, I put on a slicker and got in the rowboat and started toward the tip of land that forms one of the protecting arms of the cove. The dog eyed the foul-weather gear with foreboding; she has no taste for riding in a wet boat. A voyage of discovery breeds its own forms of evil, she reasons, and one of these is to sit in the bow of a boat with rain beating into her face. It was not yet raining, but if rain was not imminent, the idea of rain had at least entered the realm of the conceivable. Weighing the prospect of our discovering something exciting in the deep forest against the prospect of coming home wet, she threw caution to the wind and jumped into the boat as I loosened the line. City dogs grow up in ignorance, like wild trees that have not been pruned, but country dogs— and especially those living on an island—possess a deepened consciousness and a widened curiosity; they are instructed by the finest teacher in the world—the elements.

Since the tide was ebbing, I abandoned the boat at the water's edge and we struck out into the forest. It was a primeval setting. The forest was thick and dark, the floor was a tangle of brush and rotting limbs, there were no discernible paths, and even the dog had to pick her way carefully. It struck me suddenly that what I was seeing was exactly what I would have seen five thousand years ago, or even fifty thousand years ago. There were no buildings or even vestiges of any, there were no overhead wires, no billboards, no antennae, no discarded automobile tires, no Kentucky Fried Chicken containers, nor any of the other manifestations of civilization. So far as the forest was concerned, I could easily have been a man of the late Pleistocene age carrying a paleolithic tool instead of a Swiss army knife, and accompanied by a brute that had taken to sleeping on the floor of my cave. The only incongruities, the only things inharmonious with time, were the clothing and objects on my person, the fillings in my teeth, and the collar on the neck of the dog. It was an eerie feeling but not an unpleasant one. I'm not at all sure that the period in which I live represents the apex of civilization; in fact, I suspect that it isn't. There is substantial evidence pointing to the likelihood that the fifth century B.C.—the Age of Pericles—far surpassed the twentieth century in greatness. It possessed no television or zip codes, but it offered the world the greatest architects (could the Parthenon be built with union labor today?), the greatest philosophers, the greatest mathematicians, the greatest dramatists, the greatest historians, and for all we know the greatest artists this planet has ever known. Moreover, the Periclean Period in Greece celebrated life, not death. (The Egyptians left tombs; the Greeks left theaters.)

Don't tell me, I know I've wandered off the path, but this is what can happen when you walk with a dog under sullen skies in a deep Maine forest and you let both the dog and your mind off the leash. An immense oak tree, scarred by lightning, suddenly blocks my way, and I realize that it was already many years away from an acorn when two men met at Appomattox to solve one of the hundreds—thousands?—of disagreements that human beings are willing to fight over and die in great numbers to settle. There are rustlings in the fallen leaves everywhere as squirrels and chipmunks and other forest animals scamper away from these two strange creatures that are noisily invading their world, a world that has its own dangers since we are all—every one of us—prey, sharing the common destiny of becoming links in the food chain if only to worms. But now the dog is vibrantly alive and so am I and we push on through the matted undergrowth. The dog hears something that my ears are incapable of picking up, and she darts quickly out of sight, leaping high over logs and ignoring commands to return. I am afraid she will tangle with a porcupine and return with a faceful of quills, but she doesn't. In a minute I come upon her, staring balefully up at a tree on a limb of which sits a red squirrel, its tail twitching triumphantly. The squirrel knows the dog cannot climb the tree and the dog knows it, but she isn't happy with the knowledge at all. She wants to wait a while—maybe the tree will fall over—but I go on without her, and soon she catches up. Welcome to the world of reality, a world where birds fly, squirrels climb trees, and dogs stay on the ground.

An hour or so later, I could see a clearing ahead and we emerged from the forest to the rocky coast of the sea. A fog was drifting in from the ocean; already Ragged Island had been swallowed up. We walked back to the boat skirting the water's edge. Stranded on the sand twenty feet from the sea, the boat had to be tugged to where it would float again.

It had begun to rain, very gently, and I bent over the oars. The walk had reinforced my belief in the majesty of nature and the possibilities of life, a life full of purpose and wonder, but I could only speculate on what it had meant to the dog, other than a pleasant romp in the woods. Life to her was a constant excitement. The rain became steadier and I rowed faster, back to the twentieth century. But if there is a hopeful ring in the air, and at times there seems to be, it lies in the lessons that can be learned in that forest, not in nuclear fission or "Miami Vice" or in subdivisions called Formica Oaks.

I Know All of Her Tricks

A dog enlarges or diminishes a man's personality, a statement that will be hotly refuted by many dog owners but I ask you to take my word for it. Moreover—and this is really throwing caution to the wind—the kind of dog that a man possesses says something about the man's ambition and his ultimate destination. I won't go into specific breeds because I know what's prudent and what's downright adventurous, but I will wander around this subject a bit because if there is one thing that I know a lot about it is a dog. Human beings are too complicated; depending upon prevailing circumstances the same person can be mean or generous, trustworthy or dishonest, grumpy or cheerful, active or passive, forthright or devious. But the dog is constant, and that's why there are so many of them around. One has to have something steady to grasp, even if it serves only as a point of orientation in an insecure and untidy world.

My neighbor, the lobsterman, takes a sort of perverse pleasure in his dog's almost total lack of intelligence. Intellectually, the dog is only slightly above a plant, and the day never goes by that my neighbor doesn't boast about the dog's dumbness. A few days ago he told me the dog jumped off his boat, but once in the water couldn't make up its mind whether to swim to shore or swim back to the boat.

"What happened?" I asked, because the lobsterman had turned away as though that was the end of the story.

"He damned near drowned," the lobsterman said cheerfully. "I had to turn the boat around and pick him up. Should have left him there."

The last comment, of course, was thrown in just to blur the facts. He and his dog are inseparable, joined by an emotional tie as durable as anchor chain. The dog is dumb all right, but there is a steadfastness in its dumbness that can always be counted on, and this is reassuring to my friend. If the dog did something sensible, it would be an act of vandalism and, I think, the lobsterman would find it unsettling.

There is an antic quality to Margaret, my boxer, that delights me, largely because she thinks she is constantly outsmarting me, which isn't true. (Don't look at me like that.) I know all of her tricks, some of which are peculiarly her own and some of which are characteristic of the boxer breed. Boxers are all bossy, especially the females, and while they are often wrong about things they are never in doubt. I have had four boxers and no doubt has ever resided in the minds of any of them that they were far more capable of making the big decisions in life than I am. Furthermore, they have a determination that would make Margaret Thatcher look indecisive and faltering. Struggling with my boxer over who has the upper hand on this island takes a lot out of both of us, yet this resolute and unyielding characteristic of hers is one of the constants that I find reassuring, just as the lobsterman finds a sort of stability in his dog's witlessness.

Dogs are smarter than most people think, and the fact that they have gotten where they are pretty much bears this out. Horses sleep in stables, pigs inhabit pens, chickens roost in henhouses, and Margaret sleeps at the foot of my bed, often with an afghan thrown over her. A few days ago I saw that we had run out of dog food, so I whipped up a cheese omelette for her. I wanted that omelette myself. Thousands of years ago when humans inhabited caves, dogs took a look at those cheerful fires and sniffed the odor of roast venison, and came to the conclusion that mankind was going somewhere and this was the group to throw in with. No other animal had the sense to look down the road that far.

Margaret's foremost anxiety is to be separated from me at any time and while I tell myself this is a demonstration of her love, it really isn't. In her heart she is convinced that I may not be able to hack it on my own and, until that is proven to her, the safe thing is for her to always accompany me. When I leave her in the car for a short period while I go to the mall to shop, I always come back to see her seated at the wheel and gazing anxiously through the windshield. She has given me a certain length of time to complete some absurd human errand and if I'm not back by then, she intends to come looking for me.

Last weekend I went to Washington—I wanted to see the Lincoln Memorial once more before the Japanese bought it—and when I returned I was given the usual deep-freeze by Margaret, who, as is customary, wanted me to taste the full flavor of her discontent at what she considered a major betrayal. A child, in the rush of pleasure at a reunion, would have welcomed me back, but not Margaret. Anyone strolling down the highway of life with a boxer will find the road straight and narrow, and woe to him or her who wishes to wander off to examine some miracle that has taken place in the forest or who wants to stand alone on a rock and smell the northeast wind in the summertime.

Margaret wears the mantle of the matriarch and the lobsterman's dog wears a dunce's cap but, as I said at the opening of this piece, that says more about the owners than it does about the dogs. Right?

Let It Go

I held the copy of the book in my hand a long time recently trying to decide whether I would keep it or throw it away, knowing that a man who throws books away is in for trouble. The title of this book was *Why Franklin D. Roosevelt Can Never Be Elected President,* the author of the book was Watson Littlejohn, and it was published in 1931. Moreover, it was in mint condition. I am mentioning this latter fact because I think you can foresee my decision and I am looking about for all the support I can discover to buttress a very difficult choice. While Mr. Littlejohn's opinion on political matters may not be eagerly sought out these days, assuming that he is still alive and has kept his hand in the forecasting game, the fact is I don't recall having ever read the book and it goes against my articles of faith to toss out an unread book merely because of—let's face it fairly—an unfortunate title. I am not trying to hang the ill-fitting robes of justice and morality around my own shoulders; it's just that I have a hard time coming to grips with the trashing of a book merely because its appeal cannot be described as universal. The circumstance that I have written several such books myself creates a thicket that I don't care to enter at this time.

There are always tough, practical details in discarding possessions (Where will I put them? What will replace them? Will their loss cause me unhappiness?) but the perilous stage of the whole process comes early in the game for me when one has to say something must go or something must stay. Here is where I falter and stumble; those in my family who have an admiration for accelerated obsolescence are given the edge right there. While I'm trying to weigh values in a sensible way, the object goes in the wheelbarrow to be carted to the dock.

I think it's only accidental that one makes the proper decision about discarding something (stop me if I'm wrong about this) since there is no certain way to foretell that some future use may or may not develop. Samuel Goldwyn, whose way with words was often a strange compound of wisdom and absurdity, once warned: "Do not forecast—especially about the future." Me, I string along with Goldwyn. Look what happened to Mr. Littlejohn.

The Attic Fights Back

There comes a time in a man's life when memories are burdensome, a thought that stole into my consciousness a few days ago when I stopped at a roadside flea market looking for a five-gallon water jug in which I can transport drinking water to the island. I have a water jug, as I write this, but a fleeting glance at history reminds me that I break one on an average of every two years, and that they are becoming scarcer and more expensive as time goes by. I have always found the stale smell of "collectibles"—the new word for trash—slightly depressing, but the flea market in which I paused recently stirred up some memories that were, to say the least, unsettling.

The first object that caught my eye was a brass spittoon in such excellent condition that I was immediately transported in memory back to a courthouse in Virginia where, as a newspaper reporter, I spent a large part of every day listening to witnesses under oath lie about what they had seen or hadn't seen. The circuit court judge, a stout, white-haired gentleman whose jurisprudential dignity did not foreclose for him the pleasure of chewing tobacco as he listened to the interminable arguments going on in his courtroom, would regularly lob a discharge at the spittoon and would just as regularly miss it. The spittoon rested on a circular rubber mat, and the judge's trajectory either fell short of the mark or else described such a spirited arc that it barely hit the mat on the far side. Often I've seen a witness pause in testimony, as the eyes of the entire courtroom followed what appeared to be a promising shot, only to see everyone sink back in unspoken disappointment when the target remained unsullied. One day, during a break in the murder trial, I asked the judge if he actually tried to miss the spittoon or whether his aim were actually faulty. He looked at me gravely for a moment. "You're getting very close to contempt of court, son," he said, not unkindly. I let the matter drop.

Moving along through the flea market, I passed over a straight razor with a discolored ivory handle, a "Win-With-Wilkie" button, a four-color postcard depicting floodwaters on the Monongahela River, and paused to examine a copy of *Confidential* Magazine containing an article on "The Wife That Clark Gable Forgot." The magazines, it turned out, were my undoing; before I knew it I had purchased *Motion Picture* Magazine for June, 1931 ("Hollywood's Most Exciting New Personality—William Powell"), a 1947 copy of *Life* with Warlord of Mazelaine, a boxer who had won at Westminster, on the cover, and a copy of *Liberty* featuring the life story of Tris Speaker. To show his appreciation for a spender, the proprietor threw in a "Capehart for Senator" button.

Copper aspic molds, usually in the shape of a fish, slow down a fast-moving flea market, in my opinion, and I've often wondered if anybody has actually used one. They are found, in most flea markets, on the same table with the clear pink wine glasses and the matching boudoir lamps with scalloped shades. I can pass these at a full trot, but I stop short at the sheet-music rack. "Put Your Arms Around Me Honey," from the motion picture *Coney Island,* starring Betty Grable, George Montgomery, and Cesar Romero, is a hard one to pass up, while "You Brought A New Kind of Love to Me," from the Paramount picture *The Big Pond,* starring Maurice Chevalier and Claudette Colbert, brought me to a full stop. Needless to say, both had ukelele arrangements. I had nothing against "Deep Night" (words by Rudy Vallee, music by Charlie Henderson); it's only that two pieces of sheet music seemed enough, especially since I don't own a piano.

The enchantment—if that's not too strong a word to describe one's interest in a display of this kind— lies in the richness of the memories brought to mind. When I came to the movie posters I anticipated no problem but when I saw a stirring technicolor tableau advertising Cecil B. DeMille's *Union Pacific* (a Paramount presentation with Barbara Stanwyck and Joel McCrea, also featuring Akim Tamiroff and Brian Donlevy,) I knew I was in trouble and that I would be late getting home. How could anyone in his right mind pass up a poster of Jane Wyman and Rock Hudson in *All That Heaven Allows,* with Conrad Nagel? For all my fine talk about sales resistance, I was no match for those posters of movies that in my youth I had not seen once, but four or five times.

I stood for a long time in front of the Quick Comfort refrigerator. It's strange how an object of this kind can cause one to flounder in a swamp of nostalgia. My childhood home had had a Quick Comfort, and it had been my job to empty that drip pan every morning and each night. I knew exactly the sound that the hinged door at the the bottom of the refrigerator would make after I dropped it, a sound that I hadn't heard for over half a century. And when I lifted the top door to the chamber where the ice was placed, I smelled again the musty odor of ice melting in wet newspaper. I didn't open the food compartment; I didn't have to. I knew where the butter went, the iced tea, the cold string beans left over from dinner.

I heard a voice asking me if I wanted to make an offer for the Quick Comfort, and I came back to reality with a rush. "No," I said, "I guess I don't." I wanted to ask if the iceman still came around every day with a fifty-pound block in his tongs, but I knew the answer to that.

Impulsive Decisions

Something that has been unchanged since childhood is the whisper of adventure that sounds in the ear when I prepare for a journey of some kind, and although my work has led me into some odd and forgotten corners of the world, this *frisson* of travel is never so strongly felt as when I prepare to return to Maine to reopen my island home after I have been away for some time. It came to me quite unexpectedly a few weeks ago when I was on a small island in the Andaman Sea just off the coast of Thailand. I was in a street market, jostled by an endless parade of Thais, Malaysians, Chinese, and Burmese, when my eye picked out a piece of material on a stall that I knew instantly I wanted as a cover for a table that I set up on my Maine sundeck for lunch when the weather is right. A recollection of Maine rushed back to me, a recollection that was as refreshing as a summer shower, not because the Maine island is so great but probably because it is so small. A man's world shouldn't be too big; it should be a size that fits loosely and comfortably, or as Abraham Lincoln said when a woman spoke critically of his long legs, "A man's legs should be long enough to reach the ground."

During the winter when I am often away from Maine, my plans for home improvements frequently never get out of the drawing-board stage because one thought leads to another and the first thing you know I am being led down the primrose path by the greatest seducer of them all—thoughts of home. A new side porch being planned will require the replacement of the big rhododendron bush, and I get out the photograph album to see if the space will accommodate both, and if it is not that photograph that causes my eyes to glaze over it is the one on the next page or even the next. I am a hopeless addict where a photo album is concerned. One photograph and I am a drunkard returning to the bottle; I must see them all, and the delicious trance lasts through the final page when I close up the album and float away, completely lost in a drama that has no characters at all, only a stage setting and a well-worn one at that.

Right now I am preparing for my return to Maine and I could—if it were necessary—pack and be on the interstate within two hours, with the dog in the back seat, but I'm too smart for that. Yes, entirely too smart. Life doesn't pass out too many pleasures like this, and I intend to make the most of it. This afternoon, for example, I will go to the liquor store to pick up a few empty cartons for packing that Thai fabric that's going on the lunch table, as well as the rug I bought in Mexico, and the peck of Vidalia onions which I found irresistible in Georgia. People who have never tasted a Vidalia onion have my deepest sympathy; alone among the onions of the world it offers the admirer of fine onions everything one's heart could yearn for. Baked for an hour at 350 degrees, with its core scooped out and replaced with a spoonful of butter and a single bouillon cube, it could decorate a banquet for the *Chevaliers du Tastevin*.

As the astute reader can discern, I'm sinking more helplessly into this subject even as I write. There are the clothes that must be sorted out, and I've only this moment decided that discarding the tattered jeans was hasty and ill-considered because they will be just the thing for crawling under the Boston whaler when I scrape the hull. The lesson here, of course, is not to make decisions too impulsively. I hope I can keep that in mind when I get to the phonograph records and tapes, and especially when I start culling books. How many times last summer did I search futilely for Housman's *A Shropshire Lad*?

There is no doubt but that a man in the position that I occupy at this moment is highly vulnerable, considering the fragility of the human spirit and the careless, eccentric shape of life itself. My possessions lie strewn about me on the floor of the garage waiting to be stowed away in the car, but my mind has raced disquietingly ahead and is already at work rearranging things in the living room, adding a new porch, uprooting a fine and loyal rhododendron plant, and preparing to eat lunch off a gaudy tablecloth that even I—in a rational moment—must acknowledge would more appropriately grace a table on the other side of the world from Maine.

I envy the dog; her conflicts are all fundamental ones. She wants to be with me, she wants her two squares a day, and she wants plenty of shut-eye, preferably on my bed and without too much squirming around on my part. The possessions on the floor of the garage are all pretty much nonsense, she thinks, with the possible exclusion of her dinner bowl. Her affairs are tidy in a way that mine will never be; to a writer everything is likely to be indispensable to one degree or another, and to have to decide which of two items to retain and which to abandon drags the writer to the brink of an abyss. The only sensible thing to do is to back away, and retain both. The car begins to get crowded but if you can no longer see out of the back window there is always the side-view mirror. Once on the Connecticut turnpike I was stopped by a state trooper, who walked slowly around the car shaking his head in disbelief. "Did you ever think about hiring a truck?" he asked. He was not unfriendly, only unknowing. How can you explain to a law officer a professional need for such a fine adjustment of the selectivity process that it is often beyond the management of even a truly creative person? Believe me, Officer, I would like to live a self-contained life like that dog in the back seat, although maybe you can't see her because of the potted palm and the leaf-blowing machine.

Search and Destroy

This is starting out as a casual report of getting back to my island after an absence of several months and finding a critical need to clean up and reorganize my study, and I'm going to try to prevent it from becoming a sermon. I'm an evangelical man by nature, and when I discover something for myself, I foolishly assume that no one else has ever stumbled across it before and that it is my solemn duty to prevent the community from continuing to think in small, conventional terms and to have them join me in letting their thoughts range widely. The state of my study is a parochial problem, I will admit that, but the sorry state of affairs there and the seeds of bad habits that have been sown have a wider and perhaps even universal application. Accordingly, the text of today's sermon is "If You Haven't Used It During the Past Three Months, Throw It Away."

My study is a one-room building situated in the forest a short walk from the house, but before the leaves get too heavy there is a fine view of the sea all the way across to Yarmouth Island. A number of lobster buoys which have washed up on the shore over the years have been hung on the back wall, the only one without a window, while in front there is a ridiculously tiny porch, onto which I move my typewriter on warm days. This makes the finest working space imaginable, the envy of any urban writer, but it also contains the causes of a decline in productivity on days when the porch is used. There is, for one thing, the mockingbird who roosts in the oak tree, and whose song is not deflected or distorted by any concrete or glass building. Then there are the cormorants whose ability to hold their breath while blithely exploring underwater can seize and rivet my attention anytime. And there are so many interesting things going on there, that I find myself frequently going down to the rocks to get a better look.

All of this had to do with the outside of the study. Inside, it is a mess, a real nightmare. A man would work in such an environment only in desperation, and then by promising himself that after the job at hand is completed, the workroom would be tidied up, that never again would the quality of work be adversely affected by the chaos in which it was produced. When I unlocked the door to my study upon my return to the island a few days ago, I realized that the time had come to put the house in better order, that I was standing on the threshold of something more ambitious, more daring than anything I had undertaken in many years. It is to my credit, I believe, that once the decision had been made—even though impulsively—I fell to work.

The problem, simply stated, is the inability to discard, to throw away worthless articles. A minor weakness and annoyance to some people, it can paralyze others. Upending a large carton of magazines, I began to throw things into the box in a manner bordering on hysteria. A threadbare rug from Mexico went first, then a 1964 *Guide Michelin*, a stack of *New York Times Book Reviews*, a 1970 desk diary which, when opened at random reminded me that on January 5, I was to have lunch with Stewart Udall, the Secretary of the Interior at 12:30, followed by an Alsatian wine tasting at 3:30. Then with the carton overflowing I began throwing things haphazardly on the ground and into the bayberry bushes. Once out of the study, I decided an article was forever gone; it could not be brought back. Books, wall decorations, pamphlets, old magazines, ancient pipes, photographs, all cascaded through the front door. Recklessness had taken over and judgement was suspended; a moment's hesitation, I knew, could undo everything. When one is seeking an untroubled world of order and peace, there is no room for sentiment. Self-confidence comes quickly, rushing in like a spring tide, only to be followed by audacity. If I had permitted myself a loving moment's recall of some trophy, the momentum would have been lost. Out—without a pause—went a copy of *Why Franklin D. Roosevelt Can Never Be President*, its dust jacket scarcely soiled.

At what point in my disposal activities I developed the Three Months theory, I can't say, but I know that during the long afternoon of dispersal I toyed first with a year since the item had been last used as a cut-off date, and almost immediately whittled it to six months. Some of the things I had never used—the cobra-skin belt from India, the recording of Indonesian music, the letter-opener engraved with the name of a bank in Philadelphia—and although any of them would have functioned as well today as they would have at the time of acquisition, I could foresee no occasion in the future that would require me to wear a cobra-skin belt. These things had dug in, so to speak, and ruthlessness was required to send them on their way again. I cut the time down to three months, and while I knew that this was calling it close, I did it without batting an eye. Courage, risk, and venture are what made this country great.

Well, my own life is uncluttered now, but the study is so bare that I find it austere and forlorn, a little difficult to work in. It was cool this morning but I moved the typewriter out to the porch anyway. There will be something going on over at Yarmouth Island almost any time now, and I can only thank God that Yarmouth Island was beyond my reach when the outflow of my possessions reached flood tide.

Pack Rat Mentality

The ways of the man of Maine are often puzzling to those of us who were unfortunate enough to have been born elsewhere but who had the judgment to settle here once the true prizes of Maine were discerned. But a city man coming suddenly to the Maine coast, as I did, drops so quickly into the Maine way of life that he is often stunned to discover himself reacting in a way that is alien to his normal behavior. Maine frugality—the inability to discard anything that may have some use a little further down the road—infiltrated my character so subtly that I was totally unconscious of having abandoned my city-bred profligacy until my daughter, wandering over the island on a summer visit, came back from the boathouse to tell me it sheltered a disgraceful collection of junk. "You never had a pack rat mentality before," she said scoldingly. "What has happened to you?" I wanted to tell her I had become a Mainer, but it seemed to lack the substance of an adequate answer. I gathered I was on probation until something was done about the boathouse, so I walked down to the end of the island to take a look at it. She was right; I have seen more orderly junkyards.

What even the most discerning and fair-minded mainland reader doesn't know, of course, is that an island ecology possesses a stricture unknown elsewhere. Whatever comes on an island, *sooner or later,* must go off the island. Long ago I learned to unwrap packages on the mainland wharf to avoid lugging wrapping materials back across the water; there is even a receptacle at the end of the pier for junk mail, unwanted magazines, occasional soft-drink cans, and any unclassifiable detritus the need for which on the island cannot be proven. I have even shaken down guests before letting them on the boat, much like the electronic eye screening passengers for an airline boarding, to make sure they are not transporting something that can just as easily be left in the car. I am going out of my way to make this point clear because it contains a measure of justification for the untidy state of my boathouse. Some things are put there to await transportation back to the mainland, an in-transit limbo so to speak, and it should not be assumed even by meddlesome relatives, that this is a permanent state. I said as much to my daughter when I got back to the house, but she shot me a withering glance. "It is the same as it was last summer," she said, "only worse." There was a serious flaw in grammar there, if not logic, but I let it pass.

During the early afternoon I took two boatloads of items of varying degrees of usefulness over to the mainland, transferred the cargo to my neighbor's pick-up truck and drove it to the township dump. There was only one person there when I arrived, an elderly man poking with a stick through some castoff pipe and plumbing equipment. When I pulled a mattress off the truck, his eyes lit up and he came over quickly to lend me a hand. "That's not a bad mattress," he said. "Why don't we just toss it on my flatbed truck?" I nodded assent, and we swung it on the truck bed. He came back with me and eyed the contents of my truck. "That looks like a right solid little table there," he said, "and I need one just about that size. Do those two buckets leak?" I said that one did and one didn't. "I'll take them both," he said. "I can mend the one that has a hole in it." In the next few minutes, we transferred almost everything from my truck to his. "I can't get any use out of those paintbrushes," he said, "and there's not enough of that linoleum to do anybody any good. Looks like you haven't got anything else I can use." He climbed into his flatbed and started the motor. "See you around," he said.

I got in the borrowed truck and sat there, brooding uneasily. I didn't feel relieved, as I should have, of ridding the island of rubbish and clutter. I was aswim in a sea of doubts and misgivings; the mattress was fair, the one bucket was good, and the table was exceptional and getting better all the time. A fresh coat of paint and it would have been as good as new. I had bent over to turn on the ignition, when a large truck pulled in beside me and the driver alighted. The truck was loaded with barrels. Before the man had pulled down the tailgate,

I was out of my truck and standing beside him. "Will any of those barrels hold earth?" I asked. The man glanced at me casually. "That's about all they would hold," he said. "You'd have to saw them in half."

I tried to appear indifferent, but I couldn't easily conceal my excitement. Only this spring I had sought to buy some barrels in which I could plant lettuce and maybe even some strawberries. Nothing grew in the soil of the island; it was too acid. "I'll take a couple off your hands," I said nonchalantly. In my mind's eye I could see one overflowing with lettuce in the early summer, the other filled with healthy strawberry plants. "Better make it three," I added, fresh basil rising in my thoughts. "I can pick you out three pretty sound ones," the man said, climbing up into the truck. He lowered three over the end and I took them to my neighbor's truck. I got in and started the motor. "See you around," I said.

There was no radio in the truck, but it didn't matter. I whistled all the way back to the wharf.

What Did You Mean?

I don't wear my dislikes on my sleeve, but there should be no doubt of the depth of my hatred for tortured grammar and occupational phrases. English is a fine language, it is adjustable to fit any situation, it is precise when precision is required and loose when there is room to fool around in, and it can accommodate the user who finds the need to occasionally slip outside normal speech for purposes of emphasis or to let a little air into a temper tantrum. (Good profanity, for example, requires only 1) originality, 2) avoidance of repetition, and 3) sustained cadence.)

The government, from local township through county, state, federal and probably even United Nations levels, has emerged as the greatest enemy of clear and simple English that the language has ever faced. The irony here is that government regulations call for clarity, for easy understanding, yet they are usually so prolix and contradictory, that one is often left, as in seeking to assemble some mechanical device from the instruction pamphlet, with an extra wheel and no place to put it. I have spoken in these pages before, and usually irately, about Augusta's inability to tell the citizens of Maine what it expects of them, most recently in the matter of where to go to get a motorboat permit certificate. My instruction sheet offered three options, none of which applied to me under even the most generous interpretations, leaving me a choice of either operating an outlaw vessel or moving from the state.

Right now I am engaged in what appears to be a losing battle with Computerspeak. For example, I don't know what "byte" is and moreover I don't give a damn. What facts I can't store in my head, I usually jot down. I know my parents' names, and my wife's and my children's names, my Social Security number, the first verse of *The Star Spangled Banner*, my college fraternity handshake, the names of all the boxers I have had, and I know my age (it was ten) when I first sassed my father. He had asked me to turn the thermostat back and I replied, "If you want the thermostat turned back, turn it back yourself." I recall also how the matter concluded. I don't need a computer.

I am the politest and most apologetic of people. I impose no obsessive exactness upon my acquaintances. But I scorn the patronizing superficiality of the business world with its in-group buzzwords like "automagical" (anything that happens automatically), or "mediagenic" (something that attracts the news media), or "disincentivize" (lacking in motivation) or "subadult" (child), or "pre-enjoyed." The latter means— would I make this up?—used car.

Get Me a Translator

I keep forgetting how ridiculous and absurd legal language is. I have just received a letter from a Maine district attorney, a letter written to me in reply to a question I had asked, and it was written in such tortured and labyrinthine legalese that I had to reread it three times in search of its real meaning. I finally concluded that it had no real meaning; the district attorney was contriving to tell me nothing and he had put his reply in legalese since it served very well his quest for an ambiguous and evasive answer.

It is my contention that legal language should be confined to courts—if permitted at all—and not be introduced into the flow of normal communication. In the first place, legalese is anything but a fluid and expressive form of communication; it is tired, studded with cliches, unimaginative, and totally lacking in spontaneity. Lawyers like legalese for a variety of reasons but chiefly because they shrink, as individuals, from novelty. All legal work looks toward the past and never toward the future; to a lawyer there is no such thing as a new law, only old laws gallantly meeting new situations. Since they live in the past in their search for precedents, I suppose it is normal that their speech should be locked into the time frame of their outlook.

Communication is the transmission of thoughts and—in a world where a great deal of confusion exists—we should do what we can to reduce the confusion and not introduce new barriers to understanding. It is my own feeling that we should all write in exactly the same manner that we speak, and it isn't difficult once you get the hang of it. When the district attorney emerged from the thickets of "above-named" and "alleged" "mistaken assumptions," he wrote, "I have determined there is a pending investigation . . . into the matter." Why he ignored the principles of plain English, I can't imagine, but it certainly would have been simpler and more to the point had he written: "The matter is being investigated." As I said, the letter was obviously written because a reply was required but I was told as little as possible. Had the district attorney written back that he would be obliged if I kept my nose out of his business, I would have felt better. That's the kind of direct answer I can deal with; we would both know where we stood in the matter, which is more than I can say about the situation as it is.

Gustave Flaubert, the French novelist, spoke wisely when he said: "Whenever you can shorten a sentence, do. And one always can." When we speak, we almost always avoid compound sentences. It is only when we write that we swell up and get pompous, lawyers and doctors more so than most. When a man is corresponding with his government, he invariably is in a bad frame of mind to begin with and his fuse is likely to be short. He doesn't want to get any answers that are evasive or couched in legalese. He wants the facts, and damned few of those.

Many years ago I came into possession of a book called *The Art of Readable Writing*, by Rudolf Flesch, and was so captivated by two points the author made that I have never forgotten them. One was a list of what he called "empty" words—participles, prepositions, conjunctions, adverbs—that had worked their way into the structure of the language and which he said made up more than 50 percent of all words commonly used. The list included "for the purpose of" (for), "for the reason that" (since, because), "in order to" (to), "in the neighborhood of" (about), "with a view to" (to), "with the result that" (so that), and a few dozen more, all of which were enemies of simplicity and clear speech. The other thing I recall from the book was the author's vigorous defense of ending sentences with prepositions, which he said unfailingly turned stiff prose into idiomatic prose. I love a good prepositional ending, and was delighted to read that the President of the National Council of Teachers of English had said that "a preposition is a good word to end a sentence with."

My own concern over abuse of the English language came at a very early age when I was taken by my mother each Sunday to St. Luke's Episcopal Church in a small town in Virginia. My mother sang in the church choir, and a popular hymn at the time was one that went "And He walks with me, and He talks with me, and He tells me I am his own . . ." I never cared for the hymn because I never knew who Andy was, although I thought about him a lot, searching for clues. I felt then that something was wrong; that Andy should have been identified. Peter DeVries, the novelist, must have suffered from a similar bewilderment as a child. In one of his books he told of having heard, for the first time, a hymn called "Oh, What A Cross I Bear." What was so unusual, he wondered, about a cross-eyed bear that a hymn should have been written about it?

Do Sound Bites Need Stitches?

The weight of opinion may be against me on this subject but I feel a fateful moment in history occurred recently in Brooklyn when a federal judge ordered a government agency to rewrite one of its directives in understandable English instead of the incomprehensible rhetoric which the federal government admires so fulsomely. State and county governments—including Maine—have unblushingly followed the tortured and twisting trail leading from Washington in this regard, despite Augusta's disarming way of suggesting by a casual shrug that it can't imagine how it got mixed up in all of this. I would prefer my state government to spend less time trying to outwit me and more time telling me exactly what it expects from me, and I doubt that I stand alone in that attitude. Readers with good memory may recall that a year ago I wrote a rather testy piece in this magazine because the state government had given me several contradictory instructions for registering my motor boat. Whoever had written the instructions was clearly smitten with the conditional construction and the extravagant use of qualifiers; there were *ifs* scattered throughout the directive as though they were raining down from heaven. I got the impression that the author of these instructions was determined to avoid a flat-out assertion at any cost. A set of instructions—or a law, for that matter—can be written so that an average man or woman can understand it. If this can't be done, then the need for the law very likely is lacking, and I say the hell with it.

Lawyers (stop me if I'm wrong about this) like legal language not only because it feeds their sense of whimsy, but also they are greatly heartened by its exclusionary character. Since laws are written by lawyers, they find it to their advantage that others cannot successfully navigate legal waters on their own. My notion of a fine deliverer of laws was Moses, a man who never employed an unnecessary word and who understood the virtue of clarity. "Thou shalt not kill" is about as clear as a law can be and doesn't leave much room for a murderer to cop an insanity plea or for a hunter to claim that he was thinning out the herd for the herd's own good. The laws which Moses passed on to the people of Israel all rang with the clarity of a bell and while recent times may have seen considerable slippage in public support for some of the decrees—those dealing with covetousness and adultery come to mind—this in no way reflects upon the simplicity of the injunctions themselves.

This subject is particularly timely now since we have recently emerged from an election during which hypocritical oratory took possession of the land. The television sound bite replaced discussion; sincerity and truth fled the stage. The male candidate whose eyes grew misty at the thought of how women's rights had been trampled on over the years often turned out to be the defendant in a class action suit brought by the women in his office who for years had been seeking equal pay for equal work. Words became tricky, meanings were ambiguous, thoughts were evasive, style was distrustful, the politician—ever nimble—left behind sound, but little substance.

The ordinary people of America give our language its currency and keep it alive, the theater gives it resonance, and the government and the politician give it vagueness. The Brooklyn judge gave the latter the back of his hand. "The language used," the judge wrote in his opinion, "does not qualify as English." The people in Augusta didn't seem notably concerned that I was unable to fight my way out of the tangle of rhetoric and get my boat registered. A pleasant lady telephoned to say that I could do one of several things depending upon the circumstances, and my mind began to wander right there. Multiple choices confuse me. I asked if we could narrow it down to just one procedure, but she said she was afraid it was not that simple. "Where you go to get your boat registered depends upon a number of things," she went on, not unkindly. "You have to decide which of the different circumstances fit your case." I introduced the possibility that none of the procedures may fit my case, but she was ready for that. "Then we will have to think up a new procedure for you," she said agreeably, and hung up. I decided then to take the matter up with the highest authority on Maine legal matters that I knew—my neighbor, the lobsterman. He was hosing down the deck of his boat after he had taken his day's catch ashore. "Drive over to the Harpswell town office," he said, without looking up. "It's only a mile down the road. Give them ten dollars and they'll give you a sticker." That's all there was to it. I was back with the sticker in thirty minutes.

God-Fearing Atheist

If the garage sale isn't Maine's number-one growth industry, then the antiques business must be. I wouldn't know a genuine antique if I saw one, but I know that a lot of things said to be antiques in the roadside shops look to me like attic trash crowding its luck. Vendors of some of the questionable stuff have become a little wary themselves at describing certain items as genuine antiques and have devised a variety of new terms which imply that what an object may lack in age it more than makes up for in its value as a curiosity. That lets a little fresh air into a crowded room. "Yesterday's treasures" went a long way down the road of suggestion without really promising anything, and it caught on quickly. Nobody bothered to ask when "yesterday" was, and the term smacked of some kind of hidden value. It was an ideal solution, but it was too good; it soon became overused. It was then that the term collectible was coined, a term even more ambiguous than "yesterday's treasures" because what one person collects another may pay to have carted away.

Collectible has had a good run and has served the trade well—in fact many dealers don't want to give it up—but I notice that it is gently being pushed aside by "modern antiques." There is a remarkable quality to this term because it is a prime example of what is known in English grammar as an oxymoron, a conjunction of contradictory terms. Among some oxymorons that rush to mind are "mournful optimist," "plastic glass," "studied indifference," "pretty ugly," and "down escalator." My neighbor, the lobsterman, never fails to delight me when I tell him something that he already knows, and he accuses me of telling him "old news," which as an oxymoron possesses the clarity of a bell.

Phasing out of current usage a term that has outlived its usefulness because of a steady accumulation of unappealing associations has proved fairly successful in recent years. It's a way of declaring nomenclatural bankruptcy, of starting all over thanks to Chapter 11, with a new name and no burdensome debts. When the word strike, used in a labor context either as a verb or a noun, became an abrasive term to the general public and one associated with inconvenience, organized labor dropped the word quickly and substituted "job action." To perceive labor through its new wrapping is to see it as less inclined to keep a man from getting home to his dinner, or to keep an airline from flying, or to refuse to collect garbage. A "job action" is much nicer than a strike; it is tidier by far, more acceptable, and it somehow doesn't seem to involve the public.

I won't put a specific date on the time that *prison* or *slammer* became unmentionable, but I know the term "correctional facility" is now in general use and seems to be the way the media has been instructed to refer to the place where criminals are kept. I don't know what happened to *penitentiary* either but I can guess. Having the word *penitentiary* drop out of use seems a shame, in a way, because in its purest sense it was rather nice, coming from the Latin *penitentiarius* or where one brooded repentance. Whether Willie Sutton, the bank robber, spent his time repenting or planning a new sting after his release no one can say, but I seriously doubt that he considered himself to be in a "correctional facility."

Dope used to be just that, but now it has mellowed into "controlled substance," and what twenty-five years ago was a "dope fiend" or *junkie* is now an "addictive personality." New York City was no more hospitable to its influx of immigrants from Puerto Rico than California and the Southwest was to its Mexicans, and soon both Puerto Rican and Mexican became words one used not unaccompanied by a vague feeling of guilt. Obviously a fresh beginning was needed here, and the word *Hispanic* was devised to make everything new and wholesome again.

I don't know whether the obsolescence and erasure of an old usage always accomplishes its end or not, but I'm sympathetic in general with the theory. If nothing else, it suggests that something is wrong. E.B. White put it better when he wrote that man's inventions, directed always onward and upward, have an odd way of leading back to man himself, as a rabbit track in snow leads eventually to the rabbit. Anyway, where I am concerned this is an unbiased opinion coming from a God-fearing atheist, which involves the use of two oxymorons in a row and I can't do better than that.

Can You Say That in English?

Being of an apologetic rather than a controversial nature, I normally leave matters of this kind to those who have a taste for skirmishing with authority, but I received a letter a few days ago from the Maine Department of Inland Fisheries and Wildlife and although I've read the letter over and over during the few days it has been in my possession the highest praise I can bestow upon it is to say that, at its best, it is the most chaotic and convoluted bit of writing I have ever encountered. It is so confusing that, in its way, it possesses a certain fascination. One lingers with it, as one does with a difficult puzzle, hoping that sooner or later the key that will unlock the mystery will turn up.

I have had some unfriendly things to say in these pages, in earlier times, about the language of law or legalese ("the party of the first part grants and conveys to the party of the second part, for one dollar and other valuable considerations, that parcel . . .") as well as journalese (". . . according to White House sources that insisted upon anonymity when questioned about . . ."), but of all the pressures brought against the English language the most threatening, in my opinion, has been the language of government or "gobbledygook" as it has come to be known. Here obscurity thrives; government writers fear lucidity and step around the clear sentence as though it threatened their very lives. Connoisseurs of first-rate, world-class gobbledygook must on no account miss the Department of Inland Fisheries and Wildlife's letter on "1987 Boat Registration & Excise Tax." It must be read to be believed since no description could convey the full obscurity of the text nor the unparalleled success of the Department in withholding the meaning of the letter.

I won't go into basic grammar, but I would like to say a word or two about conditional sentences since it was here that the author lost control of the situation. A conditional sentence, of course, is one that leaves the reader holding the bag. Something may or may not happen, and the words if and may are invariably present but not nearly so frequent, I hasten to add, as they appear in the letter I am holding where they fall like a gentle summer rain indiscriminately across the landscape. As I said, I have studied this letter quite closely since I own a boat that requires registration and I had hoped to find out exactly what the new procedure may be, but I got into a nasty tangle in the first paragraph and never quite recovered my balance.

The writer of the letter gets off to a bad start by flinging a couple of conditional sentences at me ("this Department may establish local boat registration agents . . ." and ". . . local registrations may charge a fee . . .") but from that point on it was just maybe this and maybe that. Obscurity may have a place in poetry, but I don't have a great tolerance for it when I am reading something that is supposed to instruct me. In this case I wanted to know more than just that the Department *might possibly* establish registration agents. Did they in fact do it? And while they are at it, I'd like to know if local agents will charge a fee or are just permitted to do so if they feel like it.

In Paragraph Four the reader really walks into a thicket, and the going gets tough. "If your town is participating in this program," the letter continues, but I am thrown off at this point because I don't know whether my town is in on this caper or not. The next paragraph tells you what to do if your town is not participating, tossing in another conditional sentence just for the hell of it: "... or you may take your renewal to another town for validation." It's not clear what benefits, if any, will accrue from the exercise of that option. On the next page, moreover, the reader is told that "Maine residents pay the tax to the town in which they reside," a simple enough declarative sentence but one that seems to blow away the earlier instructions about what to do "if your town is not participating in the local registration program."

E.B. White once declared that Americans, perhaps more than other people, were impressed by what they didn't understand, and on that basis the 1987 Boat Registration letter may become a monument which we may all look up to with great respect. (Where did I get those two *mays*? Has the Department of Inland Fisheries and Wildlife got me writing conditional sentences now?)

I had never worried before about my boat registration; the procedure was simple and involved nothing more than sending in a check every couple of years and, when the decal arrived, plastering it on the bow of my whaler. Now I'm nervous and uneasy about the whole thing, wondering if my town is participating and whether or not I would be better off to take the renewal form to another town for validation. What was once commonplace is now roundabout and cursed with strange options and contradictions. You know what I'm thinking about doing? I know it sounds like I'm taking the cowardly way out, but I'm thinking about selling that boat.

Old-Fashioned Lying

An election year has us all in a nervous and unstable state and since we expect almost anything from politicians we tend to keep our thermostat of surprise fixed at a fairly low setting. Even so, there was something curiously unsettling in a news article a few days ago, where a New York City politician seemed to berate God for His part in the robbery of an icon from a Greek Orthodox Church in Queens. "We don't know why the Lord allowed this to happen" was the accusing remark that grabbed my attention, a petulant utterance that struck me as impious if nothing else.

The curtain has just gone up on the election-year circus, and if this is the theme of the overture then we are in for quite an unpleasant year. So far as I know, however, my congressman is still campaigning on a secular level, and I trust he will continue to recognize the line where his authority ends and God's begins.

I would like to call attention to one or two other subjects I have recently encountered that have caused a further darkening of spirit. It's impossible to discuss the low level to which American taste has descended without wondering if things would have been better without rock and roll music, and its punk and rap offshoots. All three seem to have generally lowered our cultural standards, much as a lowered net makes a tennis game easier. Those whose memories go back to pre-rock music will recall a band called Shep Fields and his Rippling Rhythm, which was pretty bad, and Lawrence Welk and his Champagne Music, which was worse, but I recently heard a rap band called Dogvomit, which was worse than any of them. The point I am making, as the discerning reader already sees, is that at the very least the names of the earlier bands, if not their music, spoke to us in a way that did not cause involuntary recoil. Dogvomit, and the Sewer Works Crew, another rap band of current popularity, seem to be headed in a direction which, if followed, raises the probability that these may be among the last groups whose names appear on CD labels but not in family magazines.

In this country an unjustified bias has always been shown to novelty, but I believe this is less true in Maine than in any other region. Call Mainers eccentric if you wish, but they lack this general adoration for trend-setters and, figuratively speaking, more often than not are inclined to tap a coin against the counter to see if it gives off a spurious sound. Prevailing orthodoxy is always mercifully brief—like the Macy's Thanksgiving Day Parade, there is always a new spectacle ready to turn the corner and come into view—and Maine's apostasy strikes me as one of the state's most admirable qualities. Mainers recognize that what is called new is almost invariably old; the reappearance of the familiar in some gaudy new clothes. In the current recession large businesses are laying off workers but they are calling this "down-sizing". It sounds better than "firing," and if it sounds better, it must be better, although not to those down-sized. During the Eisenhower administration, the spin doctors came up with "reduction in force" or "rif" which seemed to please everyone except those who were riffed. It would be fascinating to know who gains what from this word game. It reminds me of the recommendation a chap once made for his doctor: "He's one of the sweetest men alive. He even touches up the X-rays to make his patients feel better."

The computer world, whose voice has spoken with a strange new vocabulary, has come up with "liveware" which is computer-speak for "human being." This troubles me, perhaps unduly, for it seems to lower the human being to a pitiable condition—a minor figure strutting across the world's scientific stage—and I can't see a sensitive man or woman viewing this as anything but disquieting. The computer nerds, those teen-age wizards who would rather hack into the Pentagon's secrets than play basketball, are now known as "techno-weenies," but whether this term is loaded with admiration or contempt I am not qualified to say. In my own youth I would not like to have been known as a techno-weenie, but since I am typing these words on a L.C. Smith, circa 1942, standard typewriter, I doubt that my opinion is widely sought on any subject.

But getting back to the matter of using words to conceal true meaning, I would like to say that I have a soft spot in my heart for old-fashioned lying because it was often done openly and in the best of spirits. Take the 1933 Chicago World's Fair, for example, which was remembered, if at all, for Sally Rand's nude fan dance, inspired, she explained, by "watching white herons flying in the moonlight above my grandfather's farm." Sally was lying through her teeth about those night-flying white herons, but it helped her act and we remember her a half-century later as liveware of perpetual springtime.

Eco-Echo

Perhaps the greatest sins of all the sins are committed against nature because the harm done is not merely felt by one's neighbors or one's countrymen but by the whole world. We are locked together in a fight so that survival; the Brazilian peasant burning tress in the Matta Grosso is lessening the ability of the atmosphere to cleanse itself of carbon dioxide so that the Italian or Swede can breathe clean air, and the reckless use of fluorocarbons in air conditioning New York offices is enlarging holes in the ozone layer over Antarctica. "...and therefore never send to know for whom the bell tolls," wrote the poet John Donne; "it tolls for thee." I think I share a quiet place at sundown on my island with only a blue heron, but unfortunately I share it also with Japanese fishermen setting out mile-long nets that ensnare not just tuna but also dolphin by the thousands. We love our children but are doing everything we can to leave them a blackened cinder on which to make their home.

  Americans delude themselves easily. We feel noble when we talk about the *need* to reverse the destructive drive of industry in polluting streams, of loggers clear-cutting great forests, of toxic wastes being buried in shallow graves, as though in admitting error in the past we are achieving something substantial for the future. The President of the United States sees nothing strange in calling himself the Environment

President and then seeking to re-define the nation's wetlands in a way that would circumvent the Clean Water Act and open up over half of our marshlands to development of shopping malls, golf courses, and housing subdivisions. We say, therefore we are, as shadow becomes substance. The President is probably not aware that he is an inexperienced and maladroit actor in an outdated drama that has no relevance to the late twentieth century.

I once read that if you would tell a child about the hollowness of some of the conventions he or she will be back in ten minutes using this information against you. There lies our hope: if we don't save the planet for our children they may save what's left of it for themselves.

Nature's Database

Like most Mainers, I long ago developed the gift of skepticism, the fires of which I had thought I had kept reasonably well-banked until I read a few nights ago that Maine's wild plant and animal life was to be given a "computerized data base." I'm not sure what that is, since I possess a very poor grasp of high-tech *patois*, but I regard computers with the same suspicion that early pioneers regarded Indians and I'm inclined to put the wagons in a circle at the first sight of an arrow. The Nature Conservancy, which claims me as one of its more feverishly ardent members, has concluded that its ecological life-history information in Maine can best be handled if stored in computers, and for all I know they are right. It's just that the mention of computers causes a knee-jerk reaction with me, and if I continue to keep the plant and animal life on this island on our normal face-to-face basis—an arrangement we have mutually worked out over the years—it is not so much a manifestation of distrust of The Nature Conservancy as it is my own unwillingness to turn over to computers certain functions which I think the good Lord intended to hold onto for Himself. In nature things work out if you leave them alone; it is only when man meddles too much that the system ultimately falls apart.

I am told that fewer than forty kinds of amphibians and reptiles exist in the State of Maine, and of that two score or less, certainly only a few inhabit my island. If I can't keep the comings and goings of one garter snake in mind, I shouldn't be living alone on an island. I saw him only once last summer, a tiny fellow about a foot in length, when he wriggled out from under the house to catch a little snooze in the sun. He was gone a half-hour later when I came out of the kitchen to see if I could tempt him with a few bread crumbs, but, as you can see, I have the information about this snake well within retrieval reach. I suppose a computer print-out would read something like this: "Snake appeared 10:19 A.M., July 19th. Laid in sun eighteen minutes, apparently asleep. Breath normal. Slight eye flicker. Disappeared. Whereabouts unknown. Bread crumbs ignored, later eaten by two blue jays and one grackle." That's more information than is needed; it's like the government's appetite for details on its printed forms. As any reader can plainly see, I'm going out of my way to demonstrate that I can be as tendentious as The Nature Conservancy; maybe more so.

So far as other amphibians and reptiles are concerned, I don't remember ever having seen any turtles around, but frogs and salamanders occasionally come out from heavy underbrush or from under rotting boards, and while I've never kept any notes on their habits, I'd know where to locate one if the need ever arose. I think a computer would err on the side of being too helpful. A healthy salamander—and certainly a *happy* one—is the salamander who is left alone under a rotting log in the forest. Moving a log to conduct a census or to observe the salamander going about his daily occupation only sets a salamander's teeth on edge, and puts the whole community in a state of turmoil. A nice, peaceful log suddenly becomes Beirut.

Where ecologically rare plants are concerned, my own need for a computer file diminishes to the point of disappearance. I have a great attachment to lady-slippers—the small wild orchids that blossom on the forest floor in early June—and I keep a reliable census each year to see if my flock increases. The spring of 1984 saw the total reach seventeen, although like other pollsters I should admit to a margin of error of plus or minus 3 percent If only to be fashionable and in tune with the times. I would say my statistics on the lady-slipper situation are as reliable and up-to-date as any computer could provide. Of course, the procomputer people would say that I could die suddenly and take my lady-slipper statistics with me, but my answer to that lies in the frequency with which my bank and travel agency tell me that their computers are "down" and that I must come back later. Human mortality, in my book, offers no less security than a capricious computer.

In throwing in their lot with the computer crowd, I'm sure The Nature Conservancy is convinced their decision will have a telling effect on wildlife protection. As usual on matters of this kind, I will stick with the status quo. A man living on an island has a mysterious relationship with that scrap of land surrounded by the sea, and with all of the plants and animals on it. The land is not so much a place to live—an address, so to speak—as it is a way of life, and the owner rejoices when he and nature combine to achieve the fulfillment to which all parties there aspire. On an island a closeness prevails, and I would feel somehow cheated if my occasional encounters with the garter snake were reduced to a computer inventory. Personal confrontation is the thing, whether it's with a salamander or a snake or a Northeast storm. Living is feeling, not a message read on a computer print-out.

Biodegrading

Environmentalists say there is a strong possibility that the babies now being born may be the last generation to dine on lobster or be able to drink unfiltered water, and while this may be true it is also true that these major anxieties are often a matter of individual preference. There is some catas-trophe on the horizon most of the time and the lobster situation—if I can believe my neighbors who are mostly lobstermen—is certainly one of them. But before the lobster becomes as scarce and as expensive as caviar, I think the people of Maine are going to have to face a threat to their salva-tion from plastic bottles which are filling up their shorelines and floating back and forth on tidal currents that once flowed clear. This is a creeping contamination that is facing us right now and not a problem a generation away.

Walking along a shoreline, especially when the clouds are low and a sharp, moist breeze is blowing in from the sea, is a more insistent thing with me than almost any recreation I can think of. People are fond of calling a solitary walker a "loner," and this may be true but I see no need to apologize for finding pleasure in a brisk walk on a blustery day, accompanied or unaccompanied. I recently ran across a speech of Cyrano de Bergerac's that impressed me so much that I memorized it (I can handle three lines, beyond that I'm in trouble) and I would like to share it at this time. Cyrano said: "Oh, to sing, to laugh, to dream, to walk in my own way and be alone; free, with an eye to see things as they are." But what my eye sees now is a shoreline littered with plastic objects—bottles, cans, containers of all kinds, and all possessing an inestimable life span. Sometimes these objects get buried in the sand temporarily, but so far as I can tell they never wear out. Salt water is an unsurpassed corroding agent—"It can corrode a rock," my lobsterman neighbor says—but plastic seems to thrive on it. Where rock ledges and beaches were once filled with driftwood, they are now covered with plastic containers. Even oil slicks are eventually cleaned up by natural forces, but for the first time man has created something that nature can't handle.

An additional factor, which has soured me on the matter of plastic waste, is that my boxer, Margaret, finds plastic objects which have been washed ashore on the island to be enormously appealing and superb for chewing and chasing. Her eyes will light up at the sight of a Clorox bottle with the keenness they would show for a porterhouse steak. After a real low tide, the area around my backdoor looks like the deck of the Islip, New York, garbage scow that was rejected by four countries and seven states. Accordingly, I have become an unwilling conduit for getting plastic objects to the local dump. A few weeks ago the dump supervisor remarked to me: "You use quite a lot of Clorox, don't you, Mr. Stinnett?" His curiosity was understandable, but I was in no mood to discuss the matter. Once a plastic bottle is tossed into the sea, it has no ownership, its origin is irrelevant, it has total disregard for ownership boundaries, and it is impartially offensive. A high tide or a strong wind may dislodge it, but it drifts to another shore. It never disappears completely.

I have wandered Maine shorelines more extensively than the average man, and I have learned something about plastic containers. The most frequently encountered are, of course, Clorox bottles, but the pumpkin-colored Pennzoil container is more durable, heavier, and more unsightly on the beach. When the sun strikes a Pennzoil container at just the right angle of reflection, it can be seen from a considerable distance. For a long time I mistakenly believed that a discarded rubber boot, half-buried in the sand, was the most stubborn object to the biodegradable forces of nature, but I have since recanted and taken a more tolerant view of the rubber boot. It sticks around a long time after its welcome has worn thin, but it does disappear in time. I have never seen a Pennzoil bottle break down, which is a fine tribute to its shelf character but something else again when it washes ashore empty of everything but sea water.

E.B. White, a few years before his death, wrote that the dirty state of affairs on earth was getting worse, not better. Since White's voice was stilled, contamination has continued at a faster pace, in new ways, and with new excuses. American industry has found public relations cheaper than safe disposal of industrial wastes. If our rivers, our seas, and our air are being turned into waste dumps, the public-relations specialists bending over their typewriters in their steel and glass towers in Manhattan hasten to assure us that the accumulation of plastic bottles on the shores of Maine are nothing more than a yardstick of progress. Who wants to block progress? Well, my hand is raised. I want to block it.

Drinking Water

Few of us manage to explain a lapse in service with the charming innocence of the young man from the Drinking Water Laboratory in Augusta who cheerfully told me on the telephone that I had received no reply to my request for a sample kit because "we have been running a little behind recently, but I think we will be caught up again pretty soon." There was a pleasant, convivial feeling in his tone of voice, one that seemed to enfold me into the little conspiracy to defend the delay, and for the moment I felt that my state government and I were joining hands in making the best of a situation that had somehow gotten out of our grasp. But motoring back to the island in my boat, the warmth of this new relationship began to chill. What, I thought, if surface water had gotten into my well and was causing its discoloration; would I get hepatitis, or something worse? Was there anything worse? By the time that I got back to the island and had tied up the boat, the thought that was uppermost in my mind was the need to make a few final decisions of a very grave nature.

What had happened, to take it from the top, was that my well water had suddenly taken on the color of iced tea, and my neighbor on the mainland with whom I discuss practical matters of this kind, suggested that I send in a sample to the testing laboratory and see if it were safe to drink. I took a deep drink of my neighbor's water—a symbolic act, I suppose, to fine-tune my imagination into thinking it would tide me over until my own situation had cleared up—and went back to the island where I wrote a letter to the Drinking Water Laboratory requesting a sample kit. (I was told the laboratory wisely refused to take water sent in just any old bottle.) Three weeks later I had received only silence from Augusta, a silence that was chilling to a man with a feverish imagination who had difficulty separating fact from fancy. That day I got off a letter to both the Department of Environmental Protection and to the governor, urging them to get this kit moving to me while there was still time.

The commissioner of the Department of Environmental Protection promptly washed his hands of the entire matter, advising me in a letter that while the department administers many programs concerned with water quality, it does not handle the testing of drinking water. I felt I detected a note of satisfaction in the commissioner's letter, but my spirits rose when I saw that he had sent a copy of his letter to the governor. At least, I reasoned, there was an awareness in Augusta now that my welfare was at stake, and while my survival may not be teetering on the fulcrum of bureaucratic inaction, the way was being cleared—slowly perhaps— for sending me a drinking-water testing kit.

One can never be certain how an official like the governor comes to arrive at a decision, but I assume that he prodded the young man who eventually called to say that his office was running a bit behind the volume of requests. The commissioner of the Department of Environmental Protection sent copies of his letter not only to the governor but also to the director, Budget and Finance, of the Department of Environmental Protection and to the director, Division of Health Engineering, Department of Human Services. These two latter officials may have contributed to the decision that was reached and I hope I am not ignoring some valuable contribution either or both made in my behalf, but I feel that it was the governor's intercession that broke the roadblock. The occasions when a man feels it necessary to confront his state government should be rare and exceptional since the relationship between the governing and the governed is so precariously poised. It is under these circumstances that I am giving all credit to the governor in the hope of containing this controversy and not allowing other state agencies to get involved in it. I believe the governor will appreciate that.

Writers, as a group, are likely to be paranoid, working in isolation as they do, and my next anxiety came from the sudden suspicion that perhaps the cheerful young man had to decide on the basis of potential contribution to the state welfare which occupational groups should have priority since requests were obviously outrunning available drinking-water kits. Any writer of sound mind would realize instantly that in a triage situation of this nature, he or she would be sent to the end of the line since a writer's contribution to the Gross National Product—whatever that is—is negligible. In other words, the writer knows, deep in his heart, that drinking-water kits don't go to the whimsical, the undisciplined, the dreamer. What is worse, I can't take this sort of thing to the governor and awaken his support.

Well, it's been two months now, and I'm still bringing drinking water over from my neighbor's well on the mainland. His water looked a little rusty this morning, but I think I'll wait another day before I call his attention to it.

Happy Earth Day

The people of Maine, like those of other states, are convinced that whatever is new is bound to be much better than whatever is old, and all one has to do to find proof of this is to walk along a beach or wetland on the coast of Maine to see what people are discarding. For some reason,

Maine people still regard their beaches and coasts to be the prime disposal area of unwanted junk. I have just read a *Wall Street Journal* report on national beach cleanup activity which revealed some peculiarities in state dumping: Oregon, which has a bottle bill, had fewer bottles than other states; syringes were most prevalent in Texas, but New York and Delaware were not far behind. Massachusetts had the most sewage-associated trash, and Louisiana had the most garbage from ship's galleys. Almost everything showed up in one state or another, including nine messages in bottles, one of which read, "Help me. I'm lost at sea. If you find me, I will grant you one wish."

I have run a few private tests along Quohog Bay in Maine, and it is my conviction that plastic containers outnumber everything else in this state and they are also the most stubbornly durable. But last fall I came upon my first microwave oven, and was startled to realize that we were so deeply into the microwave age that already we were tossing out the early models. A generation of appliances in a high-tech society is getting briefer and briefer, and I am afraid only small minds like mine balk at dismissing those that are practical, precise, lucid, and comfortably functional. The last time I moved—some years ago—a large carton containing kitchen appliances failed to arrive, and while I don't know what it contained I still look for consolation, and regard its loss as a wound that has never healed. To grieve for the ghost appliances of a misdirected box may strike some people as insanity, but they are the people who consider technology the king, who don't know the comforting grasp of a fine old screwdriver or who can appreciate a functionally sound frying pan which derives its loyalty from its ability to distribute heat evenly. If I found that chap who was lost at sea, the wish I would have him grant me would be just such a utensil.

But I'm drifting off into fantasy now, and I intended this piece to be a sort of historical pageant of American consumerism and environmental oversight. Conservatism has always found a friend in me, and while there are many things a whole lot worse than tossing away usable objects, I have never cottoned to the notion that a household is functionally sounder by reason of its shiny newness. No, sir! That new, complicated coffee-maker, with its filters and thermostats and hidden intestines, ought to produce a cup of coffee as good as the old percolator. If it doesn't, you're likely to stumble over it the next time you walk along the beach. The old percolator is awkward, its physical appearance is almost comic, and one has to keep an eye on it even if the other is on the "Today Show." If left unattended, it gets instant revenge by bubbling over into froth at the spout, and quite often putting the fire out. But it fills an awakening house with a wonderful odor, and the coffee comes out hot the way coffee should. Throw it away if you want to, but it all comes down to what a man or woman wants when they pick up a coffee pot.

I think it might be a good idea if all adult Mainers took a walk along their nearest beach to see, first, what a mess they have made, and secondly, what extravagant habits they have slipped into. I visit the beach with a certain amount of regularity to get driftwood for my fireplace and, I must confess, I occasionally bring home a usable section of rope, or a board of an interesting shape, or a flower pot that was thoughtlessly thrown out with the flower. There is a minor rodent drive in all of us, which I feel is no cause for shame. When I last visited the beach it was early summer, and I was surprised to see how the scene had shifted, how the stage was set for the summer of 1991. Gone was the immense log from which I had once sawed sections, driven by a winter storm to some farther shore, and gone, too, were the three automobile tires that I had grown to loathe, and the half of a doghouse that my boxer, Margaret, had always found interesting and worth a thorough sniffing. The change of scenery had involved the scattering of the usual broken lobster traps, a boot half-buried in the sand, more sheets of plastic than I cared to count, a variety of metal containers rusting away, and twenty, thirty, forty— how far along the beach do you intend to walk?—plastic oil containers. The latter were not rusting away; man is biodegradable, but plastic containers are not.

There are personal signals of public unhappiness with our environmental practices, but as long as we take great glee in throwing things away we must find some place to throw them. Four and a half tons of nonrecyclable litter were left in Central Park, New York, after the celebration of Earth Day. This raises serious questions. But the most important, it seems to me now, is the Biblical one of who has the right to cast the first stone?

Killing Is Good for Animals?

The world's brew is bitter enough these days without hunting season, the beginning of which always seems to be celebrated by some new development that others appear able to take in their stride but which causes me to stumble. Right now I'm trying to forget an item I read in a newspaper, an item that caused me to put the paper down and lick my lips nervously. Since then my appetite has fallen off, I spend a lot of time drumming my fingers on the desk, and I'm not sleeping too well. It was the most disturbing news story I've encountered since I read a few years ago that the state of South Carolina faced the need to install a new electric chair because the old one was considered unsafe.

The new item told how police had raided a cockfight in a town in upstate New York, seized sixty-two gamecocks, and arrested over a hundred spectators. The spectators were all fined and the gamecocks were turned over to the local animal shelter. So far so good, but now get this: "They (the birds) were prepared and served today as part of a chicken dinner at the children's center." My problem is trying to decide if cockfighting is less humane than being prepared and served, regardless of how good the chestnut dressing may be. I hope I'm not too set in my ways to get into the spirit of this thing, and I promise to try. The next time I'm driving in the country and I see a fender-happy pheasant wandering in a circle beside the road, I know what to do. I'll telephone the animal shelter, and then hurry home to chill a nice dry Medoc.

This piece started out about the hunting season and took an unexpected detour, but I will now come back to the original subject. I care a great deal about animals, and I think their continued existence in the ravaged environment we have created is almost a miracle. Highway slaughter alone, it would seem, is sufficiently thorough to eliminate animal life in this country eventually, and perhaps sooner than we think. Whether animal life is essential to human welfare I cannot say, but it's a close call. A walk in the forest with no likelihood of ever seeing a squirrel or a rabbit or a deer strikes me as an empty and melancholy experience. I've never met a deer I didn't like, but I can't say the same about hunters. Killing animals for sport is part of man's gradual degradation of the environment, and sooner or later we will pass the point of no return, and evidence is mounting that we may already have passed that point.

Hunters steadfastly maintain that killing animals is good for the herd, it kills off the culls, but they have not told the truth about this. When a hunter gets his sights set on a moose he doesn't know if it is a cull or the healthiest bull in the woods, nor does he care. He wants something on the fender of his car when he returns home, and I find it difficult to buy his contention that he has gone into the woods for conservation purposes. Does he close up his business and go into the woods to feed deer and moose when there is deep snow on the ground? Nature or the Lord, or both, managed wildlife propagation in a fairly satisfactory way long before the Maine Department of Inland Fisheries and Wildlife entered the management picture and long before Maine hunters decided the best way to increase the deer and moose population was to kill as many of them as possible.

My distaste for hunters goes back to an experience I had a number of years ago when I lived on a farm in Bucks County, Pennsylvania.

Seeing four hunters in my front yard, I went out and informed them that I didn't like hunting and I wanted them to leave. "My advice to you," one of the hunters said, "is to get back in that house where you belong. I've told you once, and I'm not going to tell you again."

If I seem too extreme in my views on the rights of animals, I would like to tell a story, a quiet story, told to me by the late Rachel Carson, whose powerful book *Silent Spring* sounded the first general warning that we were destroying the planet on which we live. Miss Carson told me of the small laboratory she maintained in her home near Boothbay Harbor, and how she brought up from the tidal pools small samples of water to observe, under a microscope, the tiny creatures that inhabited it. "Of course," Miss Carson said, "I always returned the little samples of water back to the sea after I had finished my studies." I couldn't restrain a smile, and I said that the balance of nature would hardly be upset by whether or not she returned a spoonful of water to the sea. She was silent a moment, and then said very gravely: "If those tiny creatures are going to survive, I must return them at the same tide level from which I removed them. That means I must set my alarm clock, put on a robe, and with a flashlight make my way down to the tide pools. I think it's worth it."

Moose Trap

I have a lot of answers that I would like the questions to. One of these involves the matter of moose now said to be wandering along the highways of Maine at night where they are struck by speeding automobiles, often with more damage to the car and its occupants than to the moose. The question here is probably this: since the moose is a throwback to the Pleistocene Period and not a strikingly intelligent one at that, shouldn't the driver of the vehicle assume the major share of the responsibility for avoiding these collisions? Drivers of automobiles are believed to be a great deal smarter than moose, although this is an assumption that I am not always sure is supported by the facts. The moose looks like something waiting for a jump-start, but the automobile or truck driver is bubbling over with confidence, purpose, and impatience; he doesn't always know where he is going but he knows that he has got to hurry to get there.

Massachusetts drivers, of course, are something else again, and must be dealt with under a totally different code of highway behavior, much as the people of Louisiana have found the Napoleonic Code more to their way of life than the usual state constitutions. There are a lot of odd news items jostling for attention in the Boston newspapers, but one that remains in my memory is the police report of a head-on collision in a Boston car wash. Having lived for a while—precariously—in Boston, I know exactly how it happened, as does anyone who has spent much time on Massachusetts highways. The average Massachusetts driver, whether man or woman, starts blowing the horn of the vehicle even before the ignition is turned on. Boston is the only city I know of where the pedestrian must automatically look in both directions before crossing a one-way street, and traffic lights in Massachusetts are considered to be suggestive only.

Maine drivers are much less lunatic, quite sane mostly, but it is not unusual that some become giddy with knowledge of the power at their whim and it takes a moose in the headlights to bring them quickly into touch with reality. The moose is an animal with a glorious past but an utterly hopeless future; only conservationists really care about the animal. Now that it threatens the automobile by its nocturnal wandering, the moose may well be ebbing from the scene at a pace equal to that of this century.

"If you hit a moose head on, you just take its legs out from under it and you won't see it till it comes through the windshield," said Howard C. Nowell, of the New Hampshire Fish and Game Department. According to Mr. Nowell, the number of moose collisions in his state increased from forty-nine in 1985 to 170 last year, and the two-pronged question here seems to be is the problem getting worse (yes) and what can be done to stop it other than driving more carefully (not a hell of a lot)?

I can't say I've never seen a moose I didn't like because I haven't seen enough to make a sensible judgment. I saw one a few years ago when I was going down the Snake River in the Grand Tetons of Wyoming, and a couple of summers ago I saw one dive off a rock ledge in front of my island and swim across the mouth of the cove to emerge on a rocky bank and disappear into a forest. I liked these two moose very much and saw no reason to be inhospitable to either of them. The Snake River moose was drinking, but paused politely to gaze curiously at the boat I was in and then lowered its head to continue drinking. I had the feeling that each of us, in our own way, was meeting in a manner of mutual forbearance; there was a lot of sky, a lot of mountains, and a lot of river, and neither of us had any reason to feel crowded or out of place.

The situation with the other moose of my acquaintance was somewhat different and the stage was much smaller and more constrictive. But here too the moose was intent upon some errand of its own, and disregarded me as being unimportant in the scheme of moose affairs, a situation that pleased me in a way I find difficult to explain. The sight of a moose swimming across my cove was exciting and provided a splendid interlude in an otherwise boring day; I wish he would do it more frequently and he could certainly count on no interference on my part.

Like Mainers, the people of New Hampshire get quickly to the heart of a situation. The editor of a weekly newspaper in an area where there have been collisions between vehicles and moose compared the problem to a sharp corner of a highway. "I never saw a corner that killed anybody," he said. "It's the people who don't turn that get killed. I don't blame the moose. I fault the people who think they have a God-given right to drive sixty miles per hour through the woods."

The third question, I guess, is why do moose come into towns and congested areas, but an answer to that already occupies the field. Rural real-estate developments and suburban sprawl have diminished normal moose living space, and the homeless and disoriented animals wander aimlessly, much as the homeless people of large cities sleep in cardboard boxes in subway stations and parks. What a moose needs is not what it is now getting, any more than the cardboard box is what the homeless man needs. In the soft air of a late summer night, a moose may think a stroll down a country road is just the right thing to take its mind off its problems, and it's only when the brilliant shaft of light from an onrushing vehicle blinds it that it realizes in the jungle of its fear and shock that something is terribly wrong. Well, something is.

Maine as Culprit

I am a fine, brave, and taciturn man, but I let out a gasp of pained astonishment the other evening when I read that every man, woman, and child in Maine threw out nearly five pounds of trash every day. Brooding about a thing like that can turn the most even-tempered of us into a Type A personality overnight. What has happened to the famous frugality of Maine people? Are Mainers become recreational shoppers, buying things just to kill time? If they are throwing five pounds of trash what—excuse me for choking up—are they keeping?

The blue heron that fishes lethargically at low tide along the rock ledge in front of my island has gotten off his schedule lately and is showing up in an erratic pattern, and I wonder if this is because he's finding too many plastic Clorox and motor-oil containers washing up on the ledge and he can no longer tell if he's striking at a minnow or a bottle. The heron is indifferent about the percentage of our state's wealth that goes down the drain in the form of waste and food for the overfed; his interest is in an uncluttered shoreline and some seawater clean enough to permit him to catch a shiner that flashes into his line of vision. The heron's affairs are in tidy order: all he wants is a clean place to fish and a spruce tree in which to roost. It is man's state of affairs that is messy beyond belief. I am suddenly concerned about those qualities we have always admired in ourselves as Mainers—our thrift, our diligence, our abhorrence of extravagance, our industriousness. What sort of basic mismanagement has brought an end to all of this?

I take my waste to the Strawberry Creek Recycling Center on the mainland once a week, but aside from the newspapers I don't come near the implausible Maine norm. I read the *New York Times* every day, but if I keep encountering news such as this bulletin on Maine waste I may stop that and go to bed early instead. I'm not an excitable man, but more and more I find myself stirring up a little drink when I get back to the island after a trip to town, a town that seems to get more crowded with shoppers every day, and I'm suddenly aware that when my boxer races ahead of me to get in the boat it's always for the trip home and not for the trip over to the mainland.

I don't know if you are ready for what I'm going to tell you now, but I feel a sense of responsibility to lay out all the facts on this whole matter of Maine's increasing discard of waste. According to The Natural Resources Council of Maine, an organization I admire immensely and whose statistics I accept as I accept the Gospel, the residents of Carrabassett Valley throw away forty-seven pounds of waste per resident per day. Don't ask me any questions about this because I don't know the answers, but I gather that it isn't destined to be a valley much longer. By the time you read this it may be Mount Carrabassett.

If I seem to be singling out Maine as the primary culprit in the destruction of New England and its coastline, I would like to say here that while this state is doing just about all that it can do to make a mess of its waters it is still a feeble influence alongside the U.S. Navy, whose ships discard an estimated 5.4 tons of plastic a day into the ocean. The navy says it is sorry about this, real sorry, but they keep on doing it and say they cannot stop until 1992. It would seem to me that if someone, say the President of the United States for example, would order the navy to stop this foolishness tomorrow then it could be done, but I have a poor grasp of the federal government's ability to do the sensible thing, and you should consider my opinion in this matter worthless.

There is a lot of talk about cleaning up Maine's seacoast but everybody seems to be biding their time until they are forced to do something and the force hasn't yet appeared on the scene. Well, that's not exactly true because last fall some volunteers working on the coastal program of the State Planning Office collected over 13,000 pounds of garbage and trash that had been dumped on shore locations, and while this cleaned up only 120 miles of a 3,500-mile coastline, it was a step in the right direction and showed that a lot of Mainers have this thing on their minds and are already mourning the loss of clean water and clean shores. Most of the trash picked up by the volunteers was plastic, including the yoke that holds the six-pack that chokes the birds to death, and the plastic bags that the sea turtles eat thinking they are jellyfish, and the plastic containers which lie at tide level and which will outlast all of us since they are not as biodegradable as man. Apparently the navy's plastic waste has not yet reached our shores because the volunteer crews identified the waste as stuff obviously thrown overboard from sailboats and other recreational vessels, from commercial fishermen, and from beachgoers who feel that a picnic is a one-way trip for containers. Other interesting items found include a television set, a carpet, a bedspring, and a pocketbook. The latter was empty, as empty as the beach was empty of beauty, as unnatural as a lone power pole that supplants a spruce tree, as forbidding as the clump of ruffled feathers and the six-pack yoke that lies half-buried in the sand.

Ozone Layer Blues

Probably the most demoralizing form of human activity is trying to talk someone around to your own social and political beliefs. Now that world communism can no longer be feared, I would like to see the countries of the world hold hands and try to save what's left of the ozone layer, but the minds of men (and women, too—by all means women, too) are still too cramped to see the planet as it really is and if the truth is faced we would have to acknowledge that we all miss the communist menace just a little. I had an idea I was willing to offer the world to help ease us out of our former obsession with communism, but it may well be too little and too late. (Most of my plans for saving the world, or at least that part of Maine where I live, have fallen on very barren soil indeed largely because, I am told, my plans are ultimately unworkable; they start promisingly but end inconclusively.)

Since I have now built an almost unbearable suspense in regard to the loss of communism as an obsession and my proposal for dealing with it, I suppose I must outline my idea at this time. Before we can abandon communism entirely we must elevate the character of the substitute, and if the substitute is another form of communism—just as shifty, just as unpredictable—then we have something we can all rally around to oppose. I am speaking here of the Marxist society of bees, a culture just as boring, just as dogmatic as the Leninist system, complete with all of the platitudinous litany of the brotherhood of man and the creation of a classless society based upon solidarity and the harmonious satisfaction of all of our needs. Bee Marxism meets life bravely, but, when the Red Dawn comes to the bee culture we may find it is made of sterner stuff than that which lighted the sky over Leninist Soviet Russia and Eastern Europe.

Personally, I resent the patronizing air of bees, their treacherous swarming and their sullen dispositions, and if it weren't for honey I think you would find more signs of zeal creeping into my comments on the terrors of bee communism and the unhappy ways of politics in bee colonies. So far as I am concerned, Bee Marxism makes Soviet communism seem like a day at the Magic Kingdom.

It should be obvious by now that this is all introduction to something else either very sinister or very hopeful. It is the latter, I am pleased to say, and it comes from a report of the Green Index released by the Institute of Southern Studies in Durham, North Carolina, which analyzes and rates the various states' encouragement of a healthy environment. The Green Index probes 256 different indicators and top marks were given to Oregon, first, and Maine, second, among fifty states. (You probably want to know which state came in last, and I'll tell you now and get it over with, so we can get on with the study: Alabama came in last. Texas, Mississippi, Arkansas, and Louisiana joined Alabama at the bottom of the charts, which says something about the South which I had just as soon not be said since my roots are in Virginia and I still hold an affection for the area.) Maine has good reason to be proud of its location almost at the top of the list of states since the index weighed air- and water-pollution measures, toxic and other waste disposal, energy use, population density, and especially strict environmental laws. Where the latter is concerned, California led the pack, with Oregon second.

You might wonder what the Green Index has to do with TV, and normally so would I since it takes an extraordinary television show to cause me to lay aside a book or a newspaper. But I saw one the other day. I gave the screen full attention when I heard a panel leader ask his guests to tell the audience what things from their pasts they now miss the most. The first guest called on spoke up almost instantly. He missed the old bands, he said, especially Jan Garber, Enoch Light, Guy Lombardo, and Ben Bernie and All the Lads. I nodded appreciatively; I would have added Jimmy Dorsey myself, but I wasn't asked. The next chap said he missed most the sweaty excitement of the boxing ring, and declared he would pay a sizable sum just to see the Jack Sharkey–Max Schmeling fight again. This was obviously over the heads of the other panel members, who looked confused. "Sharkey beat Schmeling in 1932 at the old Garden," the panelist said, not bothering to conceal his disgust at his colleagues' ignorance.

A lady panelist said she missed Greer Garson, Loretta Young, and Paul Muni. This restored group harmony, and everyone nodded agreement. The next panelist said she missed the dulcet, syrupy platitudes of the late Senator Everett Dirksen, of Illinois. "Nobody could say absolutely nothing as beautifully as he could," she recalled wistfully. "Where have all the wonderful speakers gone?" Only one panelist was left, an elderly lady who looked uneasy and who licked her lips nervously when the gaze of the host and other panelists turned on her. "What do you miss the most?" the host asked gently. The lady hesitated. "I miss most," she said in a low voice, "the ozone layer."

A gentle lady sticks a foot out to trip everybody up, but these are busy days for gentle ladies and we wish there were more of them. Getting back to my plan, it is this: in a peculiarly turbulent time, let's vent our national anger by trying to convert the bees to a capitalist economy—leaving the honey pretty much as it is now—and let's try to get a gentle lady on every television panel show. Can we have a show of hands on this proposal?

The Wonder of It All

To be natural is such a very difficult pose to keep up," wrote Oscar Wilde a hundred years ago. The old boy was better known for offending London society by picking odd sexual fruit from orchards in which it was felt he had no right to roam than for his epigrams, but the latter sparkle even today despite the corrosive effect of time. Writers today are preoccupied with what they want to say—their small sermons—and not with ways of expressing it. Wilde was of the tradition of London wits who considered style as important as the idea itself, a concept that Marshall McLuhan tried—and failed—to obliterate a few years ago with his "the media is the message" nonsense that was quickly shot down in flames.

Already I'm wandering from my subject. If Wilde's essays, plays, and novels smelled of London clubs and taverns, it did not lessen the validity of his central theme and that's what I'm struggling to get back to. To be natural and to discover delight in natural things is a prize not easy to come by in this period where fashion prevails over everything else and where Eddie Murphy's obscenities have made him a very rich man. There was a time, and not very long ago, when trying to sneak even an oath into a movie script was like trying to sneak a sunrise past a rooster, but now ten-year-olds in movie houses laugh heartily at language that wouldn't be tolerated in a lumber camp. What brings this up is a small volume I've come upon recently and which I don't remember having ever read although its author is one of my favorite writers. The book is called *The Sense of Wonder* and the author is Rachel Carson, the brilliant lady whose *Silent Spring* first warned us that we were poisoning the planet on which we live.

Miss Carson touches words like a harpist touching strings. Not only is her spirit bright and filled with the love of life itself but her touch is sure. That she spent a large part of her life in Maine—at a shoreside spot not far from my island—must be irrelevant; she would have been Rachel Carson in a New Mexican desert or on a Nebraskan plain. She opens her essay— which is what the book really amounts to—on a stormy autumn night when she took her twenty-month-old nephew, wrapped in a blanket, down to the beach (this was in Maine) in rainy darkness. Miss Carson doesn't fool around with lengthy introductions; the toilsome business of writing which plagues so many of us who write only seems to send her soaring aloft quickly like a plane taking off on a short runway. She wastes no more than a sentence to describe the lonely, rain-swept beach where big waves came thundering in and where dimly-seen shapes boomed and shouted and threw great handfuls of froth at her and the infant in her arms. Then: "Together we laughed for pure joy—he a baby meeting for the first time the wild tumult of Oceanus, I with the salt of half a lifetime of sea love in me. But I think we felt the same spine-tingling response to the vast, roaring ocean and the wild night around us." Wow! This is the Christmas present for those who love the sea, for those who love Maine, for those who love life itself. I can't tell you whether the book is gentle or exhausting or, perhaps, both, but I will say it is wonderful, and that takes us back to the title of this slim volume itself.

The wonders of nature and of simple things seem to be making a comeback, to be touching people who are weary of the sound of endless traffic, of sirens screaming in the night, of twelve-year-old kids shooting each other in order to get a better street corner on which to deal drugs, of high school principals being stabbed to death in hallways, of leveraged buy-outs, of the unashamed hypocrisy of politics, of Eddie Murphy's obscenities, and the growing sterility of the human spirit. I have written before, in this magazine, of Maine's increasing popularity with people from other states, and I believe this is a manifestation of general unhappiness with the empty vacuum of urban life and the terrible realization that the state of the human condition is becoming one of numbness, of failed communication, of high insensibility, and—the most lamentable of all—of indifference. Life has never been a carnival but neither has it—in my lifetime—been such a release of disorder and despair as that which now seems to have us in its grip. Maine, and the other placid spots on the nation's map, seem to be tugging at the hearts of people who have a bellyful of rock music, cynicism, greed, public corruption, unruly crowds, bottomless despair, and life without dreams. There are signs everywhere pointing to this, and I feel obliged to use Maine as an example because I see eyes light up when I say that my home is in Maine. I do not think of Maine as Shangri-La, as somewhere over the rainbow, but more and more I realize that other people do, that they see it as offering a way of life that has largely ceased to be.

Miss Carson ends her essay with a promise of a fulfilled life not from greed and acquisition but from "something infinitely healing" in the true beauties and mysteries of the earth. These lasting pleasures, she writes, "are available to anyone who will place himself (or herself) under the influence of earth, sea, and sky and their amazing life." I trust Miss Carson, and I wish she were here now to teach this generation a lot of what they have forgotten. Or never knew.

Closed Ecosystem

At a time when we are confronted on all sides by things that are mediocre or worse, it is refreshing to come across something which is genuinely good or genuinely bad, and we point to the *Providence Journal-Bulletin* as one of the former. The Providence newspaper has endeared itself to me by an editorial it recently published that said:

"Island dwellers, much more than mainlanders, understand that we live in a closed ecosystem. On islands, the inhabitants are forced to live with the environmental consequences of every thoughtful and thoughtless act and know that resources must be carefully conserved; that problems brought from off-island cannot easily be sent back; and that anything destroyed on the island is lost forever. As a result, islands and islanders can teach us a lot about living in another closed ecosystem—the Earth."

Well. Nothing tricky or sentimental there, nothing political, nothing promotional, just the facts stated tersely. It's too easy to get poetical about island life, but the Providence newspaper resisted the temptation. The late Richard Bissel, the Dubuque chap who gave up his family's pajama factory forty years or so ago to go to New York to write *The Pajama Game*, *Damn Yankees*, and other musical hits and books, bought a summer place on a small island near Boothbay Harbor. The house was called "Green Shutters," obviously because of its window decorations, and he referred to the place in a rapturous way in numerous magazine articles. But as he started fixing the place up, I noticed it began to appear as "Green Shudders" in his writing, a subtle transformation of attitude. That sort of thing is not rare on islands.

I have been twenty-three years on this island, and while I never think of it as being a "closed ecosystem" I realize that—in a miniscule way—it is certainly that. Underscoring what has become known as the "extinction crisis" on Earth, scientists and environmentalists now estimate that one species becomes extinct every hour of every day, which causes my thoughts to race to the matter of snakes on this island when the matter of a separate ecosystem is mentioned. There were snakes here when I first took over the island, not many and certainly not harmful ones. But occasionally I encountered one when I lifted an old board or rock, and I am unable to say which of us found the encounter more disturbing. Snake sightings grew more and more infrequent as the years went on, although I never killed any, and the last snake I saw here was about six years ago when a small garter snake wriggled out from under the house to lie in the sun near the kitchen door. That, I assume now, was the dinosaur of Hamloaf Island. The *Providence Journal-Bulletin* would tell you that I can teach the mainland public a lot as a result of this and other encounters with wildlife on my closed ecosystem, and while I appreciate the high trust placed in me by the editors of the paper I am not sure it is deserved. There was neither a thoughtful nor a thoughtless act on my part in the snake survival matter, but my hands were not so clean where the chipmunk was concerned.

In the early days of this column, I wrote frequently of the chipmunk, an engagingly obnoxious little rodent called "L.B.," who was here when I arrived and who tolerated my intrusion upon his island only because I absentmindedly left Oreo cookies on the kitchen counter and he valued Oreos more than life itself, which it almost came to, in the end. Over a period of two or three years, L.B. made my nights a living hell searching for Oreos in the dark. Champagne glasses were knocked from shelves, entrance holes were chewed into cabinets, and finally only a lead-lined ammo box from a navy surplus depot could be used for holding pastries overnight. It was when L.B. chewed a hole in the door to my daughter's room and beside it another hole to use as an exit that I decided he had to go. I caught him in a Havahart trap and exiled him to another island, which in reality meant that he only traded one ecosystem for another. Perhaps this whole episode with the chipmunk is irrelevant to the subject, but as you can see I feel my innocence is unproven and I'd just as soon that none of this got back to the *Providence Journal-Bulletin*. This is not an episode from the past that I prefer to drown in drink, but neither do I emerge as a bulwark against environmental irresponsibility.

I read somewhere the other day that ecological systems that won't support wildlife won't long support us either, and I believe it is true. What I am going to try to do, though, is disprove the newspaper's contention that anything destroyed on an island is lost forever. I'm going to take my Havahart trap over to that island and catch a chipmunk to bring back here. It will prove that ecological destruction can be reversed, and it will set an example which if followed widely will clear a man who is heavily encumbered with the baggage of guilt, and at the same time help make the world young again.

Zeitgeist

I like the mail that I get from readers even when they tend to scold, such as the letter that arrived today. The writer who said my work was always interesting is endeared to me by his amiable error, but he then went on to suggest that I should be more careful to stick to "the pure and simple truth" about modern progress. The truth is rarely pure and almost never simple, in the first place, and I think life would be very tedious if it were either. *Modern* and *progress* are antithetical words and should seldom, if ever, be used together.

I'm more than willing to step outside and settle this matter now. For example, I see nothing in rock music, with a very few exceptions and I can't recall one at the moment, that can engage the sensibilities of a mature adult. It is crude, unbelievably primitive, totally lacking in any tonal subtlety, largely dissonant, and at its best becomes monotonous after a thirty-second exposure. I will skip over the requirement that rock musicians must look as degenerate as possible, usually shirtless, and always with scraggly facial hair and dark glasses. The lyrics (*lyrics?*) accompanying rock music are usually one simple sentence repeated over and over until the vocalist becomes exhausted or the hall is rented to another group, whichever comes first. The saxophone, the clarinet, the trumpet, and the trombone of earlier music are now museum instruments; only the amplified guitar thundering chords remains as the music of our time.

I got tired of Trivial Pursuit the first rainy weekend on the island when I had guests from New York, and I'm supremely indifferent to what is on those cards, singly or in categories. I like, even less, the later games spun off from Trivial Pursuit, especially the one dealing with Wall Street, junk bonds, and insider trading. I don't really like walking in the rain but I must say there are worse things than getting wet.

I remember when election years were fun, with candidates speaking from the observation cars of trains. Lies were told without malice and claims were made that staggered the imagination, but throughout it all the proven rascality of the candidates went unspoken, and an air of friendly collegiality prevailed. I yearn for those days because I genuinely feel that the governments put in office by those elections were more efficient than those we have today, and I spend a lot of time wondering how and why the Chief of Staff of the White House has managed to become a more powerful figure than the President, whoever it might be.

In days gone by, trains ran late, some so late that they barely preceded the next train, but the fare structure of train travel made sense and no such absurdities existed as the "yield management" of airlines where there are nine passengers seated abreast, each going to the same destination, each eating the same meals, each watching the same movie but each one paying a different fare.

There are many other aspects of contemporary life that are one hundred percent wrong and not to be tolerated by decent individuals. Corporate dishonesty is one of them. And acting any different from the way I do is another.

Today's Specials

Like a lot of people who always thought lobsters hung around the place where they were eventually trapped, I was startled a few days ago to read that lobsters have gotten as travel conscious as the rest of us and that some of them log up to as many as 100 miles or more a year. Considering the lobster's size, 100 miles is no weekend jaunt to New Jersey to see the folks; it is equivalent, I am told, of my leaving Maine for a trip to Florida, a trip I seriously considered taking, incidentally, during the two months of rain and fog that made up in Maine what we laughingly called spring this year.

The University of Maine Sea Grant College, which is the source of my recently acquired information about the mobility of lobsters, didn't mention that the strong dollar was an influencing element in lobsters' travels, and my own feeling, which in no way reflects that of the Sea Grant College, is that lobsters have far more concern about the price-per-pound of lobsters than anything else. The strength of *that* dollar determines how aggressively lobsters will be fished, and that, I imagine, is the most unsettling concern in a lobster's life.

Just kicking this subject around a little so the Sea Grant College can have the benefit of my own findings, I would think that the mass movement of Americans this summer and fall to Europe—the greatest in history according to the number of U.S. passports issued—may have something of a beneficial effect upon those lobsters who decide to loaf around the place locally and put off travel until this winter or even next year. In the first place, those Americans going abroad will come back agreeably encumbered with knowledge of foreign foods, and will be in a hurry to display their new taste and worldliness to their friends. Quiche and croissants and pizza and souvlaki are a few of these discoveries which have since bored us to death, and at the annual banquet of the chamber of commerce when the Beef Wellington is brought in there is still a gasp of awe as memories are stirred, although for the life of me I have never been able to discern the slightest virtue in the dish.

An awful lot of nonsense has been brought back from Europe by Americans intent upon squeezing a little European culture through Customs, and in the forefront of the quest is the lust—no weaker word would be appropriate—for the "darling little street café." I like to eat outside as well as the next man if the weather is mild and the site is serene, but a dusty table situated two feet from truck traffic is not my notion of an *al fresco* adventure. During my lifetime I have traveled a great deal because it is a necessity in my work, and I find that while I occasionally pause at a street cafe in a foreign city for a drink or a snack I almost never go out looking for one, and I long ago came to terms with the knowledge that I would always take dinner in a restaurant where the food arrived hot, where I could see what I was eating, and where the flatulence of traffic was an off-stage hum and not part of the immediate drama. While I am on the subject of European cuisine, I would like to pause for a moment and discuss the matter of food served *flambé*. In my opinion, which is not humble, *flambé* is not cuisine, but theater. Serving a dish on fire does nothing to improve its taste, although it does catch the eye. I once read in a stylish food magazine an exhortation to hostesses to serve after-dinner brandy in scooped-out orange peel; the brandy would be lighted and the drink would be served flaming. I don't know about you, but I wouldn't touch that thing with tongs. I remember the article said that when this drink was brought to the table, with the house lights dimmed, there would be a chorus of *ahhhhhs* from the guests. I would say those sounds the hostess hears are more likely to be sirens, and I know where the equipment is headed. A few drops spilled and you're being measured for a new suit tomorrow.

There are a few other things I would like to add to the record, such as the chap who spends a weekend in Paris and Rome and comes home calling them "Paree" and Roma, but I'll forego the temptation. I would like to return for a moment to the subject of Beef Wellington, because I don't think people hate it enough and I want to do anything I can to diminish the notion that it is worth the fuss made over it. Once at an extravagant dinner in one of the big Las Vegas hotels, a gambler sitting next to me predicted that the main course would be Beef Wellington. Five-to-one were the best odds he would lay on the sun rising, but he offered to give longer odds on that Beef Wellington and, of course, he would have won.

It may appear that I have strayed from the subject of traveling lobsters, but I really haven't. Out of the vast sea of ill-assorted customs and tastes brought back by Americans from European vacations this summer, the fondness for lobster will not be one of them if my memory of the price of lobster on the menus of Paris is reliable. We may be in for a feverish wave of *steak au poivre* or *vitello tonnato*, but the lobsters of Maine can rest comfortably with the knowledge that they will not be the next food fad. With this worry out of the way and with the approach of fall, the lobster with a taste for wandering can begin preparing for his or her winter trip. *Bon voyage*, and watch out for traps and hijackers!

Sinking Feeling

A few days ago while driving on a back road I saw a name emblazoned on the mailbox of a small farm, and I wish to advise the farmers and suburbanites of Maine who have not yet named their places to forget the whole thing. It's all been said. The name of this farm was "Psychottage."

The change of seasons has a fine effect upon me; I start reorganizing right and left, tying up loose ends left over from last season and checking on things that, for the moment anyway, I had let drop from sight. One of the things from which I want to blow the dust, right now, is the whole subject of the time we live in and the customs and attitudes that reflect that time. Psychottage probably started my thoughts off in this direction and I suddenly began to wonder what happened to names like Chestnut Lawn or Deep Run Farm or Oak Grove. But even as I ask, I sense a sinking feeling and I know that whatever answer comes forth will have a hollow ring, like the character in the Peter deVries novel who asked a friend why man felt so compelled to actually reach the moon. "Because," the friend replied, "I feel we've been put on this earth for a purpose."

As everybody knows who reads this page, I don't avoid controversial subjects, but it may well be that in seeking to focus light on some of the absurdities of the present day I may be getting back in step with the mainstream of current thought, rather than confronting it. I stayed totally aloof during the Coca-Cola civil war, not because of any newly discovered restraint on my part but rather because I grew up in a period when Nehi Grape was the drink for the discriminating young chap about town. If Nehi Grape wasn't at hand, I fell back upon a bottled lime soda which I realize now was a primary emetic but whose sickeningly sweet taste at that time struck me as all a man could yearn for in a soft drink. I was somewhat startled, though, to discover the *New York Times* welcoming back the old Coke, as well as approving—or seeming to approve—the return of "There She Is . . ." to the Miss America Beauty Pageant. I'm not sure how far the *New York Times* goes in its approval of the return of these irreplaceables to the American scene, but I gather the newspaper found them more than just fit to print. Moreover, the *Times* said that consumers it had queried also wanted the Ford Model A returned as well as drugstores with soda fountains. Now we're getting somewhere.

I dislike elbowing my way into this discussion without being invited to, but I've waited a long time for this subject to come up. I have nothing against radio serials or brass thumbtacks, two other bits of Americana which the *Times* had unearthed, but I think they should come much further down the list. I don't mean to challenge the *Times'* priorities violently; it's just that they are inhaling the unfamiliar draught of approval and being new to the sensation they are making the customary mistakes of the inexperienced.

Personally, I would like to exchange correspondence with someone who, like me, has had the measles, whooping cough, or the mumps. There aren't many of us left, and it would be good if we could get together like World War I veterans and swap experiences. In a world full of inhibition, depression, anorexia, schizophrenia, bulimia, and conversion hysteria, it may even be a good influence. My attention was brought to this subject recently when I offered myself for a physical examination and instead of a kindly old physician with a blood pressure gauge, there was a doctor, a nurse, and a computer. Although the nurse operated the computer and has the only official report of the proceedings, my recollection of it was that I was checked for Babinski, Romberg, and Osgood Rheinmann's Disease, among others. "This tests the integrity of the nervous system," the doctor said, holding up a pin. "Whenever you feel a pinprick say 'Pin'." He sank the pin into my thigh.

I said, "Ouch."

The nurse punched a key on the computer and the printout read: "Uncooperative and refuses to take direction." Possessing the kind of mind that erases unpleasant experiences, I don't remember much of the examination but I clearly recall that when the doctor told me to put on a robe and go down the hall to the Dental Lab, I went even further. I went all the way to the taxi stand.

I have no doubt that the *Times* discovered—as they reported—one consumer who already was mourning the departure of the Montgomery Ward catalog, but for my money I'd like to see, just once more, a kindly old family doctor who would put the thermometer under my tongue and get out his stethoscope. Maybe he wouldn't have been keeping up with medical progress, but when I left I would feel like a million dollars. After taxes.

Awesome

I was reading a story in the newspaper the other day about the gentrification of Portland and suddenly realized that *gentrification* and *gentrify* were this year's fashionable new worlds. Americans love trends, worship trends, live in terms of trends, and fashion long ago thrust Americans into a search for trendy new words. Remember *ambience*? That was the new word in 1978. *Androgynous* was 1980. Remember *supportive* which Americans thought in 1979 was a much finer word than the verb *support*? Last year the new word was *awesome*, which was not so much a discovery as it was a reclamation of a workable old word. But suddenly last year things were awesome which had just been noteworthy before.

The English language has been gutted by many fires but it has remained a durable thing in spite of its abuse, and its resilience has been— well, I may as well say it, unfashionable as it now is—awesome. Right now we are tolerating a level of obscenity in motion pictures, in television, in fiction, and indeed around our own dinner tables, that a quarter of a century ago would hardly have been put up with in a lumber camp. This indulgence has spread outward from New York and Hollywood and other urban centers which are usually the wellsprings of fashion and trendsetting to Maine and to other areas normally more resistant to leniency in these matters. Television has brought about a new homogeneity in American taste and custom, leveling state and regional boundaries. Cracker barrel and hayseed humor have disappeared in mountain and rural areas, where the people now laugh at the same jokes that produce applause in Las Vegas. This could be both fortunate and unfortunate, since good taste as well as the awful could be spread by television, although the likelihood of the former occurring at this moment seems minimal.

Yet good taste is persistent and abides in strange places. From Minnesota came *Lake Wobegon Days*, which made its way to the top of the best-seller list without a dirty word, soaring up over the steamy fiction of Jackie Collins and Sidney Sheldon.

Trendiness, obeisance to fashion, bothers me since it involves the surrender of one's own judgement in all ad hoc matters in favor of the current absurdity sweeping the country, and the suspension of reason for whatever exciting cause and for whatever length of time is an exceedingly risky thing. Hitlers, Abu Nidals, and Kaddafis thrive on this sort of thing; today's eccentric may be tomorrow's genius, but he may also be Joe McCarthy riding into town with an amplified guitar. The success of Bhagwan Rajneesh, a simple-minded old man with a liking for young women and Rolls Royces, in building up an army of disciples almost overnight should have set off a ripple of apprehension in the land but it didn't. The element of comedy, always a deterrent in endeavors of madness, fortunately intruded and quickly defused the Bhagwan's dream of an empire. The group of misguided believers, seeking after an illusive Nirvana, melted away when the old fellow was revealed as comic rather than omnipotent. Laughter is about the best purgative there is.

New York City and Los Angeles set most of the trends in this country and if they both seem painfully unimaginative, it is because true value has very little to do with public acceptance. The chic restaurants of New York's East Side and Beverly Hills' Rodeo Drive thrive on a success that has very little to do with good food. What is more to the point is the extent that the captains and waiters maintain high standards of insolence toward the customers. A place that treats its customers badly must be good, and it is to the diner's credit to be accepted at all. This sort of thing led, ten years or so ago, to Yogi Berra's famous remark about a New York restaurant when he said, "Nobody goes there anymore. It's too crowded."

There is a fierce independence in the people of Maine, and they possess a natural skepticism. I've eaten in almost every restaurant in my neighborhood, and I haven't encountered any that would stay in business long if they substituted arrogance and disdain for reasonably good food, and that includes Portland where gentrification is now underway.

Virulent and Contagious

I make my living at the unsubstantial business of writing, which I suppose adds very little to the Gross National Product, but what few people know is that on the side I run a one-man search-and-destroy commando unit against trendiness or whatever is chic. Actually I shouldn't be in Maine at all because a guerrilla activity of this kind should be carried out behind enemy lines, which would place me in either New York or Los Angeles, but since I despise both cities, having lived in one and visited often in the other, my strategy is to occupy a comfortable outpost here from which I can throw rocks to my heart's content. Trendiness has never established much of a foothold in Maine, so I am really a late comer to the fight, but I feel that my emergence now from covert activity marks the beginning of a new phase in the struggle. Never forget that Maine has a fuzzy sort of adjancency—I prefer to think of it as a frontier—with Massachusetts, and Boston over the past decade has been precariously balanced on the slippery slope of fashion. The modish little restaurants on Newbury Street specializing in mimosa cocktails and alfalfa sprouts, the foreign film houses in Cambridge with their retrospective festivals of *The Cabinet of Dr. Caligari,* and the mass substitution of the words *boutique* and *maison* for *shop* in the halls of Copley Place, all make me feel that Boston is perhaps irretrievably lost, having moved so far into the world of chic that it cannot scramble back. A man I know, you might even call him a scout, told me recently that on Tremont Street he had seen a store advertising "general merchandise," but I don't believe him. I had spent a sleepless night and I think he was only trying to make me feel better.

The *New York Times* turned up a very interesting man the other day and I commend him to historians. His name is Anthony R. Cucci and he is the mayor of Jersey City. When he was told that he had been selected as one of the world's best-dressed men, the color drained from his face. Mr. Cucci said that he would need time to assess the political damage of his being placed on the list. "I have not ruled out the possibility that this honor is a political smear tactic," he said. The more I read about Mr. Cucci, the better I liked him. "I go for the polyester blends that hold up," he went on in a way that must have struck terror in the hearts of the Fashion Foundation of America people who compiled the list. "I have never been to Europe," he added. This latter revelation must have hurt the Fashion Foundation most of all, since in chic circles anything European is infinitely better than anything American simply because it is European.

I hope my readers don't see me as a sort of modern-day Joseph McCarthy seeing communists under every bed, but I admit to a certain uneasiness when I drive through some of the coastal towns in southern Maine and read the cute names of the summer shops, the cafes, and the bed-and-breakfast inns. As I said, I consider Maine's southern flank adjoining Massachusetts via New Hampshire's I-95 corridor to be an unprotected area, knowing trendiness to be both virulent and contagious. If Maine becomes chic, it will creep in under the cover of darkness from the south. Please remember where you read this.

What I must warn you against now is a mutant development that has taken root in the eastern part of the United States and which, like most offshoots from parental strains, is all the more dangerous because the real is sometimes difficult to identify from the spurious. I am speaking of the "old-fashioned" country store, the "old-fashioned" ice-cream parlor, and the "old-fashioned" café, all of which are very chic. The country store sells hard candy, yellow cheese, and potholders with off-color inscriptions on them, while the ice-cream parlors offer such flavors as chive, Oreo cookie, and cantaloupe, all of which are priced at $3.50 for one scoop. Most of the old-fashioned cafés have *Arkansas* or *Texas* in their names and, I am afraid, larceny in their hearts. All are terribly cute.

The appeal of Maine, of course, is that it stands alone on the Atlantic coast as a rugged, fiercely independent state inhabited by people of great common sense and practicality who will tolerate a little foolishness but not too much. It is possible, but I think unlikely, that the state would go to any great length to embrace the prevailing taste and become vain, feckless, transparent, sterile, and devoid of basic humanity. People come to Maine because of its singularity and not because of its similarity, since it still possesses the prizes of silence and beauty which have largely been driven from the world.

Today has been a fine day in every respect, with small, white clouds drifting in an indigo sky. Though a faint memory of the day still lingers in the west, the first stars are showing and it's going to one of those evenings that makes Maine the changeless enchantress that she is. On an evening like this, I would like to wander down to the dock and have a casual chat with some stranger over a couple of bottles of beer. Somebody like Mayor Anthony R. Cucci, of Jersey City, for example.

Aerobics, Computers, Pasta

New Yorkers, as anyone knows who reads these essays regularly, fascinate me endlessly, largely because they are the most self-conscious people in the world. They live in a close community totally dedicated to fashion; the restaurant turning away overflow today will have a FOR RENT sign on the door tomorrow. A friend from New York,

one who is engaged in advertising—the trendiest of all trendy occupations—spent a weekend with me on the island recently and in a far-
reaching conversation over drinks one evening gave me a cycloramic
view of what is currently chic in New York. "There are only three things
that occupy the thoughts of New York people in the autumn of 1988," my
friend said, and I bent forward to receive this information, much as one
would lean forward to get a little insider-trading information from a
leveraged-takeover specialist. "The three most important things right
now are aerobics, computers, and pasta. Nothing else really matters."

Wow! Aerobics, computers, and pasta. Well, New Yorkers are
not alone in their conviction that computers are the miracle that will
save the world, but I think in most places across the country a
computer is recognized as a business tool and not the true heartbeat
of life. Frankly, I despise computers, my dislike for them beginning a
few years ago when my bank couldn't take my deposit because, as the
teller told me, "the computer is down." (It is my suspicion that "the
computer is down" is taking its place beside "the check is in the mail"
as one of the chief all-purpose evasions of our time.) I reminded the
teller that I was seeking to make a deposit in a bank, not in a computer,
and she looked at me as though I were rejecting the Old Testament.

I must say, in defense of New York people, that they possess no
dream of bringing perfect understanding to the rest of the world. This is
probably because they feel there is very little world outside of New York,
and what little exists is too insignificant to worry over. Generally speaking, the New Yorker goes about his or her business with a sense of
detachment from the rest of the world, enjoying the great drama that is
being played out there. This should surprise no one; why should one go
to a play and read a newspaper instead of watching the stage? New York's
considered opinion is that there is too big a separation between Manhattan and what lies to the west of the Hudson River to ever bridge the gap.
I have often wondered what would happen if the rest of the United
States adopted this egocentric attitude and refused to get sidetracked by
concern for what the other cities were doing, but I finally reached the
conclusion that the nation would then be made up of an accumulation of
spiteful, scornful, and crotchety little entities and that much of the fun of
being an American would vanish.

A few days after my guests had returned to New York, I decided
to run a test to determine how Maine related to the preoccupation of
New Yorkers with aerobics, computers, and pasta. I caught my
neighbor from the mainland shortly after he had brought in his
lobsterboat for the day, and was hosing down the deck before going
home. I asked him if he thought much about computers, pasta, and
aerobics. "What's that last?" he asked, turning off the hose. "Aerobics,"

I said. "It's a form of exercise that speeds up the heart action." He looked at me as if I were either insane or totally drunk. "Exercise," he said, as though the word itself hadn't occurred to him for many years. "Friend, if I can sit at the wheel of that pickup truck long enough to get home safely I'll be lucky. Please don't mention the word *exercise* in my presence if you can help it."

The French-Canadian carpenter who was doing some work on the house didn't even reply when I told him about computer fetishism on Manhattan Island. He shot me a glance freighted with disbelief, and then turned to his work. "I've heard everything." he muttered.

Well, that left pasta. For a long time around Maine, the only pasta one encountered was spaghetti buried under tomato sauce and occasionally enlivened by meatballs or clam sauce. I see in the supermarkets now that the pasta horizon has been greatly widened by the appearance of fettuccine, linguine, angel hair, tortellini, and other butterflies, shells, and rings the need for which had not been established locally until the past four or five years. I asked a Boothbay Harbor restaurant owner how he felt about the public clamor for pasta dishes, and he rubbed his hands in satisfaction. "Simply great," he said. "I make more money on a pasta plate than anything else on the menu. Seafood used to show the biggest profit margin, but no more. Diners have moved away from red meat because of health reasons, and the slack is being taken up by pasta. Wonderful. It's money in the bank for restaurants."

It was at this point that I concluded my poll, having discovered, with two or three percentage points plus or minus for error, what I wanted to know. Maine people can take aerobics, computers, and pasta or they can leave them alone. But they have learned that pasta is better for the old ticker than a lot of red meat, and if they stick with pasta there is a good chance they can forget all about aerobics—and computers.

Couch Potatoes

One of mankind's most cherished dreams is that it can count on continuity, that things will go along pretty much as they are going now. Well, dream on, friends and neighbors, because when you awaken you will find things changing so fast that not only will you be unable to predict the future but you will have trouble keeping up with the present. That's where I come in, and you're lucky to have me to fall back on.

The goal of this column, if you have not read it before, is to excite good humor and at the same time free you from the bothersome need of keeping up with what is currently *chic*. (This is as good a time as any to point out that fashion requires you to sprinkle as many French words and phrases in your letters and conversation as you can think of, and don't worry unduly about using them correctly. The other person seldom knows more than you do. When I was a much younger man I lived for a period in a French city on a street that was named after a French general, who was considered locally to have been a national disaster, but my address on the back of the letters I mailed home built up a great deal of credit in my social account.)

The unusual always attracts attention. Take the currently fashionable term *couch potato*, which has the potato growers in Maine in a petulant state, feeling as they do that it somehow demeans the potato. I would like to write about the couch potato with enthusiasm, but I can't because the term is rather tiresome in all of its aspects. A couch potato is someone who sits around all day watching television. The term was already in wide use among the trendsetters, but it fell into common *patois* (notice that French word?) when the three major television networks broadcast a public service announcement of the American Pediatric Academy saying that children who watch too much television become couch potatoes. That was bad enough but it got worse—from the Maine potato growers' point of view—when *couch potato* was defined as someone who became obese, boring, and dense. There was hell to pay after that. But to show how fashionable terms sweep the country, there is at this moment in California an organization known as The Couch Potatoes, dedicated to television, which claims chapters in fifty states. When asked about the Maine chapter, the organization requested a little more time to assemble its facts. Knowing how quickly fashion crests and then recedes, it probably hasn't as much time for this job as it would like to think it does.

New York, of course, is a wellspring of American fashion, and a friend of mine there advises me that we are now in what is known as The Retro Period, and that I should take it from there. I admit to some difficulty—living as I do on an island in Maine—navigating fashionable waters on my own, and I pressed for details. "It's going backwards," she explained patiently. "Go back as far as you like, only keep it simple. Forget *nouvelle cuisine*; the fashionable thing to eat now is meatloaf with mashed potatoes. Keep out of singles' bars—they're dead. I'll send you a new book that's out now on the subject of lunch boxes, like we used to carry as kids. There are Howdy Doody lunch boxes, Lone Ranger lunch boxes, Barbie Doll lunch boxes. See what I mean?"

Realizing I had a poor grasp on the central thread of this thing, I asked for more examples. "One thing is sure," she went on, "and that is it must be something from the past, something that goes on after all occasion for it has disappeared. In sports, the fashionable thing is bowling. Get the group together, have a few drinks, and go bowling."

"What does the group drink?" I asked feebly, struggling to impress an authority with my eagerness to see this thing through.

"Beer," she replied. "It's the fashionable new drink. Drink a few bottles of beer and go bowling. Or to the pool hall and shoot some pool. That's the new rage."

"Wow!" I exclaimed involuntarily. "Pool? Are you sure?"

"Pool's the thing but so is baseball," she said evenly. "And your saying 'wow' was good and old-fashioned. You're catching on."

When I asked if there was a statistically significant increase in baseball, she interrupted me. "Forget that kind of talk," she said. "Remember we're going back to a simpler time. We're dressing simpler, more in the blue-collar class. Comfy shoes. Leather jackets. Old aviator's jackets are priceless. If you can find an apron with 'I like Ike' on it, you're in clover. Nostalgia's back."

I was trying to assimilate this, but there was more. "And the best thing of all," my friend concluded, "is one doesn't have to apologize for cocooning."

My expression must have revealed my ignorance. "*Cocooning*," she explained, "is nesting. It's when you come home from the office and choose not to go out for dinner. On Sundays you cocoon by sitting in front of the fire and reading. Or watching TV. I know *cocoon* is a noun, but in The Retro Period it's used also as a verb."

I had the feeling we had come full circle. If you cocoon enough you will likely become a couch potato, but I didn't say anything. It was as though somebody had pushed the rewind button on New Year's Eve just before midnight.

Black Plate Special

I often feel that I'm lagging in life's race because the things that are happening these days are so dynamic that I'm usually way over my head just contemplating them. I know my outlook is conservative where new styles and customs are concerned, and I don't like to mess around with new developments that I don't understand. But I came across something in a magazine the other day that so intrigued me that I couldn't pass it by, although my better judgment would normally have sounded an alert. What the magazine article said, in effect, was that black is now the fashionable color for food and if anyone has a hankering for social success, he or she had better get with it.

On occasions of this kind I always go to the kitchen and pour myself a drink and then carry the glass down to the dock where I can think things over. Different people, when faced with something perplexing, seek out a sort of secure place for a cautionary examination of the problem at hand, and I have found my dock ideal for picking out the broader meaning of issues that bring me close to the edge of desperation. When I return to the house I am sometimes more confused than ever, sometimes exhilarated, sometimes I feel entrapped, and sometimes I go back just to get a refill.

This was a prickly proposition, this sudden emergence of the need for specific color in one's food. I decided I had better lean against the ramp and get comfortable because there were no easy answers in sight and I suspected that my involvement in this matter was inescapable.

The woman who wrote the article had come forward in a straightforward if blithe manner. "People seem to like food in unusual colors," she quoted a chef as saying, "and black has the most drama. Chefs are doing black pasta for the visual effect." But the new style doesn't stop with black pasta. The writer goes on to say that black rice, black beans, black olives, black truffles, and even black seaweed are showing up on restaurant menus everywhere, and of course the whole concept is being picked up by hostesses who want to set a table that is fashionable in every respect. There is even black popcorn for those trendsetters who like to nibble on something socially acceptable while watching a movie on the VCR.

Before going further, I should mention that I am hardly a novice in matters of this sort. I passed up participation in the National Pea Council's drive to step up the reported average of eleven peas eaten each day by every man, woman, and child in the United States, not because I was indifferent to the Pea Council's problem but because I had a premonition that something more critical was likely to happen in the food world and I wanted to be ready for it. I was later drawn, somewhat against my better judgment, into a minor controversy kindled by a ladies' magazine over making a coffee cup by turning an orange peel inside out. "After-dinner coffee aflame in orange cups will make your dinner unforgettable," the author had written. "Saturate a cube of sugar in a spoon with brandy, light, and float in the coffee. Then stand back for the *oohs* and *aahs* when you enter the darkened room with the flaming orange cups."

I've never lifted an orange peel full of flaming coffee, and I would do so only with tongs and, if available, I'd like an insulated glove. You could pick out a man who has drunk coffee in this way, I believe, by a nervous and shifty gaze, by the fact that he's wearing a new suit, and I think you would find that he had very short hair.

The author of the article chose her words with uncanny accuracy; I don't know anything that would make a meal more "unforgettable" than some flaming coffee in the lap. The really smart guests, I believe, would get their coats and slip out as soon as the lights go dim because that's the tip-off that something unusual is in the works and that it will involve fire. Forget about the *oohs* and *aahs* too. Once a few of those orange peels collapse, the hostess isn't going to hear *oohs* and *aahs* but she's going to hear words that wouldn't be tolerated in a lumber camp.

California, as you may have guessed, is on its toes where black food is concerned, the Fog City Diner of San Francisco featuring a black chili, and the general word is around Los Angeles to the effect that black symbolizes luxury and that black edibles should therefore be held in high esteem. Not only does black provide a sophisticated color, but it also implies a rich concentration of flavor, in the opinion of the lady who wrote the article. It has suddenly occurred to me that food that is burned black while the chef is reading one of the fashionable gourmet magazines could now find new use and social status, although its concentration of flavor may be a little too rich for even the most sophisticated palate.

I always thought that an egg sunny-side-up on a piece of toast was a splendid sight on the breakfast table, but I realize now it's an obsolete setting and one that does no credit to anyone. I was on the dock wondering how to get around the rigid and arbitrary disciplines I now face in regard to the color of foods when a thought occurred to me that may make my zeal for green spinach, yellow squash, and red tomatoes still possible of attainment. I'm just thinking out loud now, but suppose I ate all of my meals in the dark?

Power Appetizers

At precisely 1:15 P.M. on a recent rainy Thursday, John Fairchild, publisher of a fashion periodical called *Women's Wear Daily*, sat down at his customary table in the Four Seasons Restaurant in New York City and ordered a baked potato. The request sent tremors throughout the food and fashion world.

I have too weak a character to apologize to the potato growers of Maine for the remarks I made on this page a few months ago about the "couch potato," a trendy description of those who lie around most of the day watching television. The lifespan of fashionable slang being as fleeting as it is, the term fell from use almost before my comments were published and aside from some minor muttering I don't think the potato people felt their product had suffered from an unflattering association. Now I have cheerful news for all of those bound to the potato by economic or emotional ties. When Mr. Fairchild orders a baked potato, *everybody* orders a baked potato.

New York, and to a slightly lesser extent Los Angeles, sets the style for this country, and where they lead, we all follow. The day after Mr. Fairchild's request, those who had been in the restaurant at the time of the apocalypse all ordered a baked potato as their first course, as did others who had heard on the street what Mr. Fairchild had done. Rumors sweeping across the city became garbled, and it was only to be expected that in the ensuing days a few hapless individuals would mistakenly order French fries, but aside from deep humiliation on their part when they learned the truth, the day that had begun under the gray blanket of mist and a heavy overcast was destined to become historic.

The *New York Times*, bowing respectfully in the direction of Mr. Fairchild, immediately gave almost a full page to the discovery of the potato. Since there is not a hell of a lot that can be said about a baked potato, other than that it's baked, the *Times'* writers found it uphill going in their effort to stretch out the story to the limit that had been assigned to it. One writer, apparently told to deal with the baked potato as a "power appetizer" so to speak, ambled along courageously with a discourse on changing tastes and told how the weather vane was caused to spin wildly as the wind, and Mr. Fairchild, veered. The chef of the Four Seasons, as you can imagine, was interviewed as to the kind of potato Mr. Fairchild had eaten (Russet Burbank), and he added that after baking he let it stand at room temperature for fifteen minutes "to relax and finish baking." A tense or nervous potato, one assumes, results from failure of the chef to allow for that fifteen minutes of relaxation, but I'm only thinking out loud now and I don't want to give the impression that I'm still quoting from the *Times*. However, now that the subject of tension has arisen, I think it only fair to say that some uneasiness may occur when the Four Seasons diner glances at the check and discovers that his or her baked potato cost $8.50. I don't know how the Maine potato grower feels about that division of spoils.

The extent that Mr. Fairchild's discovery of the baked potato has been amplified and extended far beyond the fashion world of Manhattan is revealed in the announcement by Harper & Row, the book publishers, that they are rushing into print a potato cookbook which an impatient public can acquire in 1990. How quickly Mr. Fairchild may tire of the potato nobody can say, but I suspect the publishers would be assuming an untenable risk if they delayed publication after that date. I would hate to see the book come out on the day that Mr. Fairchild went to the Four Seasons and ordered braised leeks.

The summer of 1989 was a dismal one for Maine lobstermen who saw the price of lobsters decline to the point where the cost of bait and fuel made lobstering anything but profitable. You can see right now what I'm going to propose. Mr. Fairchild cannot be bought—you may be sure too many people have tried that already—but if he were told that the whole economy of the State of Maine hung precariously on his ordering a 1¼ -pound lobster, with melted butter, could he refuse? Maybe with a baked potato on the side?

Mr. Fairchild's world is inhabited largely by those people who from insecurity or ignorance are incapable of making *ad hoc* judgments. They accept an appreciation system devised by the people they admire, in this case Mr. Fairchild. If he wants a baked potato, they all want a baked potato because in that direction lies social salvation. In all fairness, however, it must be said that Mr. Fairchild's dilemma is common enough. As a trend-setter it is his obligation to live on the edge of history, but it is also his obligation not to fall off which is another way of saying that where lobsters are concerned he has to watch his cholesterol like the rest of us. Never forget, death is nature's way of telling us to slow down a little.

Color Me Conventional

I'll read anything; movable type was invented for me. The other day I was idly leafing through a new magazine and I was suddenly struck by what the inventive genius of the fashion world could produce when unselfishly pooled. Is there anyone here—I'm going to ask for a show of hands—who remembers when colors were simply yellow or blue or red or green or purple? Well, they aren't anymore, so the quicker you can erase all of that obsolete nonsense from your mind, the sooner you can take your place among the mall-smart, thoroughly up-to-date thinkers qualified to lead us into the on-rushing twenty-first century. *Green*, for example, is part of the untidy clutter of what passed as a color designation in the primitive civilization of the century now coming to a close. In place of *green* you are to use *spruce*—

easy enough for Mainers—or *vine* (a little darker), or *sage* if you want to let a little air into it. How I wish I could claim that last phrase as my own, but in all honesty I must say that I took it verbatim from the magazine. But the time will come, at some dinner party this summer, when it will roll off my lips without attribution and I can even now foresee the glances of admiration it will invoke.

The late Irvin S. Cobb had a reputation for disliking his fellow writers, a distaste he carried to the point where it even embraced the writer of epitaphs (an epitaph, he declared, is a belated advertisement for a line of goods that has been permanently discontinued). I have seldom numbered writers among the occupational groups I most admire, knowing that the flimsy business they are in rarely leads them down paths of rectitude, but seeing now the problems they face in dealing with the simple subject of colors—how a term may be obsolete by the time it is printed—creates a bond of sympathy I had not previously known. *Green* is a word that once brought to mind a certain color but now the word is *Mediterranean*; does that do the same thing? Maybe it does, maybe it doesn't. The brain spins in what might be called conventional circles, and it leads us to think in conventional terms. Like breathing, it is a habit difficult to break and in the long run may be just as risky.

Another magazine I chanced to glance at told a related though somewhat different story. The fashionable thing, I read, is to describe colors in terms of food. "Well-known foods," the article asserted, "convey the true tonal quality of colors in a way the old terms could never equal. Purple is one thing but isn't eggplant more precise?" A *cantaloupe* shirt was shown to drive home the point, while a pair of boysenberry shorts completed the ensemble. I didn't mind the canta- loupe shirt, but I wouldn't have touched the boysenberry shorts with tongs. A leek blazer, further along, caused me to stop in my tracks. I know for a fact that leeks are green at the top but white at the bulb, and here we faced a needlessly complex situation which can throw a widely ranging mind back into abandoned conventional thinking. I glanced at the blazer to see if it were green or white, and it was neither. Forced to follow the *patois* of current fashion, I would say, if you will forgive me, it was a sort of vomit green. I'm not attempting to blaze any new trails here, believe me, but just trying to follow the new trend as I see it.

I wish I could say that the matter ends here, but it doesn't. I had scarcely begun to think in terms of an oatmeal sweatshirt, spearmint slacks, and spinach pullover with a yam collar when the matter of color designation took an unexpected turn. A catalog arrived, urging me to cling no longer to foods as a designation of colors (hell, I had just started), but instead to "create comfortable conceptions" arising within my own personality. They promised to match a color to whatever word I sent in with my order, and to speed up the process they jump-started me with a few samples. Would I like a knit polo shirt in either *lagoon* or *wicker*? Or a *kelp* undershirt? Or *lawn* shorts with a *parakeet* belt? These conceptions may have been comfortable for others but they were not comfortable to me. I always thought a parakeet was a bird clothed in Day-Glo feathers of wild disorder, and the thought of wearing something of that nature around my waist was a little like asking me to pose buck naked on the roof of the Municipal Building. I won't do it.

Well, if this whole scene lacks reality, let me end on a prospect more pleasing to those of you—and to me—who still think in small, conventional terms and can feel complacent about it. I got out my L.L. Bean catalog (1990 Summer) and nervously opened it up at random. A Maine hand on the wheel, when a ship is in troubled water, brings reassurance. There it was—Bean's Sport Sweaters, in red, white, green, yellow, and light blue. A feathery sensation came over me, that wonderful feeling when you step outdoors after a thunderstorm, and the world seems fresh, and clean, and young again, and the sky is as light blue as those sweaters. Do you know what I mean?

Dog Spa

Difficult isn't really the right word to use in discussing the relationship between a man and his dog because the dog can't speak for itself and we end up with only one side of the debate. In a piece I wrote here recently I made a few observations about dog owners that were critically evaluated in an insensitive way by some readers, so in pursuing the subject further I am trying to be disarmingly simple and to draw no conclusions.

The unusual always arrests attention, and the intensity of the appeal seems to stand or fall by the degree of its relationship to absurdity or outrage. That a thing is good or bad is a side issue, little more than the icing on the cake. When I first read about the Marin County, California, vacation homes for dogs, my initial reaction was to telephone one of the places to see if they were—in the patois of the times—for real, but after reading the entire item I concluded that the news item was legitimate. Let me explain that Marin County is that area at the end of the Golden Gate Bridge across the bay from San Francisco, and that earthquakes are, perhaps, the least of the natural and unnatural phenomena that keep the local people awake nights. It is a yeasty atmosphere, with plenty going on all the time. The news item admittedly is a small sample of Marin County behavior, but I think it suggests how delicately the forces of reason in the area are balanced.

Boarding a dog in a kennel while the owners are away is a fairly commonplace thing in this country but it is barbaric by Marin County standards. One vacation home for dogs—forget the word kennel—specializes in taped messages from the dog owners which are played daily to the individual guests, with care taken, I assume, not to let other dogs overhear some extremely private message or personal nickname that would make the dog the laughingstock of the exercise run, once it was whispered around and became common knowledge.

A second Marin County dog spa—this one in a place called Larkspur—features private baths, TV sets, and beds with fur throws for those chilly evenings when the heat hasn't yet been turned up. I worry about the problems presented by television though, since dogs can't handle the remote, and I'm not sure what a guest does when he or she has seen that particular episode of "Roseanne" and isn't interested in a rerun. I know that nothing is perfect but I'm not sure dogs realize that some may be inclined to turn surly when forced to watch the news while "Cheers" is getting chuckles in an adjoining compartment.

Moving for the moment from such things as matched component stereos and Jacuzzis, I would like to bring up the unpleasant matter of social status, since you can be sure there is ultimately a serpent in every paradise. In yet another Larkspur vacation home, dogs who "get along" with other dogs may mix socially, but I am curious about how much equal opportunity exists in the matter of "getting along," and how much democracy prevails at the water trough, which I see as a sort of singles bar. To be blunt, I would like to know how a member of a minority—a real mutt, for example—would be treated in this environment. And there is still another, larger question which comes up concerning sex but I have not been totally dispossessed of my sanity and I would like to be excluded from the loop—as President Bush likes to say—when the subject arises.

Important events are seldom singular, so I was not surprised to read a few days later of another development, this one less disquieting but also involving dogs. I must direct your attention now from the baroque folkways of California to the tidy little coastal settlement of Mere Point, Maine, where an inventive man named George Bean has come up with a skunk odor-neutralizing formula that is said to make life worth living again for country people owning dogs. I have always used tomato juice, whose effectiveness is undeniably limited, and there have been times when tomato juice appeared so frequently on my shopping list that my grocer wondered if he would have to set an arbitrary limit to demands that clearly indicated addiction. Mr. Bean calls his product Skunk Kleen, a sensible name that gets right to the heart of the situation, and I want to give him credit for not coming up with something unbearably cute, something using the word *skunque*, for instance. I've learned that Mr. Bean has also developed a formula to neutralize the mating scents of female dogs and cats and he calls this—well, it could have been a lot worse—Lust Buster.

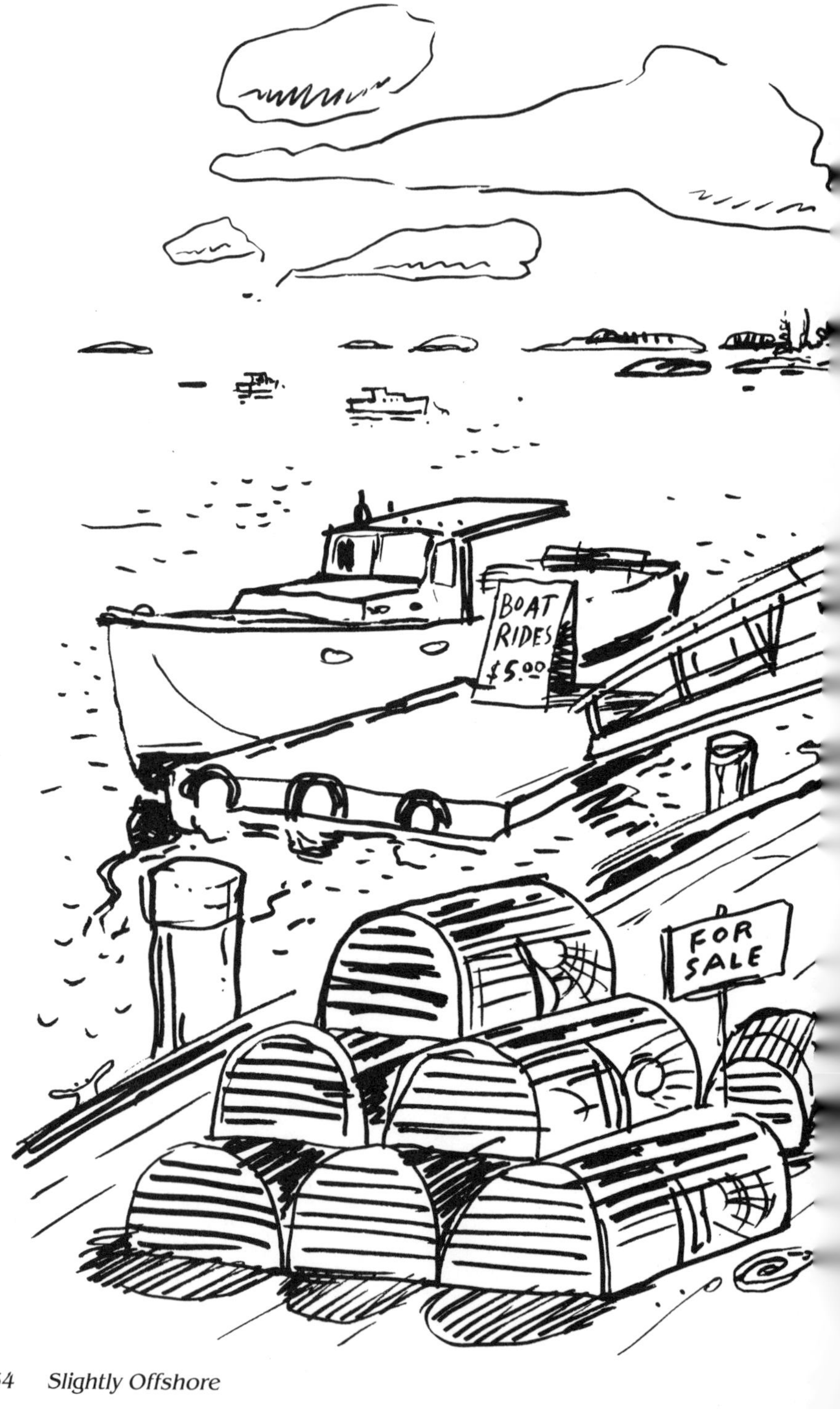
BOAT
RIDES
$5.00
FOR
SALE

Vacationland, Not Disneyland

I have been told that it was the schoolchildren at Biddeford who came up with the idea of putting a lobster on Maine license plates and I was surprised. I thought children had more sense than that; it seems the sort of foolishness that only an adult would dream up. I cling stubbornly to the view that a license plate is the identification of record of a specific automobile or other vehicle, and certainly should not be turned into a billboard carrying a marketing message. I know state legislators jostle each other in their efforts to impress voters with their pride in the state, but putting *Vacationland* on a Maine license plate accomplishes exactly nothing except, hopefully, suggesting to voters that not much is going on in Augusta. The United States Supreme Court has told me I can put adhesive tape over *Vacationland* but that doesn't work too well; after the first rainfall the tape comes lose at one end and dangles. And cops hate it; they equate it with communism, or what used to be communism. The operator of a car with *Vacationland* taped over will get a ticket for speeding before the car gets out of the driveway or into second gear, whichever comes first.

There is a delicate balance between unspoiled native charm, which is Maine's primary asset, and joining the herd in appealing to the hordes of packaged tourists for whose patronage Maine will become a different place. This is another way of saying that Maine is on the cusp between virginity and promiscuity, and sooner or later is going to have to make a decision.

Law of the Marketplace

Well, it was nice to read that familiar story in the local newspaper the other day, and I want to salute the paper for running it again on time and for not trying to bring any new angles or approaches to an article that we have all grown accustomed to and don't wish to see disturbed in any way. After observing that the life of a Maine lobsterman has always been hard, the paper predicted it was going to get even harder because mysterious changes in the sea were directing lobsters elsewhere and that the catch this year was going to be sparser than that of preceding years. The story interests me endlessly because my neighbors are all lobstermen and while I don't set out any traps myself, I lean toward the lobsterman's view of life. Actually, this places me in a situation where I don't always rest easily. When lobsters grow scarce, the price rises, and while that is a fine thing for lobstermen, it is less fine for those of us who eat lobsters, and I have finally decided that there is no evenhanded response to this disagreeable dilemma. I want my lobsterman neighbors to make all they can on what they pull from the sea, but I'm not sure I want them to make it on me. I suspect some of man's finest motives have crashed unashamedly on this shoal of self-interest, the normal human resentment against one man's good fortune becoming another man's undoing.

I make no pretense of possessing any scientific knowledge of lobsters' ways, but I think the growing scarcity of lobsters is caused less by mysterious changes in the sea than by the simple fact that the shallow waters of Maine's coves are being fished out. Hardy planters of the Massachusetts Bay Colony put a lobster in every hill of corn to serve as fertilizer, and the creatures were then so plentiful the colonists could snatch them from the eel grass without getting their feet wet. Whether the colonists had a taste for lobster or not has not been definitely established but we know they had a high regard for wild turkey and you see what happened to the wild turkey population. A decent feeling for nature seems to be the answer, but where a man's livelihood— or his appetite, to bring the responsibility home to me— is concerned, the law of the marketplace will ultimately prevail. The time may come, of course, when lobster will be as expensive as caviar, and for the same reason. Wild turkeys were replaced by tame turkeys, which may bring comfort to those who worry about the future of lobsters and that includes government scientists, the environmentalists, the State of Maine fish and wildlife experts, and people like me who are ready to melt a little butter at the drop of a hat.

Another news story which caught my eye recently was a prediction that Maine, and other U.S. vacation spots, would have a sizable increase in tourists this year because of the weakening of the U.S. dollar abroad and the growing fear of international terrorism. This fact was turned up by the U.S. Travel Data Center which said that Americans have "spent a lot on durables like home appliances and automobiles but now they've pretty much satiated the demand, and they're turning more of their discretionary dollars to vacation travel." Personally, I think the U.S. Travel Data Center is right about the increase in domestic travel, but they should drop that nonsense about appliances and automobiles which, in my opinion, is about as wrong as you can get. I travel a lot and I don't mind admitting that I'm getting nervous about sitting around European airports. But if I'm traveling abroad less, it isn't because I have too many appliances and automobiles. Only this morning I was thinking how handy it would be to have a pickup truck, and I've been fascinated for some time by the notion of bringing a VCR to this island so I can watch movies on rainy nights without getting into a wet boat and driving seven miles to Cooks Corner.

Having more tourists in Maine this summer, I suddenly realize, puts me in precisely the same position I occupy with regard to my neighbors getting more money for their lobsters. It's a fine thing for Maine's economy, no doubt about that, but already I'm worrying about where I'm going to park when I go to the post office, and how long I will have to read an ancient copy of *Sports Illustrated* while waiting for a haircut, or how I can summon the patience to drive home on Route 24 when it is choked with vacationers heading toward Bailey Island. The conflict, of course, is fundamental, but I know it will disappear in time without a trace, as it deserves to do. I will get my stamps and haircuts in the early morning while the vacationers are fishing for blues in Casco Bay, and if the traffic gets too heavy on Route 24, I'll try an alternate route which I don't care to reveal at this time. Some years ago when Mississippi was seeking to lessen its dependence upon agriculture, a state executive with a wry if undisciplined sense of honesty wrote a paper in support of an increased budget for the promotion of tourism. "One tourist equals one bale of cotton," he wrote, "and is much easier picked." It's something for Maine people to think about.

Idle vs. Idyll

If there is a youngster in the Casco Bay area who would like to make some money this summer cutting weeds and doing some painting, let him hold up his hand. Not that I'm expecting any response, because my experience during the past few weeks—during which the weeds around my place achieved what is known as maximum growth—has convinced me that all boys in the State of Maine over ten years of age are independently wealthy. Last summer, in a moment of hysterical optimism, I brought over to the island a young chap who was going off to college in the fall, and who agreed to stack a couple of cords of wood for a sum that should have paid for his first semester's tuition. A friend of my daughter's was visiting at the time, causing the youth to put on a display of apathy that not only indicated a healthy contempt for his employer but at times suggested that he did not understand how to place one log on top of another. When my daughter's friend came out on the sundeck in a bikini, all work halted. "That chick could get a wolf whistle from a missionary on his deathbed," the youth said, sitting on the logs he had already stacked. "Isn't it about time for a coffee break?"

A few days ago I drove to town to see if I could do any recruitment there. The first kid I approached was a youth of about seventeen. Obviously he was unemployed since he was sitting on the front steps of his home, staring idly at the house next door. "How'd you like to do a couple of days' work painting and burning brush?" I asked genially. "Maybe by fall you would have enough money to buy a used car."

The boy stifled a yawn. "I just traded in my Trans Am on a new convertible. And you're standing in my way. I'm trying to case that new doll that just moved in next door. Not a bombshell maybe, but she's certainly in the tactical nuke class."

It was the same with the kid on my road who works occasionally on lobsterboats in the cove. I asked if he would like to work for me on Saturdays. "Sure," he said, "if you can pay my rate. Five and a quarter an hour with a 10-percent automatic escalator clause tied to a cost-of-living increase." I made a remark I don't customarily make in the presence of young people.

There are six million unemployed people in the United States as of the last Department of Labor report, but apparently Maine's share of this total is zero. When I was a kid I thought fifty cents and a Coke was a fair price for mowing a lawn, but kids these days seem to want the toll rights to the Lincoln Tunnel. I thought once of bringing my heavy artillery back into action—involving my daughter's friend again—but while that would get a young worker to the island there was no guarantee of getting any wood stacked.

There was a time, before my friend, the lobsterman, passed away, when I had a fairly constant labor pool at my disposal since he had a half-dozen sons who were usually watching television, one of whom he would promptly dispatch to the island when he got my signal for help. The older boy was strong as an ox and used profanity that was both fierce and imaginative, but he worked diligently and usually went home early. This, I found later, was all to the good, because I had begun to discover vodka bottles in the leaves, and on one occasion when he left the island in his boat to return home he was clearly on instrument flight.

My friend, the lobsterman, would make a house call himself if the circumstances seemed to indicate a crisis situation, and on one occasion when there was trouble getting a new wharf in place, he rounded up some idlers in the neighborhood and brought them all to the island. His arrival resembled nothing so much as Gulliver wading ashore at Lilliput with the whole Blefescu fleet behind him. The English language has its pockets of poverty, so I am unable to describe the events that took place that day, but when they all departed the wharf was in place.

Two summers ago I brought over a kid from Cundys Harbor, a youth whose aptitude tests showed that his best chance for a success-ful career lay in a field in which his father held an influential position. I put him to work scraping paint from the sundeck, a job in which he failed to distinguish himself in any way. When he asked for his fourth coffee break, I decided to take him back to the mainland. As he clambered out of the boat, he said: "Remember that while one worker remains in chains, none of us can be considered free."

I guess we must all never forget that we are living in an era of passing fancy and the quick buck, but I don't know how to summarize my feelings about that. The only words that leap to mind are those I learned from the oldest son of my friend, the lobsterman, who one day mined such a rich vein of profanity that I thought it best even to send the dog back to the house.

Backwoods

Anything that portrays Maine as a pleasantly backward state peopled mostly with hayseed characters is fitten for the *New York Times* to print. A few years ago, the *Times* had a glorious day with the shutdown of the Bryant Pond hand-crank telephone system. The paper sent a reporter and a photographer to the site to interview and photograph Elden Hathaway who ran the hand-crank system, and Hathaway, slipping momentarily into character and speaking with the unmistakable sincerity which outsiders expect of Mainers, gave them what they needed for a two-column write-up.

There's something about Maine's oddities—such as clean water and unpolluted air—that bothers the *New York Times*, which prefers the commonplace stuff it is used to, such as muggings, homicide, and the theft of public funds. The *Times* sees Maine as a sort of time warp, a place where progress collides with the status quo and where the former is usually stopped dead in its tracks. Just as the *Times* classifies California under the category of Nuts and Cranks, it positions Maine in a department reserved for Backwoods and Cracker Barrel. The *Times* is happiest when things are pinned down, all neat and tidy. I've said it before and I'll say it again, I hate the very guts of a telephone and although I wasn't fortunate enough to have been a subscriber to the Bryant Pond Exchange I was greatly saddened when its service ended. If there must be a telephone, the hand-crank kind is the best of them all, where one chats briefly with Central, discusses last night's movie, inquires about the weather, exchanges a little gossip about the new librarian, and then asks to be put through to the hardware store. Somehow the human element seems to be retained here, a situation that disappears entirely in a dial call.

When Monhegan Island conducted its referendum a few years ago on whether or not to have a cable laid underwater connecting the island to the mainland, the *New York Times* gave the story coverage that a major election or a minor war would have envied. Radio messages crackled across Casco Bay, and any islander who wasn't interviewed was either drunk or bedridden. The reason I'm bringing this up now is that the *New York Times* has just discovered that ice is still sawed up on Mooselookmeguntic Lake and stored away for the summer, and this was enough to bring a special Backwoods and Cracker Barrel correspondent to Oquossoc together with Miss Madeline de Sinety, a photographer. In my mind's eye, I can see exactly what happened in the *Times* newsroom. The reporter who received the tip-off races to the news desk, his eyes glowing. "Chief, do you know how those hicks in Maine get ice for their drinks?" he asks. The news editor, bored, looks up. "Of course," he replies. "They get ice from little trays in the refrigerator. They hold them under the tap until the cubes start falling out into the sink and—"

The reporter holds up his hand. "You're all wrong," he says. "They have these fellows with long saws who go out on the ice and saw out big blocks, and they store the blocks under leaves and hay in an icehouse until July—" But the editor is already on another telephone demanding a quarter page in the Sunday edition. "I want a two-column head reading ON MAINE LAKE, ICEMEN PRACTICE A DYING CRAFT," he barks, "and lead with a two-column photo of some of these guys out on the ice sawing their brains out. Get de Sinety up there fast before the stuff melts. She's good at that backwoods stuff."

It's too bad that the writer and Miss de Sinety failed to talk to me while they were in the neighborhood, because my memories of going to the icehouse when I was a boy are still quite vivid. It was a fine thing to be sent from the house with a bucket and told to bring back a pail of ice to the house for iced tea on a summer Sunday, but there was one drawback to the chore that I didn't care for at all. Black snakes loitered beneath the insulating layer of hay and leaves because they liked the cool temperature there, and burrowing down to ice level one had to push aside several black racers which woke up in a foul frame of mind and thrashed around wildly in the semi-darkness of the icehouse. I wasn't too fond of iced tea, but I did like a little ice in my Nehi grape soda, and this provided the margin of motive I needed to carry out the errand.

Oh, well, these are high-tech days we live in, although I must say the ideal ice tray has yet to be built. There are always two cubes that refuse to budge. I suppose a man can't expect the world to stand still, but I sometimes wonder if it is really a sin against nature to resist change. There are times, today is one of them, when dislodging a black snake seems no worse to me than banging that tray around trying to dislodge those two ice cubes. If the *New York Times* would care to interview me, to talk to the real McCoy where hayseeds are concerned, almost anybody on Quahog Bay can tell them how to get to my island.

I Dare You

I am by temperament a country dweller with a fairly low regard for the staged events calculated to draw visitors to this or that city or state or region for the purpose of calling attention to the locale. So don't count on my showing up for the garden club's annual tulip show or the Colonial homes tour or the bake-off or any of these events regardless of the fine motives of the sponsoring organizations. But one was held in Maine this past spring that I missed, and all I can say is that I'll never miss it again, come hell or Hiawatha, as an old aunt of mine used to say. (On more than one occasion I pointed out to my aunt that the term was "Come hell or high water," but she insisted that didn't make sense. For over a quarter of a century now I have been examining "Come hell or Hiawatha" to see what sense *that* made, and I still seem to be overlooking something.) But to get back to the event which so captured my fancy that even today—several months after the fact—I am shaking my head in bitter disappointment over having missed what I now think of as the Maine event that more than anything sought to express the soaring spirit of the human soul and constituted a glorious attempt to reconcile art and life. I refer to Auburn's Three Stooges Festival and Convention and the pie-throwing episode of the 1988 session which one newspaper described as having "gotten a little out of hand."

I have thrown a pie—I caught my surprised target full in the face with it—and I can honestly depose herewith that although it occurred thirty years ago I can still recapture the gorgeous release of suppressed tensions and inhibitions which followed, like the clap of thunder which follows the lightning flash. There are certain experiences one encounters which are lessened by the recounting, which to one degree or another defy description, and I think pie-throwing is one of them. The beauty, the timing, the miracle of having achieved unrehearsed perfection, the shock of surprise on the part of the target, the cosmic reverberations, all of these combine in a flashpoint that lights up the universe. I am tingling just writing about it.

The Auburn Festival and Convention, which was held at the end of February, was a tribute to the three comedians and at the same time a benefit for the American Cancer Society. Miss Deborah Dolley, the society's representative at the convention, received $4,300 as benefactor. She is also said to have received a pie in the face.

My own singular experience with pie-throwing occurred, as I said, some time ago but I recall it with that strange clarity that accompanies experiences which one later realizes help form the skeletal supports of character and identity. I was entertaining a male guest, my best friend actually, for dinner in my apartment in Washington. Lacking dessert, I had telephoned a bakery around the corner and instructed them to send over a freshly baked coconut-custard pie. We had had a few drinks before dinner and a bottle of wine with the meal but neither of us was in any sense drunk which, in the light of what happened, should be emphasized at this point. When the bell rang, I went to the door, accepted the pie, and removed it from the wrapper as I approached the table. It was then that my friend made the remark that we both agreed later perhaps should not have been made. "Have you ever thrown a pie?" he asked.

I was holding the pie in my right hand, and I hefted it to get the feel of throwing something. With no warning, I felt a sudden tug at my arm, a tug that grew more overpowering by the moment. "Of course you haven't the guts to throw it," my friend went on recklessly, "and I doubt that I would, although I've always wanted to toss a pie at someone."

My arm was behind me now, and my hand was balancing the pie carefully. My friend was smiling and obviously enjoying the game of goading. He tilted his chin forward and thrust out his face. "Go ahead," he said. "I dare you." The words were hardly out of his mouth when the pie hit. I believe, too late, he realized he had gone too far. I remember his eyes widening in alarm as my arm started its forward swing. The rest is all too familiar from slapstick movies: the eyes trying to blink through the carnage on the face, the crust dropping into the lap, the chair being pushed back from the table.

Most thoughtful people will assume that anyone defending pie-throwing is living in total intellectual stupor, and I can't deny that I am balancing myself on the high wire as I write this. But humor basically is sad; the clown singing in Leoncavallo's I Pagliacci, while melodramatic even for opera, suggests how in a comic atmosphere everything burns with a fierce, unnatural flame. About 800 people—mostly but not entirely from Maine—crowded into the Quality Inn at Auburn for the Three Stooges Festival, and I doubt that there was a single innocent bystander in the house. The master of ceremonies got a pie in the face, and from that moment I gather things started moving. One of the organizers, a man from Maine, said the festival would "probably" be held again next year. Well, I'm sending in my registration fee today. If the people in Augusta want to make Maine memorable, they should take that lobster off the license plates and put pie-throwing in that space. I know what tourists like, and they can get lobsters anywhere.

The Maine Attraction

Tourists are going to swarm all over Maine this summer because the state has become very chic, in fact just about the most fashionable thing around. There is a reverse snobbery at play in all of this, of course, since Maine is plain, largely unadorned, not in the least pretentious, and the weather—certainly in the past few years—has been awful. There have been signs that this was coming but, like a summer thunderstorm, it grew quickly, and suddenly we have arrived at flash point. Department stores around the country are setting up what they call a "Maine Department," a fashionable women's dress shop in New York last fall opened a complete "Maine Floor," bookstores across the nation are filling their windows with Maine books, lobsters are appearing on menus even in Arizona, and the gift shop anywhere that doesn't stock place mats featuring Portland Head Light is in trouble.

I don't know whether I feel sorry or pleased for Louisiana, whose great days of fashion have faded with the end of the Cajun phenomenon. Frankly, I am relieved that blackened redfish have gone back to wherever they came from, and I would as soon not hear anything further from Paul Prudhomme, who in retrospect seems to have been more of a showman than a first-rate cook. And before Louisiana, Texas was the fashionable place to be, with glittering hotels and some of the world's most expensive restaurants, and dress shops where an appointment was required before one could enter. A ranch owner or an oil promoter was a man enthroned, with his cowboy hat and expensive leather boots, and the entire nation watched "Dallas" and yearned for that rich, adulterous Texas life where the skies were not cloudy all day.

What makes Maine's rise to fame and fashion all the more remarkable is the fact that so many people don't even know where it is. A friend of mine told me recently that a woman in her office announced proudly that she and her husband intended to visit Maine this summer. "We are going to Boston," the woman confided, "and once we get there we are going to try to find Maine." In a men's store in Philadelphia this past winter where I was buying a suit, the clerk pulled tight a jacket collar against my neck, smoothed the lapels, and said, "That has a nice Maine look to it." My curiosity aroused, I walked over to the mirror to take another look. The jacket had three buttons, two sleeves, and was single-breasted. Jot that down if you are seeking the Maine look.

I believe Route One north from Kittery will be as restful as a bowling alley this summer. Fashion is the greatest magnet of them all. Business will be brisk, motels and restaurants will flourish, antique shops will sell out, and the price of lobsters will spiral upward, but will Maine keep its character? I'm worried. A little earning can be a dangerous thing.

Maybe Maine has captured the nation's attention because it is so little known, so largely an unexplored land. Like some Lake Wobegon invented by Garrison Keillor, people have heard tales of small villages sleeping all winter under blizzards, of lobsterboats lost in weeklong fogs, of dour people who would make Scots look like Riviera playboys. The fact is that there is some truth in all this—but less and less every year. Things change and there is nothing the American public likes more than change. Not me. Within reasonable limits I like to keep things as they are. I crossed three coastal restaurants off my list last summer, two because the chef came out to shake hands with the guests instead of staying in the kitchen where he belonged, and one because my waiter, who asked me to call him Michael, twisted a pepper mill in the vague direction of my salad while reciting the specialties of the day, all of which were so extravagantly priced that the manager was afraid to list them on the menu. It may be slightly foolhardy of me to throw stones at this aspect of Maine, since it is the glass house that I call home, but my defense is that I like it the way it is and not tarted up to be fashionable. The influence of the passing fancy and the quick buck too often lingers.

The presence of the Bush family home at Kennebunkport, in my opinion, has very little to do with Maine's coming into fashion. The movement was detectable before Bush was elected; only a plague could have halted it. However, the division between fantasy and reality easily disappears, especially under the heat of the spotlight, and if the President spends too much time in Maine, the fashion burnout will come quicker than it normally would. Fashion, thank God, is fickle.

There has always been something beguiling about Maine's sturdy self-containment, its fierce independence from the rest of the country. Of all the states that might conceivably survive secession,

Maine, I believe, is more likely than any other to successfully go it alone. I like the story about the Bangor grade-school boy who, in writing an essay on Franklin D. Roosevelt, began by saying that "The thirty-second President, Franklin D. Roosevelt, was born out of state." Consider the errant charm of that sentence if you wish to savor the full taste of the real Maine.

Where *Is* Maine?

Since I travel almost constantly during the winter months when I am away from the island, I am going to tell you everything you wanted to know and a bit more about what people in the rest of the country know and say about Maine. This information was gathered by me in the mother of all field surveys, much of it in a coast-to-coast talk-show tour I took a few years ago to call attention to a book of mine recently published and currently overlooked.

All of the loud voices in the sampling field, old and new, are here with me in spirit, recognizing in me a giant among poll-takers: Roger Ailes, George Gallup, greying but buoyant, Elmer Roper, Teeter, Harris, Yankelovich, each with their sampling technique, their devotion to "plus or minus four points," their pre-prepared wisecracks for the sudden TV sound bite. Each of us, of course, has his own specialty. While mine is modestly limited to a single state, my colleagues deal with such broad subjects as politics, medical problems, advertising, the environment, and just plain frightening the public, such as discovering how much deadly radiation force lies hidden in a cup of coffee.

The sweep of the century carries me along on most major developments but I was surprised to find that many people haven't the slightest idea where Maine is located on the map of the United States. One talk-show host—a chap in Salt Lake City—was very enthusiastic about the state, adding that "Boston is one of my favorite cities." When I mentioned, rather gently, that Boston was in Massachusetts, he became sullen and refused to hold up the book to the camera for the usual closing freeze-frame. As the lights dimmed, he upset a cup of coffee in his haste to depart from a guest I'm sure he had mentally categorized as a smart aleck.

I am not trying to add a fresh triumph to an already illustrious career as a poll-taker when I tell you that in a newspaper interview in a suburban Chicago city, the reporter glanced at me sagely and inquired if Maine's time was four or five hours later than that of central standard time. "My hunch is that there are five hours difference between Maine and Illinois," he said. "Tell me if I'm right." I said he was right; you've got to bend the facts a little to really sell books.

The natural happening that springs to mind when watching the host of a television talk show is an April day in Maine. Anything can happen; it can start sunny, turn into heavy showers, get cold, and taper off as a snow flurry. There is a confusing combination of clear thought and cloudy tongue, which requires the guest to listen attentively if he or she has any notion of bringing the subject back to the book which the author is clutching hotly under the table. Once, in Las Vegas, the host of a morning show mentioned casually that he intended to go to New York the next day, a point of reference I quickly seized to point out that New York was only an hour's flight from Maine. He looked a bit bewildered by this offer of what appeared to be irrelevant information, but when I lifted the book from my lap and exposed it to the camera, the light of recognition came to his. "Oh yes, Maine," he said agreeably. "Maine and New Jersey, sitting there side by side, and would you believe I've never been to either one of them?" I said yes, I would believe that.

It's good to talk to a man who is streetwise from time to time, and I was pleased when I was stopped by an Inquiring Photographer in downtown Los Angeles. Since I was wearing a necktie and no dark glasses, it was easy to tell that I was from out of town, and already I had received some dirty glances from passers-by who were offended by my odd attire. "Where are you from?" the Inquiring Photographer asked loudly, hoping the microphone would pick up my reply over the roar of traffic. "Maine," I answered simply. He looked like he had been struck behind the head with the Los Angeles telephone directory. "Maine?" he repeated, licking his lips nervously. "Where in the hell is that?" I decided to let him have it. "It's 44° 49' north latitude and 66° 57' west longitude and ranks thirty-ninth in size—" but already he was moving away. "Find me a real American," I heard him say to his sound man. "When I first saw that creep I knew by his clothes he was a weirdo."

Fact and fiction continually merge. I was told recently by an acquaintance that I must be pleased with the new television series "Northern Exposure," since it was filmed in Maine "with that moose walking down the street, and all." Well, the show is about Alaska, not Maine, and I think it is filmed in the State of Washington which is felt to look more like Alaska than Alaska does. But the fact is that I do watch the show and enjoy it because it continually reminds me of Maine, with its serenity, its casual clothes, its nights compounded of mystery and fine conversation, its rugged individualism, with the lovely days of May, with the coming of the thaw in spring. It is then that I possess no unease that Maine floats like an unanchored boat in the minds of so many people. There is now an almost embarrassingly large literature associated with Maine—scarcely a travel magazine exists without a summer article on the charms of Down East—but either it isn't all read or else is filed away as though it concerned Shangri-La or Oz. I think this is a happy situation, and if I had it to do over again I think I would meet the Inquiring Photographer halfway. When he asked me where I was from I would say Oregon. Californians hate Oregon, but they know where it is.

Lobster License

As though the objectionable word *Vacationland* is not enough of a promotional slogan for Maine license plates, those of us who drive Maine vehicles will soon have to display a lobster as well. Whether all of this institutional advertising will leave enough room on the plate for numbers remains to be seen, but the state government seems to think that this double testimonial is more valuable than identifying a car that has been stolen or whose driver has committed a crime. We live a persuasive way of life these days and a moment of silence or a blank space is regarded as something unearthly which should be filled as promptly as possible. What fills the air or the blank space has come to be known as a "message," although the modifying word *advertising* has been dropped as being both needless and too likely to arouse awareness of sponsorship. A message sounds more innocent than an advertising message.

The defacement of walls, monuments, vacant buildings, and even bridges with spray-can graffiti owes its growth to this same compulsion to let no space go unadorned by a message of some sort. Observing how docile the public remains when the state prints "Vacationland" on an unused space on license plates, today's youth sees no reason why he should not use the girders of a bridge to proclaim his undying love for Linda Williams or to let the public know that the principal of the school is a nut.

Pennsylvania is pushing against the outer limits of absurdity with its slogan, "You Have a Friend in Pennsylvania," on its license plates. I should imagine that it was a very discouraging day for sane residents of the state to learn what sort of slogan their leaders had thought up for them, since it doesn't seem to make much sense regardless of how one looks at it. I suppose—I'm just thinking out loud now, mind you—the slogan wishes to give the impression that the state abounds with friendly folk, but if I lived there I think that idiotic slogan alone would cause me to be disagreeable and anything but friendly. To make a public testimonial out of your friendliness strikes me as a corruption that tends to diminish friendship and reduce its value to pretty nearly zero. Arizona has a cactus on its license plates, where Maine's lobster will undoubtedly go, and if you can tell me how a cactus can win visitors and cause people to feel kindly to a state, I would be interested in the explanation. A cactus is a prickly, physically unappealing plant, and just thinking about it causes me to want to detour around Arizona if I ever find myself in that part of the country. A lobster is just as ugly, maybe even uglier than a cactus, but it is fine to eat and has that to its advantage, although I don't see how the flavor of a lobster is going to be portrayed on a piece of tin. No, the whole thing is jingoistic, tacky, and its publicity value is highly questionable. My idea of a classy license plate is one containing the state's name, a series of numbers, and plenty of air.

New Hampshire's slogan, "Live Free or Die," is a variation of the McCarthy era's famous "Better Dead than Red" proclamation which probes a citizen's personal philosophy in a rather profound way and raises a whole complex of issues which many of us may prefer to face in private contemplation rather than in a public license plate debate. A few years ago the Supreme Court ruled that it was not illegal for a citizen—displeased with the slogan his state was demanding that he display—to cover it with adhesive tape or some other obliterating material. The freedom of silence, the court ruled, was as valid as the freedom of speech. One was free to speak or one was free to keep one's mouth shut. I may put tape over the lobster; I haven't decided yet.

Making me an advocate of Maine as a "Vacationland" leaves me wondering how this is going to help the state in any way. Will a single tourist come to Maine because he or she saw "Vacationland" on my license plate? Moreover, is it really a vacationland in the true sense of the word? My nearest neighbor hauls nearly 500 lobster traps a day and a vacation for him is a picnic with his family on the Fourth of July at Elm Island where he has a few beers, his wife sets out some sandwiches and potato salad, and his dog digs in the sand. On other days when he ties up his lobsterboat in the late afternoon he is so exhausted he hardly has energy enough to hose down the deck and walk home. Vacationland?

Slogans are designed to bring images quickly to mind and, oddly enough, Maine's choice has the unfortunate connotation for me of two of the seven deadly sins: sloth and gluttony. The more I think about it, blank space seems better and better.

Political Issues

The distinction today between the rich and the rest of us is pretty obvious except for those living on an island and here things get blurred, especially in the minds of the island owners. Sound counsel should be followed by those who live on small islands because they are apt to soar off on the wings of fantasy unless a steadier hand takes the helm. Island people dream a lot; they become convinced that the ten- or twenty-acre island is not just a home site (which it really is) but a small, well, continent, *a place on the map.* It's the map that causes the trouble. I'm a clear-thinking man and I know that I pay taxes to Harpswell Township just like the mainland dwellers, but when I glance over a map of the Casco Bay area and see my island by name, I become something else. I become sovereign authority. I travel a lot in the winter, so it's during months without an "r" in them that you have to watch out for me.

I don't understand the national economy and I'm referring to the whole enchilada. And from what I read in the papers neither does the President's Council of Economic Advisers. Like the computer people, economists have their own language, just like lawyers and doctors, which is intended mainly to keep the general public in the dark about what they are not doing. I frankly don't know the difference between being on the gold standard or being on the copper standard, nor do I really care, and the Gompertz Curve for tracking industrial production, I am convinced, is Mr. Gompertz's own plaything and has no relationship to me in any way. Later on this afternoon, I could design the Stinnett Curve which could be even more reliable since accidents of this kind often happen. A man spits out a watermelon seed, and the first thing you know there are watermelon vines everywhere.

I bring up this matter of our national economy because I want to compare it with my island economy, which shows that the federal financial structure, while wilder, more untamed than mine, is in infinitely worse shape. The federal government is some thirty trillion dollars in the red, but this sovereign island is operating slightly on the plus side of the books, even after the one-time write-off of a hefty sum for painting the house and the sauna.

What I am saying is that I think we have meekly accepted the purity of the Federal Reserve's theories although we know very well none of them would work when applied to the family budget. The genie is out of the bottle in Washington but not on Hamloaf Island. I get some comfort from that thought.

Island dwellers are wistful people always hoping that the nation will see the sense in imitating them, of focusing attention on important things like personal health, weather, the air we breathe, independence of spirit, and perhaps even a balanced checkbook.

You Asked for My Advice?

I have just received a letter from the Planning Advisory Committee of my township asking my advice on policy direction for the community over the next decade and all I can say is that they came to the right man, although my spirits are somewhat dampened by the realization that the letter was headed "Dear Resident" and was obviously run off on a duplicating machine. In the same mail I also received an insurance bill for the coming year and was startled to discover that the company—looking out for my interest every minute—had added one hundred dollars to the bottom line for broadening my coverage to include damage by volcanic eruption, damage to grave markers, and loss by theft of pewterware. If the scorched-earth psychology of the insurance company prevails, the Planning Advisory Committee should drop its concern about shoreline zoning ordinances and concentrate on more apocalyptic questions. The stakes are now much higher, I'm afraid, than the Committee realizes.

I hope I am displaying a fond affirmation of the Committee's concern over land development and educational problems of the township, but there are a few concerns of my own that I would like to call to the Committee's attention and they have nothing to do with minimum lot frontages or water setbacks. I would like to see something done about the people who feel that the most exciting way imaginable to end up an evening is to nudge over, with their automobile bumper, every mailbox on the road. The last time this was done, my mailbox was not only pushed over but was lifted from the ground and taken away. A man likes to think that his mailbox is as safe as his pewterware, but this isn't the case. I don't want the Committee to think they have asked a nut for advice on what decisions to make, but we all have our special priorities and one of mine is access to the mail. I talked to the deputy sheriff about it and he said that he knows who does it but that he can do nothing unless he witnesses the crime being committed. I suggested a stakeout, using a brand-new mailbox as bait, but he said I must be kidding. He has more to do, he says, than to sit around all night in darkness waiting for some drunk to come by and push over my mailbox. I stopped by the post office the other day and asked the postmaster what I should do about it, and he said get a new mailbox. It's things like this, Committee, that make me unsure of how much we have gained and how far we still have to go. I hope I haven't lost your attention.

Another thing that troubled me was the way the Committee questioned my occupation in their letter inviting me to help them decide the important issues facing the community in the years ahead. I was asked to circle the occupation into which I fitted, but a complication arose immediately because the occupations were divided between white collar and blue collar which is about as undemocratic a classification as you can devise. I know white collars are supposed to indicate professionals and blue collars are symbols of laborers, yet I'm a writer (a questionable profession) who invariably wears an old blue shirt when I'm at work. This could mean 1) that I'm struggling for the Ralph Lauren look, or 2) that I don't really give a damn. But in either case I come straight out of limbo with my advice and I'm sure the Committee is going to question anything I say on the grounds that my occupational classification is vague. I could part with the blue shirt—my daughter has been after me for several years to let it go— but writers are always walking a tight rope and who knows what damage this would inflict upon a man who is constantly searching for excuses not to write anyway, especially since I've now had the fear of loss of property from volcanic eruptions taken away from me.

The thing that worried me the most about the Committee's letter was in paragraph three, where I was told that "if there are differences of opinion within your household, please indicate these differences." This, so far as I am concerned, starts a whole new ball game. My boxer, Margaret, like all German dogs, has a very definite mind of her own, and not a day goes by that she doesn't back me to the wall protesting some decision I have made with which she disagrees. There are only the two of us on this island, and if you get the impression that the island government is a matriarchy, you aren't far wrong. Maybe the Committee should have sent her the letter; she is frequently in error but never in doubt. Where occupational identification is concerned she would have circled "white collar professional" and gotten on with it. Moreover, she wouldn't muddy the water, as I have, by bringing up the mailbox episode. Next to telephones she hates mail most, and it is a fortunate thing all around that the mailman doesn't have to get out of his Jeep when he makes delivery. Sometimes, if Margaret and I are at the mailbox on the mainland waiting for him, he doesn't even slow down but just throws the mail to us and keeps going. Gloom of night is one thing, but a boxer nursing a grievance is something else.

I have decided I'm going to write the Planning Advisory Committee a nice long letter, thanking them for coming to me for advice and setting out in detail what I think is the proper direction for the town to be moving during the next decade. As a citizen I can do no less. To write this letter, though, I'm going to have to put on the old blue shirt. Committee? Are you still there, Committee?

Balance of Trade

A year ago, Jon Bove was mad, so mad that he fired off a letter to President Bush, more to let off steam than anything else but also hoping that someone important enough to do something might see the letter. The chances of this happening were about the same as winning the lottery, considering the mountain of mail pouring into the White House offices every day, but it was worth a try. Jon Bove's anger was that of a man who felt that the door to the ark had been closed in his face.

I am not personally involved in Mr. Bove's problem, then nor now, but am merely serving as an unofficial historian recording the dilemma of a Maine businessman seeking to break into one of the oldest and most exclusive societies in the world—the society of international trade. Five hundred years ago Mr. Bove would have encountered the same stubborn resistance from European trade guilds that he is facing now trying to get his beer—Portland Lager—into Japan. Mr. Bove is president of Maine Coast Brewing and he says, with conviction, that his beer is good and the Japanese will like it if only he can overcome strong protectionist sentiment in that country.

I had a long chat with Mr. Bove a few days ago and I can report that his anger has cooled somewhat since last February when he first sought the help of President Bush. I don't understand marketing too well, and the marketing community doesn't care a great deal for me because I once wrote a piece saying the television drama I was waiting for was the night the decay germs would rally and defeat the toothpaste. Nevertheless, I'm going to try to bring the Portland Lager situation up to date here despite the fact that so far as the marketing world is concerned I have a price on my head. The President's attention was on something else when Mr. Bove's letter arrived, although an adviser acknowledged its receipt, but Senator Cohen was credited with bringing a new and helpful note to a gloomy situation when he got Carla Hills, the President's trade representative, interested in Maine Coast Brewing's war with the Japanese. In introducing a complicated subject like this, almost everything the writer does is wrong, like the deep-sea diver who gets an urgent message to return to the surface because the boat is sinking, and I don't want to struggle and flail about aimlessly in the intricacies of global economics. At the time that Mr. Bove took his problem to the White House, he figured that taxes imposed by the Japanese government and various other import charges would bring the cost of a case of Portland Lager in Tokyo to fifty dollars or thirteen dollars for a six-pack, and while he thought his beer was good, he wasn't sure any beer was that good.

My interest in this matter was attracted by the fact that in the parking lot of the Cooks Corner mall between Brunswick and Bath about half the automobiles seemed to be Japanese makes, but on a recent trip to Tokyo and Osaka I discovered that the sight of an American car there was about as rare as coming across a Nash or an Overland or a Willys-Knight. This situation was disturbing and puzzling to me, and the Maine Coast Brewing case, I thought, might be compact enough in size to explain how the concept of international justice was now being served. E.B. White once wrote that it was a citizen's function to air his opinions and instruct his elected officials according to his beliefs, and I take my position squarely on White's side. Statesmen are nationalist by instinct, whether they are Japanese or American, but the nationalist tendencies of the Japanese seem far more hawkish than those demonstrated by Americans where international trade is concerned.

As I said, Mr. Bove has moved from *allegro appassionato* to *andante*, a medium and more leisurely gait. I learned from our conversation that

I was not the only one who had been in Japan recently; since he wrote his letter to President Bush, he too had visited Tokyo. "I told President Bush that the Japanese open market is baloney, " Mr. Bove said, "but I have probably softened my point of view somewhat. All alcoholic drinks are extremely expensive in Japan, and the taxes for domestic products are almost as high there as they are for imports. Not quite, of course, but only a few dollars less. I'm selling a little beer now in Japan, and I'm not too uncomfortable about it all. There are trade impediments in Japan, but they are wrapped up in cultural and language differences, in inherent prejudices, and even in a certain amount of xenophobia, so the whole question of protectionist sentiment there is deeply complex."

Well, early in the spring I am going to take a bottle of Portland Lager out of the fridge and go down to the dock, where I make my big decisions sitting in the sunlight, and think this over. There are a lot of cars coming out of Japan and only a little Portland Lager going in, which may not be allowed to go on much longer. It reminds me of a speech I made a number of years ago in Toronto. Glancing around the audience, which was milling about the auditorium and bubbling with laughter and conversation, the toastmaster turned to me and asked, "Shall we let them enjoy themselves a little longer, or shall I introduce you now?"

The Indignation Is Mine

Malraux has said that form is the true expression of the artist and that to change form will often obscure what the artist has to say. My own form as a writer (admittedly we are dealing here with minimalism) is rich in indignation and although I frequently employ over-heated language, I am careful not to change because, like Wilde, I consider moderation to be a fatal thing; nothing succeeds like excess.

It strikes me that a lot of things are wrong about the way we live and to scorn the crass commercialism of our times may imply that I alone am wandering in a moral wilderness, seeing sham and injustice on every side. No, what bothers me more than anything else is fashion and trendiness, being told by the advertising and marketing people that my life will be dismal and incomplete without something that strikes me as totally useless, cheaply made, poorly planned, and disastrously engineered. I don't think Andy Warhol's talent as an artist even approached his talent for creating himself as a legend, and if Allen Ginsberg's volume "Howl" is really poetry then Keats, Byron, and Shelley were all working in some other literary dimension. Moreover, if I were a resident of, say, Boston, I would have enough sense to know that the group of millionaire athletes making up the Boston Red Sox had no real connection with the city other than the fact that the word Boston was embroidered on their uniforms, as their work clothes are called.

The other day I read that a modern poet had said at a writing seminar that he wrote poetry rather than prose because poetry filled up the page quicker. This not only appealed to my taste for whimsy, but also a fresh whiff of truth seemed to fill the air. Modern poets live carefully hidden lives, their verse revealing so little of their spirit and what they are seeking to say, that we often scarcely know they are in the room, and suddenly one comes along and blurts out a simple understandable truth. I applaud this poet and I think I will buy his book as soon as he manages to fill up enough pages to please a publisher.

Me and the Outboard Motor

The illusion of limitless horizons comes with owning a boat. Of course, a sailboat gives wings to dreams much quicker than anything else, but I've even felt the first challenge of a sea rover in a small whaler in a small cove. It is a primitive emotion at best, but it is undeniably present: the man at the helm is a man of responsibility, he must make decisions, he must know where the shoals lie, he must navigate. Handling a craft—any kind of craft—places one in a world that is foreign to the landworld, and that person becomes an actor in the ceaseless drama of the sea.

My influence and standing in Card Cove has been on the wane since it became obvious that I knew nothing about the outboard motor. My neighbors, the lobstermen, have found it amazing that a man of my age and experience—after all I have been on this island now for fifteen years—could be frustrated by anything so simple. Even ten-year-old Maine kids know when to spit in the gas tank, know when to blow on the spark plug, know when to kick the casing. The lobstermen have come out to tow me in so often that last summer one of them suggested, not unkindly, that perhaps I'd better not take my boat out of the cove the next day. "I've got to go to Augusta," he warned me. "I won't be around all day." These experiences, as ignominious as they have been, have not dampened my feeling about the sea, have not lessened my romantic notions about operating my own craft. If I don't venture out too far into Quahog Bay with my outboard, it's because I don't relish the long row back to my dock. I try to strike a balance between Joseph Conrad and William James, between the romantic and the realist.

My dog possesses full confidence in my way with the sea and doesn't hesitate to take her place in the bow, unless it is raining and then she feels that anybody who gets into a wet boat should have his or her head examined. The fact that we row home so often bothers her not in the least; in fact, when we come back into the cove under motor she sometimes glances back at me to see what has gone wrong.

Many of our boat trips take place after a day of painting. I loathe the odor of paint, and once the brushes have been cleaned and the drip cloth returned to the boathouse, I like nothing better than to take a quick run down Quahog Bay in the direction of Bailey Island. The sea air always restores my disposition, the odor of paint is blown from my clothes, and I take along a bottle or two of beer for refreshment. It is a fine way to relax after a hard day's work, and I feel as one with the sea—the dog in the bow, the wind in my face, and the widening wake of the boat trailing behind. I don't know why I am always surprised to feel the boat jerk a couple of times as the motor coughs and quits. Inevitably, I feel betrayed; it is as though the scenery has fallen on the actor at the most dramatic moment of the play. When I say *the* motor I am employing the generic article; there have been so many motors and with none of them was luck on the ascendant. One would think that I would go out of the cove in a subdued frame of mind, but this is not the case. There have been variables in different motors' attitudes towards me, but my approach to the open warfare between us is that sooner or later I will win and that today could easily be the day. Thus I always venture out on the bosom of the sea filled with a sort of shining hope. My optimism is a matter of local legend; it commands even the lobsterman's grudging admiration.

There have been times when I have made the most of a bad situation. When the motor died, I rowed to the nearest shore, pulled the boat up on the sand, the dog jumped out, and we explored the area. I never tire of walking along a Maine coast; the litter of the seafront possesses its own significance. There are always the boot half-buried in the sand, the ribs of forgotten boats, the plastic containers, the sea-washed sculpture of driftwood, the broken lobster buoys, the abandoned ropes and salt-wasted gear of passing boats. Dried driftwood, if the proper length, I toss into the boat to bring home; driftwood fires are captivating to watch since the salt and minerals from the sea often provide blue and green flames. On one rocky point of land where we once went ashore to explore I found an immense clump of wild roses in full bloom, the white blossoms filling the air with a scent so strong that the smell of the sea was obliterated, and in a freshwater marsh at the edge of the forest grew a collection of wild iris. This is the beauty of Maine that few visitors see: the tiny sand spit molded by sea and wind, the cord grass holding down the beach in the tidewater marshes, the hidden fiords embraced by rocky walls that are as they were a thousand years ago except for the lobster buoys bobbing on the surface of the deep blue water. I know a fiord like that; it lies in the passageway between Great Island and Orrs Island, and I go there sometimes on days when the clouds are hanging low over the treetops, and I lie on the rocks and lose myself in the timeless beauty of the place. I sometimes wonder if I don't listen for the dying cough of the motor with anticipation; the dog does, I'm sure.

Put on Your Party Hat

I like to stay to see how the movie or play ends, but I make an exception for the end of the year. There's too much going on once the countdown for the new year starts, too much hasty rearrangement, too much frantic search for lost documents, too many last-minute bill payments for tax credit, too much implausible tidying up of emotional disorder in order to face a clean slate on New Year's Day. It's one of those things that appeal to Americans who yearn for an official stopping and starting date for all of their enterprises and adventures. A specific date provides a happy association of astronomy, tidal flow, business commitments, fresh outlooks, forgiveness of past sins, fitness intentions, and, I suspect, the beginning or the end of romantic ventures. We all want to live a far more self-directed life than most of us can manage, and we look to New Year's Day as the time to go into a sort of Chapter 11 to eliminate old entanglements and disorder and launch us on a new life that will be solid, tidy beyond belief, and completely fulfilling.

I don't know about you, readers, but it doesn't work for me, and this is public notice that I'm giving up trying. In the first place, I'm not in the mood to forgive anyone and at the top of the list, even above the IRS, is the weatherman at the Augusta radio station who misled me with astral punctuality throughout the summer of 1986 with his prophecy of "general clearing throughout the area during the afternoon." As anyone with the memory retention of a year-old infant recalls, it didn't clear during the afternoon and, if anything, the weather turned worse all summer long. I've lived in Maine for seventeen years and I can't remember a soggier, more sodden summer, the blame for which I place squarely on the Augusta weatherman.

If the Brunswick postmaster thinks I have written off my ill will and have forgiven him, he is following an illusory path. Those frequent notes deploring the tilt of my mailbox coupled with chilling threats are engraved in my mind and are not easily shrugged off. I always thought that interfering with the delivery of mail was a serious federal offense, and acting on that assumption I made a personal visit to the post office to report that my mailbox had been pulled up and taken away. When asked where I had bought the mailbox, I gave the name of a hardware store on Maine Street. "See if they don't have another one," I was told. A sensitive man doesn't easily forget a remark of that kind.

Moreover, this year I am not going to speak to the man who comes to my wharf occasionally to buy lobsters from my friend, the lobsterman who ties up there. Noticing my boxer dog one day last August, he made the gratuitous observation that "That's the ugliest dog I ever saw. What's the matter with its lower jaw?" Admittedly, Margaret has a minor problem with the fit of her teeth when brought together, but a slight occlusive shortcoming scarcely warrants such wide-ranging and destructive criticism. I have, in my private thoughts, wondered how effective Margaret's clasp would be if that jaw were to seize the visitor's ankle, but this is just one of those interplays of fact and fancy which are common to us all. To my credit, you will notice I have said nothing about the kid he brought with him, who whined several times that he didn't want a lobster for dinner. "I want a hamburger and ketchup," he said, "and a side of fries. Maybe two hamburgers."

If I speak to the man who delivers parcels during the new year, it will be a greeting lacking all warmth, since he has devised a game that for sheer inanity sets a mark that will not be reached again in our time. Living on an island, as I do, I long ago worked out an arrangement to have packages dropped off at one of two neighbors' homes on the mainland. Whether he keeps some sort of scoreboard or whether he's a master of the laws of probability, he always keeps a step ahead of me and manages to leave the package at the house where I did not call. It is not quite the end of the year as I write this and the score stands at Deliveryman 9—Stinnett 0. I would like to outthink him once before the year ends, but my confidence is shattered and my heart is no longer in it.

The miracle of New Year's Day, of course, would be if we all considered it just another day, and didn't try so hard to make something of it. It's the misplaced effort that dismays me, the stubborn insistence that something is happening that we should all celebrate. You are a year older and your car has just depreciated $1200, if you think that's any reason to put on a paper hat and drink champagne. Now December 31, 1999—which is only a few years away – is something else again. I'm going to tie one on that night, and I hope you are all here to join me.

Sanity in an Unsettled World

A letter from a reader recently said, "Indignation seems to be your most inexhaustible resource." In all honesty, this wasn't my first brush with this charge. It was only last year that a letter reached me on my island saying, "You have a limitless capacity for indignation." I don't care to dwell excessively on this theme or any of its variations, but I would like to point out that in the period of social engineering that we are now passing through where everything has to be bland, sterile, washable, homogenous, and carrying Federal Drug Administration approval, an occasional voice expressing normal human resentment should be tolerated.

Since I have already demonstrated—as apparently I have—that I still retain a taste for a little rough-and-tumble and haven't totally acquiesced in the general march toward chastened tranquillization, I would like to offer a few lengths of the mind's string too short to otherwise use. I present these as A Few Thumbnail Rules for Remaining Sane in an Unsettled World. All are thoroughly pretested, which is the way things must be these days.

1. *Never* sit around waiting for a telephone call. I'll tell you right now it won't come.

2. Don't think you are the only one relieved when holidays are over.

3. Your assumption that most people are stupid is incorrect, but it's usually safe to act on that premise.

4. Frightening though it is, in many respects this country is on a downward slope.

5. Awareness is the character to look for in people; it is the key to everything.

6. Don't try to break any natural laws.

7. Never lose your temper unless you enjoy the excitement of total vulnerability.

8. Most people scare easily.

9. Anxiety, warranted or unwarranted, paralyzes.

10. Everybody is superstitious, regardless of their disclaimers. Coincidence is tantalizing.

It's hard to prove the potential for practical application of any rules of human behavior but if one believes in the possibilities of life, we must push past genetic blueprints and deal with common human needs.

If this is the sort of thinking stirred up by readers' mail, there are other letters that suggest only dawdling, letters that send me into that pleasant glassy-eyed state where I just want to reread the letter and let my thoughts roam. I have just received a fine letter of this kind from a lady in Zurich who read an essay I had written in this magazine about my island, and it stirred up dreamy memories of her own island on this side of the Atlantic Ocean. "It is thousands of miles away from places where I can earn a living," she writes, "but the time I have been able to spend there has been the most spiritually awakening, humbling, educational, and genuinely glorious part of my life. I was especially struck by your description of day breaking on your island as seen from your skiff. I can perch on my 'sitting rock' the entire day and watch what I've watched for weeks and just marvel at the newness of it all."

Maybe this is just island talk, like loon calling to loon over a waste of water at twilight, but I think not. Most island people I have known and especially those inhabiting Maine islands are innately humble people. The man or woman who lives on an island builds his or her isolation without meaning to and sooner or later it begins to take possession of the soul. Island life is not a simple life; the loneliness can deepen consciousness and widen curiosity, and the island dweller finds a great deal of time for contemplation. "I am a writer, too," the lady's letter continued, "and I have tried to write on my island, but I get sidetracked by the beavers or a wild rose hip or a frog that sat on my foot for two hours or the smell of wood smoke or the overpowering silence or the sight of a deer swimming from island to mainland. Is it island mentality that makes some of us question the merits of 'civilization'?"

No, I don't think it is. Henry David Thoreau never lived on an island, but he felt that most of us labor under a mistake "laying up treasures which moth and rust will corrupt and thieves break through and steal." But if Thoreau were alive today I don't think you would find him living in a condominium either, and certainly not in a real estate development.

Wait Fast

Singularity has never been a conceit of mine, although I once had a dog that yearned for a life in show business. Get out a camera and her posing and cute antics were enough to turn your stomach, and she stayed out evenings so much you might say she was in the public domain. But I have never claimed any distinctions for myself that were extraordinary in any way except perhaps one, and I would like to kick that one around a little since an arresting quality in man has always been his attitude toward himself. The distinction—or call it a characteristic if you prefer—is that I wait very fast. In fact, I wait so much faster than most people that I'm often finished waiting before they have scarcely begun. This is thought to be impatience on my part by many, but patience has very little to do with it. It's just that I like to get waiting over quickly, so I speed it up. I lived many years in Manhattan where the pace of waiting is fairly brisk but I can't honestly trace my tendency to wait fast to my years in New York. I was a fast waiter as a child.

Still green in my memory is the time in grammar school that I was kept in after hours by the principal, who believed in the value of punishment as deeply as Galileo believed in gravity. I was instructed not to read or even study but to sit there and contemplate my offense, after which the principal retired to his office. This was the sort of situation that accelerated my normal high waiting speed, and I realized almost immediately that the center was not holding. By the time I got home, the principal was on the telephone to my parents.

What one day is considered deviation might be recognized the next as perfectly normal, but I must acknowledge that I am still considerably ahead of the pack where waiting is concerned; in my mind an overload of restiveness calls for action and the sooner the better. Hardly a day goes by that I don't walk out on someone who keeps me waiting too long— doctors, dentists, garage mechanics, or store clerks. Yet I have long known that fast waiting breeds its own form of inconvenience. Quite often I have to go back the next day and try again.

I bring this matter up now because of a Maine characteristic that I first noticed with bemused detachment some years ago, but which I have now come to regard with all the jubilance of a rained-on parade.

Maine people in a queue, whether at a bank window, the post office, or any place where it is necessary to stand in line, are remarkably patient until they reach the window and then they move in, get comfortable, and prepare to stay awhile. They ask questions, they chat, they spread out papers, they tidy up and prepare to leave only to suddenly remember something else, and before you know it they have settled down again. To most Mainers there is something exhilarating about arriving at the window, something that seems to stir up old longings to visit, to reminisce, to mingle. I have always drifted erratically to the wrong lines, even when I lived in New York. In the bank when I fall into line behind a young girl, it invariably turns out that far from making a simple transaction she is making Christmas Club deposits for all of the girls on her floor at the office. The person in front of me at the stamp window of the post office is not buying a book of stamps but rather is mailing a sizeable stack of certified letters, for each of which a return receipt is requested. In a passport line, the man in front of me turns out to be Darth Vader. As you can see I've had problems outside of Maine too.

Newton's law of motion—"objects at rest stay at rest until they are pushed"—strikes me as the philosophy that should prevail in keeping Maine queues moving. At the vet's recently, a woman came out of a treatment room carrying a small dog, followed by the doctor who uneasily eyed the crowded reception room. "... And you'll never believe what little Rothschild did," the woman said, stopping in the doorway. "Rothschild stood up on her little back legs, and tried her best to reach the dog-care book in the bookcase. I know it sounds unbelievable, but, doctor you have to believe me, and wait until I tell you what happened the other night when we had company for dinner. ..."

When the man in front of me at the bank window starts to pay off a twenty-year mortgage, I quickly join another line, concluding that my first choice was one where my fast-wait capability was to be tested. This sort of thing is part of the game of chance which we all must play, and my own credentials in that area are strictly in order. It's the bank customer who only wants to cash a small check but who lingers for ten minutes of conversation toward whom I am rich in resentment. Some of us are better positioned than others to deal with this Maine trait, and I admit that a man whose waiting speed at birth was set at an extraordinarily high level is not that person. In all modesty, then, I can appear here only in the role of *amicus curiae* or friend of the court. The gentle art of sociability should not be rendered obsolete, it should just be speeded up a little, and maybe not even too much. I know as well as the next man that the light at the end of the tunnel is often the headlight of an oncoming train.

Animals Are People, Too

I'm not sure precisely what arguments hunters were advancing before the legislature this spring as to why they should be permitted to slaughter more moose in Maine this year than formerly but I assume it was a retread of the threadbare theory that the moose will starve unless herds are thinned out. This argument doesn't really fly if you follow it to the end of the line, because the hunters' interest in the moose is to kill them anyway, so the moose have a bleak future under any circumstances: they either die of hunger (which I don't believe is true) or they get their heads blown off by hunters. The National Rifle Association and the provivisectionist groups have their cliché responses, and they feel these have worked adequately in the past and there is no use rummaging around in research and trying to come up with something fresh and impressive. Needless killing is a hard thing to justify—or it should be, anyway—so the hunters and the vivisectionists don't possess too many options.

The bright spot on the horizon for those who think it is much more fun to observe animals than to slaughter them is the revulsion toward hunting and useless laboratory cruelty now being shown by the youth of the country. A second-year medical student at the University of California at San Francisco recently rebelled at a cardiovascular physiology demonstration which concluded with the injection of potassium chloride into the animal so that students could observe firsthand the chemical's lethal effects. "I don't think you have to see a dog go into convulsions in order to know a drug is toxic," said Janice Cohen, the student. "There's no advantage to using dogs in those labs. We don't have to see an unnecessary death for us to learn something."

Another interesting case has arisen in California where a fifteen-year-old biology student dislikes dissecting frogs so much that she is willing to make a federal case of it. She and her lawyer are making preparations to file a federal lawsuit against her school which has told her she must either cut up a frog or get out of biology class. The girl, whose name is Jennifer Graham, has asked the school to let her learn frog anatomy from a model or computer program instead of the real thing. "The thing about this dissection is that I'm not squeamish or emotional," Miss Graham said. "I'm not like that at all. I could sit here and watch them if I wanted to, but I don't want to have any part in it." She said that she objected to the raising of captive animals for research that involved unnecessary killing or maiming of them.

And if a new breed of animal-rights activists are surfacing in campuses across the country, questioning the educational necessity of certain procedures causing pain and death to animals, a simultaneous distaste for hunting seems to be growing among young people. Last summer five young men—three college students and two high-school seniors—were sitting on my sundeck in Maine when I startled them by inquiring how many of them liked hunting. One by one they shook their heads negatively, and when I turned to the only child there, a boy in the sixth grade, he grimaced and said, "Ugh." It was a heartening plebiscite.

Shooting a moose, it seems to me, possesses about the same amount of sportsmanship as shooting a cow, except that the moose is bigger and offers a target less difficult to miss. Last summer I was summoned outdoors by the excited call of a guest who pointed to a moose poised for a dive into the sea from a wooded ledge in front of my house. The moose hit the water clumsily and swam across the cove toward the mainland. A powerful swimmer, it moved with strong strokes, and pulled itself up the bank and disappeared into the forest. The whole performance took only a few minutes, but during that time it offered itself as a target that only a sightless person could have failed to hit. What distinction could a hunter have claimed for himself or herself by shooting anything so vulnerable and exposed? It would have required very little more skill than putting a bullet into a lobsterboat crossing the cove.

My argument against killing animals admittedly breaks down where deer are killed for freezer lockers by hunters falling outside of Reagan's famous welfare safety net, because here the capricious element of sport has given way to the sterner one of economic need and hunger. A man whose family is hungry is not a man who arrives at the scene in a Volvo station wagon and who enjoys sighting down a gun barrel at a moving target. Evidently Maine's legislators could make this distinction themselves. The bill to increase the number of moose hunting licenses from 1,000 annually to 1,500 was resoundingly defeated. Enough, the lawmakers seemed to be saying, is enough.

Yankee, Come Home

The thing I usually watch for in the newspapers which I read each evening—even on a Maine island, news manages to get through and the more alarming it is the quicker it seems to arrive—is what impact the onrushing tide of events is going to have upon me. I assume that is a proper oddity, if indeed it is an oddity at all. I see now that Venice has decided that 90,000 visitors a day are the maximum number that can be tolerated in that fragile city, and after that number is reached all others will be turned back. This development in world tourism occurred sooner than we bargained for, but it had to happen because the Americans, the Japanese, and the Germans move about the world with the speed and thoroughness of an epidemic, and the time was bound to come when some city would be compelled to say enough, hold it right there.

My suggestion is that the Venetian overflow consider Maine as a first-class second choice, if you will forgive a thicket of tangled rhetoric. In the first place, those Americans coming to Maine instead of going to Venice will avoid the terrifying collapse of the dollar which this year makes Europeans refer to American currency as "funny money." I have just returned from Venice (the announcement that 90,000 visitors would be the future limit was issued while I was there, but I detected nothing personal in the timing of the notice) and the dollar was 1,256 lire at the time. While this sounds like a lot, it really isn't; it barely buys a postage stamp. Moreover, in Maine the visitor would not have the nagging anxiety that the U.S. Secretary of the Treasury would insist that the dollar had to drop even more, thus causing tonight's dinner to cost two dollars more than it did last night. I don't understand the complexities of falling currency since the United States government is as stable one day as it is another, but in this I feel I am on the same level of ignorance as my fellow citizens and especially the Secretary of the Treasury. Yesterday things were clear and simple; the U.S. was solvent and its money was valuable. Today, our chief fiscal executive says the anemic dollar should fall some more. It is my personal belief that any man who wants to lower the value of the dollar in his own pocket ought to have a net thrown over him.

If the Venetians really mean business, those denied entry would find a first-rate welcome in Maine because the state is sparsely settled, there is plenty of room and plenty of air, and, generally speaking, the price is right. The Cipriani Hotel in Venice charges about $350 a night for a room, and while it is a fine hotel, a lot of guests are going to buckle at the knees when they are handed their bill. The Royal Danieli is perhaps a trifle less, but guests leaving the cashier's desk there are usually ashen-faced and the hand holding the bill is usually trembling. A good lobster dinner can be found all along Maine's coast for about fifteen dollars, but in Venice a meal leaning very heavily on some form of pasta can easily set an American back sixty or seventy bucks. The American outside of his or her own country has never been universally loved but the dollar has always been welcomed. Now we've got something to think about.

Well, this started out as a gentle suggestion that U.S. tourists not further offend the Venetians by crowding in where they are not wanted but come to Maine instead, but my appeal has turned into something of a sermon. I hope you don't mind. The captain of the naval escort vessel *Stark*, sailing hostile waters, apparently thought he was commanding a cruise ship because he failed to activate his defense system, thereby losing thirty-seven of his crew. It is my feeling that his next command should be the *Delta Queen* cruising the Mississippi. President Carter's attempt to imitate the Israeli's successful attack on the Entebbe airport and rescue the Iranian hostages ended with U.S. helicopters running into each other on the floor of the desert, and destroying so much of their own equipment that it all had the character—but none of the comedy—of an Abbott and Costello caper. One doesn't sleep too well these days, especially if one starts musing about American military power and the value of American money.

Bringing unpleasant things into question may be one of the results of detachment, of living on an island where one is not calmed by news of dramatic stock market rises or minute increases in the Gross National Product, whatever that may be. The Long Island garbage barge now has a leak and by the time you read this it may have sunk or its cargo may have been accepted by some sympathetic port. I have watched the odyssey of the Islip garbage with considerable interest, and I will be sorry when it leaves the front pages of the newspapers. There has been a sort of jocundity surrounding the barge's wandering, and I have grown rather fond of it. Nonetheless, while I am in favor of accepting the overflow from Venice, I draw the line at Maine accepting the Long Island refuse. Discrimination has now become an obscene word, but in its purest form it retains its value. Unlike the dollar.

Speed Trap

I read the local papers to keep up to date on what my state and my township are doing, and I gather that the summer of 1987 was not one, economically speaking, which would set any longstanding records of prosperity. It was all right, but only all right and certainly not memorable. In this context then, a bright spot in an otherwise lackluster business picture must have been the little speed trap that the sheriff of Cumberland County operated during the summer on Route 24 between Brunswick and Bailey Island. Business here held up well: low overhead, no smoke-stacks, high turnover, good repeat traffic, no delinquent payments or collection costs. A splendid little business any way you look at it, unless you are one of those people who feel that the majesty of the law is perhaps diminished by police officers furtively hiding out behind dense brush waiting to ensnare a citizen with something more on his mind than the fact that he may be bending the speed limit a bit to his advantage.

Suddenly there is the coming alive of a motor, gravel is churned up, a police car emerges from leafy concealment, blue lights revolve and blaze, and the cash register rings up another sale.

You may put full confidence in what I am saying, readers, because I was there. Early one morning during the summer I was driving into Brunswick, and I was trying to decide whether to go first to the post office and get rid of the letters or stop first at Cooks Corner for a haircut. Suddenly my contemplation was shattered by an explosion of blue lights in my rear-view mirror, and I pulled over to the shoulder and got out. My feet had scarcely touched the ground when a loud voice instructed me to get back into my car and stay there until I was told to emerge. This sounded serious. Either the police officer had been seeing too much television or I was a suspect in a homicide or a bank robbery. The officer, a sallow-faced young man with a Clint Eastwood slit-eyed gaze, motioned for me to roll down the window. He gazed at me in silence. "Give me your registration and your operator's license," he said brusquely, "and stay in the vehicle." Police officers would die before uttering the word *car*; every conveyance is a *vehicle*. I handed him both cards, my possession of which appeared to be a disappointment to him, and he sauntered back to his own car (vehicle). There ensued a wait of about fifteen minutes. I looked back once to see what he was doing, but he seemed engrossed in his bookkeeping. Then he walked leisurely back to my car and handed me a ticket. "You were doing fifty in a thirty-five-mile zone," he said flatly. "Be in Maine District Court in Bath at ten o'clock on the morning of the date listed there."

I glanced at the ticket. "It says here it was a thirty-mile zone," I said. "Which is it, thirty-five or thirty? Doesn't that make some difference in the amount of the fine?" He glared at me, the Clint Eastwood look again, but he refused to look at the ticket. "It's whatever the ticket says," he replied and went back to the police car. On my way home from Brunswick, I passed him on the side of the road again, this time having stopped a lady in a pickup truck. He was ringing up another sale. A neighbor of mine told me a few days ago that he had been nailed at one o'clock in the morning coming home from Portland. "One o'clock in the morning!" he said. "That's such a good speed trap they are operating it on a three-man swing shift."

To be quixotic about speeding makes the sensible person uneasy. Speeding is dangerous, especially around schools or suburban areas where children or dogs are liable to wander carelessly into the streets. The late Justice Cardozo once said that "Mutual forbearance is the first law of the highway," and I don't see how the matter could be stated more sensibly or more succinctly. The driver wishes to use the public highway to get where he or she is going, and to get there with promptness and dispatch, yet he must balance this need with certain restraints imposed by a regard for the safety of others. In a democracy, freedoms have a way of colliding as we have seen frequently of late where the First Amendment is concerned. Mutual forbearance, I believe, is the best way out.

A speed trap is something else again, and here the law becomes slightly sneaky and tends to go underground. An apparatus is set up—fully within the law and possessing all of the outward appearance of good motivation—to collect revenue. Its zeal is its giveaway. In the case of the Route 24 speed trap, the speed limit changes four times in a distance of slightly more than a mile, thus creating an excellent course for such an enterprise. In such rapidly changing speed areas, a driver is likely to drift from one speed to another slowly and without making an immediate adjustment, and the next thing he or she sees is the rotating blue light. No, Justice Cardozo had the answer, but just the simplicity of it makes it seem to reside on a bright and distant shore.

The Twenty-Four Hour Day

I overheard it on a televison commercial the other day, a voice telling me that by acquiring the product being advertised it would help me conserve my "most priceless and perishable asset—time." Oddly enough, I was in bed totally relaxed at the time, but the urgency of the message caused me to raise myself up on one elbow and listen. "We know the day is all too short for you," the voice said ingratiatingly, "but now we can extend it for you and provide you with even more hours of valuable and profitable time."

I dropped back into bed and thought that over for a while. They didn't mean me, I decided, they meant my dog, Margaret. My day was not too short at all; in fact, it was just about right. But Margaret has long found events getting ahead of her for lack of time, and I think she was an ideal target for the commercial. In the first place, you must realize that a boxer is a bossy, high-handed dog, constantly usurping more and more authority, and this trait alone causes them to run a little late in their daily schedule. Any power lying around unused is immediately assumed by Margaret, and since we live on an island much of the year too many seigniorial rights have passed on to her because I have grown weary of the struggle. Her day is an earnest one. Each morning she makes a careful check of the entire shoreline, then wanders down to the dock to bark threateningly at a few lobsterboats which she feels may have entered the island's territorial waters. She then takes a look at the woodpile—she started this early in the spring one year when for a few nights we were without wood for the fireplace, and the fear of another shortage still haunts her—then she walks down the path to my study, pausing from time to time to discipline some field mice she hears rustling the leaves, and throughout it all she keeps a cautious eye on the chimney. A few flying sparks falling on dry pine needles on one of those gusty island days and she knows she would have a bad situation on her hands. The fact that I'm still trying to get out of bed while this is going on—aided by a cup of coffee that I have stumbled about the kitchen trying to make—doesn't cause her to hold me in contempt so much as it strengthens her conviction that the ultimate authority of the island rests where it belongs.

I must point to one weak spot in Margaret's personality data mix—to slip momentarily into the *patois* of our time—and that is her total disregard for living off the land. She likes me to provide her with two squares a day, with a few meat scraps to add interest. A friend of mine in Detroit had a Doberman pinscher whom he described as a better forager than Sherman's army. One time the Doberman brought home a whole roast chicken, still warm, that a neighbor had recklessly put on a window-sill to cool. Another time he appeared with a workman's lunch that he had filched from some construction job on the block. The latter had so distressed my friend's wife that she had hurried to the job and asked: "Have any of you men lost your lunch?" My friend later told her that her spirit was commendable, but that to ask a gent whether he had lost his lunch was a bit too personal a question to put to a total stranger.

But I'm getting away from the matter of that television commercial and the more I think about it the more convinced I am that it was badly misdirected if they had me in mind. I make my living by writing, which involves a lot of thinking, and I long ago learned that I could think as well, perhaps even better, while lying down as I could sitting up. There is a couch in my study on the island, and I have done a great deal of my best thinking on that couch. Often I find that very intense thinking exhausts me, and I drop off to sleep, which I feel is all to the good because I awake refreshed and ready to walk up to the house and make myself a scotch on the rocks as a reward for having thought so much. A longer day—which the television commercial holds out to me—would only mean more thinking, more sleep, and more scotch, all of which run counter to my personal philosophy of avoiding excesses of any kind.

What troubles me is the commercial's rather arrogant dismissal of the appeal of indolence and, even worse, the existence of it. I see nothing freakish in the satisfaction of freedom from pressure; I think a great many people feel as I do and see nothing captivating about an extra couple of hours added to a day which in all probability was already spun out as productively as it was supposed to have been. I know I'm committing deicide when I refuse to place television on the highest planetary level, but I get cross when I'm lying in a nice warm bed and am told that I should be feeling miserable because so much is expected of me that I need two or three hours added to my day. That's for Margaret, wherever she is. Well, right now she's asleep on the couch where I will join her as soon as I finish this piece.

Recreational Shopping

In the space of just a few years—I scarcely had time to turn my back—the price of a hotel room for a single night soared from thirty-five dollars to $135 and the price of a book, not even a good one, rose from $9.95 to $19.95. These are increases of such enormity that they cause a thinking man to regard with something close to panic the way familiar things slip their anchors and are suddenly not familiar anymore. The jump in prices comes now with the speed of a swift blur, not plodding along casually as, for example, the cost of a postage stamp when it inched upward over the years from three cents to twenty-five cents.

I am painfully conscious of this right now because I have only recently returned to Maine after a lengthy trip and, as usual, I didn't come back to the island empty-handed. This is not unusual for those who dwell on an island; in fact, island owners are probably the most shameless impulse buyers of all. Certain things catch the islander's eye, like a kitten reacts to a moving string, and he and she knows instantly that the island home will never be complete without it. A hardware store to an island owner is like a bakeshop to a child; just the odor of rope, oil, and metal starts him salivating. Nearly ten years ago I elected to put the trip to the hardware store at the very bottom of all my shopping lists, knowing I would be tired by that time and eager to get back to the island, and that decision stands to this day as one of the wisest I have ever made.

My most recent arrival at the wharf on the mainland saw me unloading a new sauna stove, a mountain of linens, a fifteen-piece family of pots and pans (an overdue replacement of a shameful collection of orphan utensils which has long been the scorned core of all kitchen activity), and an assortment of miscellaneous items that suggested more than anything that I was moving in to take possession of an empty house.

Thoreau, with his obsession for the spare life and his contempt for needless acquisition, would have regarded me with ridicule had he witnessed my arrival, and he would have questioned my sanity had he known the sum in dollars—the same currency he used—that I had spent in acquiring these goods. If I remember correctly, Thoreau spent exactly $28.12 in building his house at Walden Pond, a tightly shingled and plastered house, ten feet wide by fifteen long, with a garret and a closet, a large window on each side, two trap-doors, one door at each end, and a brick fireplace. To tell Thoreau that his house would cost perhaps seven or eight thousand today would cause him to snort in derision. "I intend to build me a house which will surpass any on Main Street in Concord in grandeur and luxury," he said, gazing uncertainly into the future, "as soon as it pleases me, and it will cost no more than my present home." In this remark, Thoreau resembled the late Mayor LaGuardia of New York City, who once admitted that "when I make a mistake, it's a beaut."

What Thoreau never foresaw was the time when shopping and eating would become recreational rather than functional, and malls would replace meadows in order to accommodate the public's growing appetite for both needless acquisitions and french fries with ketchup. Since we live in a cashless society these days, acquisitions can be returned painlessly and it can even be fun if the store isn't unpleasant about taking back goods for which no cash was exchanged anyway.

But those $135 hotel rooms and the fifty-dollar lunches which have become common in most American cities are having a sobering effect, and thoughtful people are beginning to wonder where this spree of excess will all end. I haven't totaled up yet what I have paid for all of the things I have recently brought to the island, and I think I know why I keep putting it off. I'm a coward; I had rather not know. But I don't join in the prevailing assumption that everything is just splendid because money is flowing recklessly, since I consider that assumption to be arbitrary and most likely without foundation. As long as I have quoted Thoreau, I would also like to open the door to E.B. White, the late Maine philosopher and writer, who believed that most common assumptions are arbitrary ones: "that the new is better than the old, the untried superior to the tried, the complex more advantageous than the simple, the fast quicker than the slow, the big greater than the small, and the world as remodeled by Man the Architect functionally sounder and more agreeable than the world as it was before he changed everything to suit his vogues and conniptions."

I have taken to wearing my glasses nearly all the time now, even though they are a nuisance when I'm bringing the boat over to the mainland in the rain, and I'm not sure why since I see fairly well without them. But I think I'm uneasy; I'm uneasy that something is going to happen to bring books back down to $9.95 in a hurry, and when that happens I want to be sure I can see how to get back to this island and to read the books I've bought—at the new price—when I get here.

Shame

The newspapers are filled these days with the wonders of oat bran and how one's life can be lengthened by oat bran's ability to diminish the amount of cholesterol entering the human bloodstream. But there is another, larger question which comes up, it seems to me: Does man really want his life extended knowing that every day he has to scrub a pan in which oatmeal has been cooked? That's not a very reassuring glance ahead to anyone who, like me, looks upon a sink containing an oatmeal pan with exactly the same relish as one would look upon a battlefield.

A thing like oat bran has to be placed on the scales of the ultimate human equation and a decision reached according to an individual's own personal taste. E.B. White, Maine's great philosopher and writer, faced this issue with both courage and wisdom and, oddly enough, over the subject of cholesterol. Told by his doctor that eggs, bacon, butter, lobster, and oysters all contained dangerously high levels of cholesterol, White looked his physician in the eye and said, "Frankly, I like the taste of cholesterol." I hope this reply was noted by historians, as it seems to belong in the truly great body of opinion interpreting the social dilemma of America in the last years of the twentieth century.

I have no doubt that an abundance of cholesterol in the body's network of arteries can bring on strokes and heart failure, and I have no wish to supplant a scientific opinion with one born of ignorance, but I have the feeling that insufficient attention is being paid to other things that can cause strokes, things that have nothing to do with the chain of human nutrition. If indignation is my most inexhaustible resource, as I have been told, then what I am about to write will probably underscore the truth of that observation. I am bitterly resentful of what the people of Maine are doing to turn their coastline into a 3,000-mile refuse dump. That I escaped an apoplectic seizure this morning when I walked around this island, and saw what last night's high tide had deposited, can be attributed only to sound health and a steady emotional grip.

This wasn't the Maine to which I had felt blissfully wedded for twenty-one years, the state that I have written about regularly in this space for eight years extolling its beauty and serenity, the one place in the world with whose coves and inlets and bays I have been endlessly enchanted, and with whose moods and manners I have been hopelessly in love. This was a shameful Maine with a foul, trash-laden shore, one becoming deep with plastic bottles, with junk jettisoned from lobsterboats, with floating bags of garbage, with old clothes, castoff automobile tires, boots, used Styrofoam, and anything else that the people of Maine are too lazy or too indifferent to take to a municipal dump or recycling center. The tin cans and tin containers will—in time—mercifully rust away; the plastic will outlast anyone who reads this.

A few days ago my friend, the lobsterman, disembarked from his boat late in the afternoon, and I could tell by his clouded face that it had been a bad day. When I mentioned that he occasionally had to face a meager catch, he exploded. "A sheet of plastic wrapped around my propeller," he said, still choked with anger. "Do you know how long it took me to get the wheel free?" I substituted his question with another. "Who threw the plastic sheet into the water?" I asked. "I sure as hell didn't," he replied heatedly. Probably not, but I know that he— and every other Maine lobsterman—throws overboard everything that he doesn't want. It's nature's great disposal facility, free to everybody, rejecting nothing. If it sinks to the bottom, fine; if it floats ashore someplace, that's fine, too. Since these remarks are certain to bring me a letter from an indignant lobsterman, let me hasten to add that other boat owners do the same thing. The chap with the fifteen-horsepower outboard tosses the plastic container of two-cycle oil into the water after he empties it into his gas tank. Refuse from the sailboat owner's lunch—aluminum foil and all—goes into the water when the picnic is over. Old tennis sneaks go over the side, as do magazines, beer bottles, pieces of rope, a strip of tarpaulin, a greasy sweatshirt, a minnow box, the wrappings from some new piece of equipment. Why bother to take anything ashore when such a convenient junkyard lies only a yard away?

Not everything, of course, that washes up on the shore was intentionally tossed into the sea. This morning I found—stranded among some rockweed—a toy tin ferryboat, its funnels painted a gay scarlet, its superstructure bright blue. A short string attached to its bow—obviously broken—told the mute story of its disastrous parting with a grieving owner. It didn't belong with the other trash; it deserved a different fate. I turned it over carefully, poured out the water, and gave it a little push away from shore. It would complete its interrupted journey, not back to the child that lost it, but to another perhaps who still dwells in the mysterious world of boats, and of storms at sea, and of faraway shores where there are white sand and palm trees, and no bags of garbage and no automobile tires.

Resentment du Jour

These are queer times, and since I don't think fast enough to be allowed to use the telephone I have to choose a more leisurely medium such as this to express my own queerness. (I think *eccentricity* is a better word than *queerness* to be perfectly honest, but to be perfectly honest these days is in itself a form of queerness so you see how a simple declarative sentence can become a rhetorical thicket before you are done with it.) I am not going to take a stand on the cataclysmic events in Eastern Europe or the failure of the thrift banks or Iran's latest atrocity, but I would like to come out foursquare against the cord as a measurement of fireplace wood because there is nothing good I can say about it. A cord, for those who came in late, is 128 cubic feet of fuel wood in a stack measuring four by four by eight feet, and anyone who can't see the trouble right there is someone who never made a fire in a fireplace. A four-foot log is about the most useless thing in the world. It is too long to get into a fireplace and too short to fit on a sawhorse for sawing. Ten years ago I swore I would never allow a four-foot log to even wash ashore on this island, an orotund pronouncement I would prefer to forget since we all make excessive remarks under stress or anger.

If I am not urging you along at too fast a pace, I would like to turn your attention next to bird feeders, since we are solidly in the season when birds go on welfare and require a little cost-of-living adjustment or COLA as the social workers like to describe it. I would appreciate it—I say this in the kindest possible way—if you didn't write in to tell me how you managed to feed the birds without the squirrels getting most of the food, because I've tried your way and it doesn't work. The squirrel is a very cunning, Type A personality, but I am not the kind of bigot I now appear to be. The squirrel is entitled to some consideration, but I know for a fact that the squirrels on this island have every hollow tree converted into bulging granaries capable of sustaining them well into summer, if necessary, and their ruthless plundering of bird feeders is nothing but greed. One would think that an inventive society capable of devising laptop computers would not find a squirrel-proof bird feeder beyond its creative management, but we have to face facts. The score at this point is Man 0, Squirrels 1.

A book critic once described me as "a writer whose most inexhaustible resource is resentment" and I suppose I am going to have to again face this sort of slander when I bring up the next topic. I loathe those margins of postage stamps that should have been removed by the printer, especially the tiny strip beyond the perforation that is too small to get a good grip on and too big to let pass. I notice that foreign stamps, even of backward Third World countries, are neatly cropped, leading one to assume that neatness and economy have not yet won the close attention of the U.S. Postal Service, and that the agency is willing to transport unnecessarily seven tons per day of excess waste paper. That figure is my own, but feel perfectly free to use it.

I often run over in my mind the years of my youth, and one of my most delightful memories is the purchase of an ice-cream cone at the local drugstore on a summer day. My two sisters and I, each clutching a nickel in moist hands, would debate endlessly on the way to the drugstore over which flavor we would choose. My eldest sister was the pacesetter; she possessed the authority, which she exploited ruthlessly, to make the first selection, a choice that invariably was always mine as well but which I would have to relinquish since it would convey the impression that originality was beyond my grasp. Throughout my youth the drugstore only carried vanilla, chocolate, and strawberry, and since there were three of us, my destiny was to take what was left which was always vanilla. But at least ice cream was called *ice cream* and not *Naoj Eiksac* or *Wjar Frustk* or *Brfsk Jstrum*, as it is now known. And I shudder when I see such flavors as onion and corn flakes listed. I still haven't recovered a taste for vanilla but every day now it seems better and better.

Fashion rules us despotically now, even to our choice of words. Every year there is a new fashionable word, and I've kept a record of them beginning with dichotomy in 1958. The new word doesn't have to be either long or arcane (*arcane*, incidentally, was the 1981 word) and can be as short as *opt* (1984). *Suborn* was red-hot during the year of Nixon's departure from the White House (1974) when a lot of suborning was going on, while *awesome* spilled over two years (1986 and 1987). *Egregious* was the word for 1988, and, of course, *anomaly* reigned in 1989. How many remember the year that *ambience* was the word to use? (Answer: 1961.)

I'm not going to get into the subject of describing colors, as we now do, by designating them as something to eat. Just the thought of it turns me purple—I mean aubergine.

Don't Encourage Them

I like to think I'm following my own destiny but most of the time I realize that the sweep of the century carries me along with it. I want to like the world the way it is as the Twentieth Century approaches an end, but then suddenly I read in the newspaper that a dinner of Maine scallops and one Maine lobster tail cost $197 per person at the Peninsula Hotel in New York, which merely demonstrates the futility of even trying to work something out that will leave both me and the rest of the world feeling comfortable the way things are.

Among my Maine friends are a number of people generally thought to be cranks, but I'm willing to listen to them because the crank of today often turns out to be the genius of tomorrow—to possess the flaw that is the abrasive grain of sand producing the pearl—and while they may be a little odd they are, none of them, odd enough to cough up $197 for some scallops and a lobster tail. My friend, the lobsterman, tells me that he has positive proof that computer beams are causing the earth to veer from its orbit into a course closer to the sun, thus raising our temperature, and he also says that of that $197 he should be getting more than two dollars for the lobster. He's right on one count and for all I know he may be right on them both. Rachel Carson was thought to be a crank when she accused mankind of aiming pesticides at the mosquito and killing the eagle. "The 'control of nature,' " she wrote, "is a phrase conceived in arrogance, born of the Neanderthal age of biology and philosophy, when it was supposed that nature exists for the convenience of man...." Miss Carson's opinion was worse than false; it was true.

I have been told by some of my readers that it is easier to say what I am against than to define what I am for, but I dismiss the charge as being irresponsible since I am for most things. It's true I am against fashion and the irreality of sophistication, all right, and of the things I like, few (better whisper this) have to do with the passing fancy, the quick buck, and marketing aptness. Marketing—the will to dominate over another person's resistance—is the prevailing philosophy of our time. I am told that I must be in step with what's current, what's vital and alive, what the marketing people tell me is the trend I cannot ignore. The fact is, however, that I can't abide Madonna, and often wonder if she knows that in taking that name she was taking the name of the Virgin Mary.

Madonna's product is narrowly based, to say the least, but her marketing skills are honed to a fine edge, and it probably isn't necessary for her to know anything at all to appeal to those who find her fascinating. And when I am told I must be in step with the times, I suppose that I should not feel dismayed when after making a contribution to an environmental fund and an animal-welfare fund I should receive—two weeks later—requests for contributions from the National Anti-Vivisection Society, the Epilepsy Foundation of America, the Environmental Defense Fund, the American Cancer Society, the International Private Protection League, the Animal Welfare Institute, the Animal Protection Institute of America, the National Humane Education Society, the Alzheimers Association, the ASPCA, the American Diabetes Association, Wildlife Conservation International, the Human Farming Association, and In Defense of Animals, all fine organizations whose motives I admire but whose feverish traffic in mailing lists I deplore.

There seems to be a feeding frenzy here, a grab-him-before-he-gets-away attitude. Like Madonna, the marketing mentality of these groups works to diminish their humanity; one pauses to wonder if there isn't more to the charitable support of a cause than response to retailing techniques. The successful candidate for public office to-day—including the presidency—is the one behind whom stands not the most dedicated supporters but the most effective marketing strategists. Overcome resistance and the world is yours.

I would like to get back to the cranks again, because they are the sheep not easily driven. It was a gentle Maine lady who, when asked for whom she intended to vote, calmly replied: "I don't vote. It only encourages them." Me, I respond to that. Individual passion must not be disturbed or manipulated if the principle of free speech and free thought is to survive. I may question the sanity of a man who chooses to spend nearly $400 taking his wife or his date out to dinner on a lobster tail, but I must say that their choice of an entree is unassailable. The lamentable thing, in my opinion, is not that the public is willing to be sold a $400 meal, but the speed with which it accepts this new level of extravagance, the speed with which it adjusts to cynical marketing techniques.

I find that I have overlooked one other organization which solicited a contribution from me, its letter having become separated from the others. It was from the Society for the Right to Die, of 250 West 57th Street, New York, New York 10107. "Protect your final right," it urged me. That lacks something, but I'm not sure what it is. It needs, well, a good marketing touch.

If Symptoms Persist...

I'm not sure the matter of the common cold has been properly explored, the medical profession having abandoned it in its fascination with the new media ailments such as Lyme Disease and C.F.S. (otherwise known as Chronic Fatigue Syndrome or "Yuppie Flu"). The common cold strikes suddenly and cruelly, its strategy being the Clausewitzian concept of total conquest and annihilation. Don't delude yourself; the common cold wants you out of the way. Margaret, my boxer who feels I need her by my side during this period when my life hangs in the balance, is taking up much more than half of the bed. I tell her that lying on the floor beside the bed will speed my recovery, but she dismisses this as just bravery on my part; a feeble attempt to face the unknown alone. No, she knows where a dog's place is and that is on the bed where she will be ready for any emergency. Emergencies are fast-breaking where a cold is concerned.

In Virginia where I spent my boyhood, the fashionable winter disease was something called tonsilitis, which turned the throat to sandpaper but otherwise had all of the agony of the common cold which in retrospect I suspect it was anyway. Tonsilitis hit me a couple of times every winter. I looked baleful. I felt lightheaded. My nose ran wildly. My mother, murmuring that it looked "like a spell of tonsilitis," would place a palm to my forehead to confirm the diagnosis. No thermometer has ever been made that was as finely tuned for accuracy as her hand. "One hundred and one," she would say to herself, ordering me to bed. "Some aspirin and ginger ale is what you need." I don't know what modern medical science has learned about the curative powers of aspirin and ginger ale, but believe me when I say that penicillin is all right as a minor antibiotic but when the going gets tough, call in the heavy artillery which is aspirin and ginger ale. I think it is irrelevant to say whether it possesses any pathological aptness or not; it's how you think. It was Voltaire's contention that the physician amuses the patient while nature cures the disease, and I frequently think Voltaire may have been on to something.

Lying here today at death's door, I glanced through the newspaper hoping to find some happening that would sharpen my will to survive. I read that fourteen fishermen have died at sea in the past eleven months from accidents, that a new term called *vaporware* is now in use by the computer industry to describe something that has been promised but doesn't yet exist, and the Postal Service says that a space probe of Mars is one thing but getting rid of the little perforated over-hang strip on postage stamps is something else again, and as the century ebbs the goal is not yet in sight. I can't say there was anything there that would get me through the night.

For some odd reason, winter and I seem to break up around the same time. There's more than just a hint of spring in the air, and through the window a few moments ago I saw a robin resting on the eave of the roof. It looked a little ragged and unkempt—who am I to talk?—and I suppose my roof is just a sort of pit stop on its way north. Or maybe it has arrived where it is going but hasn't yet had a chance to spruce up after its long flight from Florida. There is a hazy beauty outside, but it possesses that unreality which always accompanies one's perspective from the wrong side of the window. I admit I'm what's known as a bad patient; cheerful talk from a healthy visitor does nothing whatever for me, and I often wish they would leave the books and the fruit and go home. Margaret, however, is delighted with company. She wags her tail furiously, dances about the sickroom, and urges them to linger. I'm thinking of deploying her in another room the next time a visitor calls; we seem to be working different sides of the street.

I don't know why a common cold causes one to feel that the mind lags lamentably behind the body, why familiar landmarks outside the window have no reality, but I suppose it has something to do with the fact that I was raised in the belief that a man should get up and work every day but Sunday and working requires a vertical and not a horizontal presence. Things all look differently when one is lying down, even the mind seems clearer and less cluttered. I was going to take advantage of this and compose an unpleasant letter to the Public Utilities Commission in Augusta, but frankly I'm not up to it this morning. I think I'd rather lie here and complain to whoever happens to come into the room. When you're sick, people will tolerate your moroseness and often you can make a point of something not particularly pleasant that if spoken in good health would cause resentment. To this extent, sickness is beneficial; it clears out the pipeline of indignation.

The weatherman on television has just said what we are all waiting to hear—some sunny, warm days are on the way, and while tonight the temperature will dip below freezing, tomorrow will be bright and "promising." Weathermen love that word "promising." I still ache, I feel lousy, I'm disagreeable, and you know what I think their "promising" is? I think it's not a damn thing but vaporware.

Cove Dweller

Some day I intend to explore the entire concept of the word *home* because it is such an ephemeral thing that when used by itself it has almost no specific meaning. People returning to the United States from Europe, say, refer to it as a homecoming, yet the small cove in which my island floats is home to me. The categories which constitute *home* are endless, the lines are drawn across the heart. Years ago when I had a submarine cable laid across the floor of the cove to bring electricity to the island, the Corps of Engineers made me get from every landowner on the cove's mainland their permission for this undertaking. At the time I considered this mere bureaucratic nonsense since the cable lay in the mud completely out of sight and could offend no one. Since then I have changed my mind and I am now agreeably surprised at the awareness shown by the Corps of Engineers in what is more an emotional matter than one of substance. The cove was their cove, so far as the property owners were concerned, and this out-of-sight cable snaking across the floor could have been felt to be an intrusion, a trespassing on their rights. None of them objected which, in retrospect, pleases me in an entirely different sense. It is as though I were welcomed as a member of the cove community, and the hand of fellowship had been extended.

As the years have passed, I feel more and more that the cove is home. I am curious about the occupants of the new houses that have gone up on the mainland; births, deaths, marriages and divorces of cove residents bring me grief, pleasure, or in some cases just amusement, but I am never indifferent about these events. Loyalties as well as hostilities run expectedly deep in some small societies, and if there is any wrestling of this kind for supremacy in Card Cove I uphold the ascendancy of loyalty.

Fantasy Island

I asked my neighbor, the lobsterman, what he thought of the two derelict ships which for about eight years now have been rusting away in Cundys Harbor, and he shrugged their existence off as being too trivial for comment. "They get all heated up about those old hulls over in Cundys," he replied, "but I'm lukewarm about them and getting luker every day." My neighbor holds to the refreshing view that the English language is a living thing and capable of growth if properly nourished. He has an inquisitive mind and he sizes up situations quickly. One evening while walking back from a neighborhood meeting where a local problem was discussed, he summarized the situation in one crisp sentence. "They're the kind of people who'd vote the town dry," he said, "and then move."

Too often, though, my neighbor looks to providential causes and effects. He constantly scans the sky for some apocalyptic hint of earthly doom. I hastened to forestall his fundamentalist solution to the ship problem. "The Good Lord didn't bring those ships into Cundys Harbor," I said, "and he isn't going to take them out. Think it over, and come up with something original."

One of the ships, painted a startling robin's-egg blue, has been cut up almost to the water's edge, presumably for scrap steel, while the other lies half aground in a small marshy cove in the rear of the village. Until a few years ago, they both swung at moorings some distance offshore where they were being refitted to return to sea, and it was there that they first came to my attention. Going to Cundys Harbor by boat I always passed the two ghost shops and, as it often happens, curiosity began to nourish fantasy. I never saw a living soul on either ship, but something was obviously going on; there were evidences on deck that repairs, mostly of a cosmetic nature, were being made. What appeared to be a shirt board had replaced a glass porthole on one ship, while a badly rusted steel plate, extending to the waterline, shivered in the wake of my motorboat as though the ship were breathing. I wouldn't have gone around Cape Hatteras in either of them, even with a loaded gun at my head.

I have long felt that the course of juvenile literature generally follows a dull and uninteresting channel, invariably seeking to implant some poorly concealed seed of morality in the child's mind, and in the stories I have told my grandchildren when spending the summer on the island I have usually explored a somewhat wilder shore. This hasn't always been to the liking of the boys' mother, who equates the value of my influence as little better than that of a poolroom, but the boys themselves are solidly in my corner. One day when passing the two ships I explained that they were Nazi vessels whose crews had not learned that the war had long ago ended and who hid below decks during daylight, waiting to be rescued at night by a German submarine. The story hit pay dirt instantly. "Go a little closer," said the youngest of the boys, the possessor of an imagination on a highly creative scale. "I think I smell something cooking. Probably Wiener schnitzel." I turned the wheel and came in close to the side of the smaller of the two ships, close enough to grab the hawser leading to the mooring. I cut the motor, and we sat silently in the motorboat. The boys gazed a little uneasily at the ship, and one glanced over his shoulder as if to reassure himself that our island was still in sight.

"What do they do all day?" one of the boys asked, his voice almost a whisper. I held up a warning hand, and they all leaned closer. "Mostly they sleep," I said, "but one probably stands watch. They go ashore at night to get food and reconnoiter." They leaned backward. "I think the guy on watch is listening to the radio," the younger one said. "I seem to hear music." We sat there a minute or so in silence, the boys staring at the ship. "Maybe we'd better shove off," one boy said nervously. "If the man on watch sees us, he may shoot." I pulled the cord, and the motor started. "Not during daylight," I said. "It would blow their cover." The older boy nodded his head in assent. "They couldn't take that chance," he said, but he looked over his shoulder nonetheless to bolster his conviction. There was a silence during the rest of the trip, each of the boys absorbed in his own reverie. On the return trip I kept some distance from the ghost ships; a good storyteller knows when to let suspense build on its own, knows when it's best not to crowd destiny.

The matter rested there and I had forgotten about it until it surfaced at lunch on the sundeck a couple of days later. The youngest boy, after finishing lunch, made a large sandwich which he carefully wrapped in a paper napkin. "I'm going to see if I can take this over to the Nazi ship," he explained to his mother. "Those poor Germans are probably starved for a bacon, lettuce, and tomato sandwich."

"What Germans?" his mother asked sharply. "What Nazi ship?"

I explained quickly that I was going to the kitchen to get a bottle of beer. A good storyteller also knows when the fat is in the fire.

Elegy to a Friend

I had a telephone call early this morning, telling me that my friend, the lobsterman, had died. I hadn't been aware that he was even sick, but there was nothing unusual about that; a lot of mystery enshrouded his life and he probably preferred it that way. But the shock of loss makes me incapable of realizing yet that the little house across the water from my island is no longer occupied by this man, and already I feel that a great deal of color has drained out of the cove, leaving it like a color photograph that has turned to sepia with age.

In death we often see people as heroic in size when in life they were quite ordinary. In my own vision, the lobsterman was always a little larger than life, a portrait too large for its frame. This had to be because of his nature, since in physical size he was not a large man at all and in recent years had shown signs of shrinking, of drying up. But he was always cynical, always irreverent, always smoking, always drinking a little too much, always talkative, and always helpful and considerate. Display of emotion made him uneasy; he probably likened it to some weakness of the human spirit. Last spring when I returned to the island after a long absence, he brought me six lobsters. "You're too damned cheap to buy them," he said, proffering the gift and turning to go. I knew that if I had made the slightest gesture of trying to pay him he would have been deeply offended.

Life is not easy for any person who takes his living from the sea, but my friend's life was filled with hardships that I think would have staggered most people. Although totally absorbed by the sea, he was not oblivious of those who lived by land and always in his mind was the understanding that his destiny was linked with that of people from whom he was separated by huge differences of temperament and tradition. Two years ago, in a dense fog, his outboard motor failed and he was forced to spend the night drifting aimlessly in Casco Bay. It was a chill night, filled with rain showers, and his open boat provided no shelter. After he had been found by searchers the next morning and brought home, I paid him a visit. He was sitting in his living room, smoking as usual and drinking a beer. When I commiserated with him over what must have been a sobering experience, he shrugged his shoulders as though it were commonplace. "Big problem was that I couldn't get my cigarettes lighted," he said. "My damned matches were wet."

Appearances, in the lobsterman's opinion, were shallow; he couldn't be concerned with them. His house was in a constant state of disorder and his lobster boat—before he gave it up and started hauling just a few traps in an open boat with an outboard—looked like a derelict that would sink at any moment. This grotesquely patched and repaired object—generally agreed to be the worst-looking boat in Casco Bay—now lies beached in the small yard behind his house to which it had been hauled for repairs that were never made. One day while the boat was gently nudging my wharf as the lobsterman and I were talking, I suggested that he name the boat "Pride of the Cove." He thought that over a moment in silence, then his face broke out in a grin. "Isn't she a beauty?" he asked. There was a genuine trace of pride in his voice.

A few years ago in an accident, the origin of which remains a mystery to me, he had to walk through knee-deep mud with a broken leg to reach his house. I was told by people with him at the time that the profanity set something of a new local record for sustained inventiveness, for originality, and for endurance. A day or so later, I called on him with a bottle of bourbon to wish him a speedy recovery. He was sitting up in bed, his leg proudly extended in a cast. "How do you feel?" I asked. He ignored my question. "What's in the bottle?" he inquired politely.

There was an oracular ring, both touching and authoritative, to almost all of the lobsterman's pronouncements, and while I always listened to him with unconcealed admiration, I knew in my heart that what he didn't know for sure he had no hesitation in creating out of whole cloth. But he did possess the knack of separating the true value from the spurious, he could foretell the weather with an accuracy that science has not yet been able to match, he could fix any mechanical thing that was repairable, he took pride in his distrust of local, county, state, and federal governments, and he wondered aloud, in our conversations conducted at the foot of my wharf over bottles of beer, why the world had turned out so poorly after a fair start. "People have become mean," he said once, wiping his mouth with the back of his hand and placing an empty bottle carefully on the deck of the float. "Just plain damned mean. Nobody wants to work anymore and nobody wants to help people anymore. It's everybody for himself, and that's a hell of a way to live." He was not trying to show off with any profound thoughts; he was simply responding honestly to his vision of life.

Any elegy I would ever undertake to write about this cove where

I spend a large part of my life would have to take important note of the lobsterman; he was a person of consequence who invested the place with a strange kind of subjective virtue. When I heard of his death this morning the first thought that entered my mind was the line from John Donne's haunting verse: "... and therefore never send to know for whom the bell tolls; it tolls for thee."

Unearthly Glow

Romance and the tropics have been regarded as bedfellows for so long now that I have no hope of ever dislodging the public conception of the South Seas in favor of the coast of Maine. The idea won't fly, and I'm the first to concede it, nevertheless I am convinced that the world of 1987 is still a hundred percent changeable and I am going to give it a whirl. I have spent a lot of time wandering around the islands of the South Pacific and while I would not go so far as to say that "romantic places" and "South Seas" are contradictory phrases, I would say that the average island there is anything but romantic and there are very good reasons why the people who live on them die young. Bali H'ai, like Shangri-La, is a place of steamy fiction, and I am pointing out the dirty state of affairs on most of those islands to lay the groundwork for a comparison with Maine. The warm sweet air of a summer night on coastal Maine, with the tide racing in and bringing the scent of the sea on its breath, is a wonderful thing, even if it has never invoked the memory of Dorothy Lamour clad in a sarong and leaning against a palm tree.

All of this is introduction to what happened two nights ago on my island. Shortly after dinner there had been a minor thunderstorm. It had rained hard, the clouds had lingered, the trees dripped, and one had the impression things could go either way: it could clear up or it could rain some more. If the weather couldn't make up its mind, I could and I went to bed early. It was around midnight that I awoke to find the room bathed in a strange light, one that I had certainly never seen before and strange enough to cause me to slip on trousers and a sweater and go out to the sundeck. The dog joined me there almost immediately, and I think she was as startled as I was at what was taking place. The moon was full and high in the sky, but a heavy mist hung over the water causing the moonlight to take on an unearthly white glow, as though it were being filtered through a lens that robbed it of all reality.

A man can't spend a night as rare as this one sleeping, and I put on some shoes and went down to the wharf and untied the dinghy. The motorboat rocked gently at its slip but the night wasn't right for the sound of a motor; even the sound of oars seemed out of place in the silence that hung over the cove. I wiped the dew off the seat with the palm of my hand, held the boat steady while the dog jumped in, and pushed away. The island instantly became a dark blur against a white background, and its mystery stirred me in a way that a South Pacific island could never do. There was almost no breeze, as is often the case when there is mist in the air, and the boat moved easily. Instead of pulling on the oars I pushed, thus forcing the boat backward so that I could face the direction I was going. It can be awkward if there is any chop at all, but on a flat surface the boat moves speedily.

I headed for a tiny cove on the seaward side of the island, a cove that was so small that once in it I knew there would be no room to turn around in and I would have to back out, but the spruce trees hung over it so that it had more the appearance of a grotto than an open inlet. The tide was fully in, and I pushed the boat to the back of the cove and wondered why in the seventeen years of my life on this island I had never been in this magic place at night.

But everything seemed strange now and even the shape of the island was unfamiliar to me in the white mist. I crossed the cove to a rock ledge on which I had often laid in the sunshine, and that was as exotic as though it were a piece of the moon. The dog sat behind me in the boat, so quiet that I once glanced backward to make sure she was really there. A fish broke water somewhere on my left; there was a sudden turbulence in the water, a splash, and then the ripples spread out and finally reached the boat. But there were no other sounds, not even of gulls. The blue herons, which possess an ungodly squawk when they take to the air, never show up at high tide; strolling around in the shallows at ebb tide is more to their taste.

We headed back to the wharf, the dog and I, a little later as the mist began to dissipate, and the flawless surface of the night sea settled again into its mirrored calm. The reality of the world returned as the mist lifted; spruce trees became again spruce trees, and the wharf rose out of the water when we neared it. The dog leaped to the float while I was tying the line, and together we walked up the path to the house.

I am writing this now on a bright morning, and through the open door of my study I see the sea sparkling in a way that brings delight to both the eye and the mind. But you must believe me when I say that no tropical atoll ever was cloaked in the mystery and romance that this island possessed as I saw it two nights ago.

My Beloved Island

Sometimes, when my mind is on Cruise Control, I examine the reasons that living on an island is such an appealing thing, and I've concluded there is no one reason. It is the sort of thing that is written in music and not in words.

It would be easy to say that I can define Margaret's fondness for the place, but her pleasures and mine derive from vastly different provenances. To her it means freedom from a leash or even a collar, no traffic, plenty of shut-eye on a bed of warm leaves, and long, unsupervised rambles wherever an entrancing sniff may lead her. Analysis of human responses to environment is usually murky in what it turns up, and sometimes exposing the thing to a searching light strips it of whatever appeal it once possessed. My affection for this island commenced on a late Saturday afternoon in autumn when I first stepped out of a boat and began to wander up a path through the woods to the dwelling. If such a thing as love at first sight exists, this was it. The island was small, the woods were filled with broken branches and underbrush, the house was primitive and uncomfortably rustic, the sundeck sagged, and about it all hung the feeling of abandonment. But on that Saturday afternoon I loved it, and on Monday I owned it.

I don't offer this as an epic tale or the beginning of a legend because it is neither. Rather it was the discovery of something I had always wanted without knowing that I had always wanted it. Actually, I was aghast the following Friday when I came up from New York and landed on *my* island, just to spend a weekend looking around and making plans. My son and daughter came with me and the weekend was a carnival of fresh discoveries, each one bringing a rush of new and often contradictory plans. We ran the motorboat over rock ledges shearing pins, we forgot to bring drinking water, we boiled the lobsters too long, and not understanding oil lamps we lit only candles. It was twenty-three years ago and, as you can see, I still haven't forgotten the wonder of it all.

Rich or Crazy?

I have just returned to the island after being away for a couple of months and I found that not only had two pages dropped from the calendar but a whole season had disappeared. Winter had sneaked in quietly on the heels of autumn, and my home suddenly had taken on a new and somewhat exotic personality. The leaves were down, letting in more light than I had ever seen, the plants had shriveled and turned into brown stalks, a single marigold glared defiantly from a protected corner of a leaf-blanketed flower bed, and pine needles everywhere silenced my footsteps. I stood on the sundeck—an alien—and sought to find some reassurance in a glance across the bay to Cundys Harbor, to Yarmouth Island, to Pole Island. They were all in place but they, too, were different; the haze of summer and autumn had gone and they all seemed closer, more clearly revealed, more intimately a part of my island world than I had imagined them as being. This house is about forty or forty-five years old, I estimate, and it has seen a lot of winters arrive, but this is the first time I have come upon the change so abruptly, the first time I have seen autumn disappear without a trace and the fearful grip of winter fasten around the landscape.

There are acorns everywhere—I almost slid on some when I stepped on the sundeck—and those whose faith penetrates the unknown beyond the science of meteorology assert that this portends a formidable winter, that squirrels in their unscientific way can foretell unpleasant weather and gather up the heavy harvest that nature or God—depending upon the squirrel's views on pantheism and the mysteries of life—had so generously laid about. Some people, found mostly in the group whose faith lies in the *Farmer's Almanac*, claim the only reliable indication of a severe winter can be seen in the behavior of the furry caterpillar. I am a God-fearing man, but I find that I am inclined to drift along more with the acorn crowd, although in my heart I realize this is a pagan belief that excludes the Redeemer entirely.

Winter in Maine gives an impressive performance, and although I was now only tasting the edge of it I could sense something in the wind. A couple of cords of wood had been brought over by my neighbor, the lobsterman, and tossed up on the rocks, but a glance showed that the wood occupied a temporary resting place at best and that the first angry storm would see half of it heading out to sea. Tossing wood is stoop labor at its worst, but when one reckons the total cost of the wood after $150 has been added to it for transportation from the mainland, one doesn't like to see the pile eaten away by flood tides and high waves. I live in a cove, which is somewhat protected, but I've seen storms that turned the water into a witches' brew, and there have been times when a vicious chop discouraged me from undertaking a trip to shore. I've often wondered what my neighbors on the mainland think of me, and one day I got up enough nerve to put the question to the lobsterman. "Some think you're rich," he said, "because you're always bringing stuff over to the island, and the rest think you're crazy." I digested that for a moment. "What do you think?" I asked him. He didn't hesitate. "Crazy," he said.

The next morning there was a sharp edge to the wind, and before walking around the island with the dog I rummaged in the foul-weather gear and brought out an old navy pea jacket. The lining was holding on by a couple of threads, but once I had moved my arms cautiously through the sleeves it struck me as a first-rate cover for a raw, overcast day. A half-dozen gulls were huddled together on a mussel bed exposed by low tide, and their feathers were ruffled up to protect them from the cold. I've never understood why letting air into the feathers helps insulate birds from freezing weather but everyone says it is true and I'll go along with it, but reluctantly. Taking that theory to the extreme, one would think walking around with no clothes on at all would be more comfortable than walking around dressed, which I know for a fact isn't true because the preceding night I had used the outside shower one last time and I walked out of the house with only a towel on my arm and I damned near froze.

Snow flurries come to Maine traditionally in November, and the real stuff comes in December and there's not much an islander can do to protect his house. Since the cove often freezes up solid and I have to leave, I usually drain the pipes, pull the master switch, and row ashore well before snow time, but I have been there during early snowstorms and I have liked it. A heavy snowfall is a lot like a thick fog to an islander; it diminishes a small world even more, and adds an element of snugness. The dog likes it, too; if she had a chair I'm sure she would draw it up to the fire as I do, but as it is she stretches out beside the hearth, one eye open for an errant spark. Snow muffles sound; the house is never so quiet as it is when there is a snowfall.

So I am closing my house for the winter on a day when the sky is gray, and the pine and spruce trees sway uneasily in the north wind. There is a chop in the cove, and it will get dark early. I am letting the logs in the fireplace burn down, and as soon as they are reduced to a feathery white ash I will put up the screen, lock the doors, and the dog and I will set out down the path to where the rowboat waits for us on the incoming tide. We will be back in the spring, probably on a day just like this, but the hearts of us both will be lighter because it is always more joyful to open a house one loves than to close it.

Morning Person

I've noticed that people who like to live in a carnival atmosphere always describe themselves as "night people," as though some special distinction attaches itself to them. For all I know this may be true; those who go through life letting the chips fall where they might, may actually find this world a pleasantly preposterous place to be, provided one doesn't take it too seriously. I confess to a certain amount of envy, since every day I discover something quite new to despair about, but I'm troubled by their need to be night people because I've always felt that slumber was the natural accompaniment to darkness. On this island, after dinner and some reading, interrupted perhaps by a trip to the kitchen for a small glass of Scotch to help ease me into dreamland, I'm ready for the old sackeroo. I don't want to hear the wail of police sirens, or the painful amplification of disco music, or the curses shouted at a taxicab driver who passes up a fare because he or she did not possess the instant profile of a good tipper. What I am saying is that darkness does not provide me with the marvelous release that it seems to convey to those who call themselves night people. In fact, I'm not enchanted by nighttime at all, unless it is a spectacular night of great beauty, with a September moon lighting up the cove or a midsummer storm bringing the sound of thunder rolling across the sky.

What I like—stop me if you've heard me say this before—is early morning, and the earlier the better. Then the world is fresh and young again, the birds all think they are Pavarotti, there is a perfection in the moist cobweb stretching on the loom of the spruce bough, and it is hard to imagine being anywhere but walking along a path in the forest. What I am talking about is this morning.

At this time of the year, the sun comes up early and I could see it was a good day by the pattern of sunlight on the wall. I dressed quickly and, followed by the dog who quite obviously lacked my enthusiasm for such an early awakening, started down the path to the wharf. There was an odd excitement in what I was doing and, as I gaze back at them, the days that begin this way have always stirred me strangely. Once when I was very young, my father took my two sisters, my mother, and me on a motor trip into the Blue Ridge Mountains of Virginia, and we left home very early in the morning. We were to cover about 150 miles that day and I remember my father warning us all that we would have to leave very early—"As soon as it's light enough to drive," he said solemnly—or else we wouldn't arrive at our destination before dark. The car had headlights but my father mistrusted them, and when darkness came on the day's journey ended. I remember taking things from the house to the car in the semidarkness, my heart beating wildly, and I recall the feeling of fear as we drove out of sight of my home and headed out into a strange world— my throat tightened at the thought—150 miles away. It was the dark side of the moon.

It was something like that this morning. The world glistened with such newness that the spirit soared, and if no high adventure was encountered I could always remember the loveliness, the cool shadows, the salty smell of low tide, the sound of a fish breaking water, and the endless chatter of the birds. There was a rustling in the leaves, and a chipmunk raced past me and disappeared under some rocks. A chipmunk is an alarmist with a strong sense of disaster, and I assume it was looking for breakfast and became startled to find me wandering around so early. You can't count on human beings, it was explaining to the family under the rocks, but of course you never could; humans are both unpredictable and untrustworthy.

Two blue jays appeared unexpectedly in an oak, fluttering about nervously, and my hand went to my cap to make sure it was in place. I was mugged once by a blue jay in Central Park in New York City, and I've never underestimated their hostility since. The blue jay had dived at my skull that time and I still have a small scar to prove it. They let the dog and me pass without ambush today, although I made a mental note to return to the house by another path. The dog hates to go down the ramp at low tide; her feet slide, and when she is a few feet from the bottom she makes a final sprint that takes her clear into the boat. The boat was wet from dew, and the look on her face showed that she was unhappy with the setup. This was no dog's idea of a Pepsi Day.

The original luster of an early summer morning begins to fade as the sun moves higher. We took a short boat ride, the dog snapping at an occasional mosquito and I wondering if there was water enough to get over the mussel shoal without lifting the wheel. I played it safe and tilted the motor. We walked home the long way, passing the sauna at the end of the island and coming to the front of the house. Night people, I figured, were just slipping into a sound sleep, and for some reason I felt a surge of sympathy for them. I doubted that they would ever experience the discovery of a summer dawn, the dazzling majesty of a new day being born. That's for day people, and I feel lucky to be one of them.

Name That Island

Summer days on an island, as I gaze back at them, possess a pleasant placidity but they are not empty. The fact that something is unhurried and not forced does not mean that it is unimportant, despite the souped-up philosophy of the business world. I have breathed deeply of the almost carnival air of the corporate boardroom, where rampant self-consciousness swirls around the heads of those sitting at the table and where momentous pronouncements are made only to be forgotten the next day, and I can say now that scraping the hull of my Boston Whaler is a more productive work than most of the days spent in that boardroom. By temperament, I am an island dweller; the belief that island people are reclusive and unsociable is a degrading idea. I like the solitude that this island offers me, but it is like music or Chinese food or travel—I don't want it all the time. I invite a lot of people to visit me here because I need companionship as often as I need solitude, and I consider myself fortunate that I can enjoy both.

I live on what is known as Hamloaf Island, a small forested piece of land jutting up in the middle of Card Cove, which is a minor indentation of Quahog Bay which is a minor indentation of Casco Bay which, itself, is a very minor indentation in the North Atlantic Ocean. I can get in a boat at my wharf and sail to New Zealand, if I cared to, but mostly I sail to

Cundy's Harbor to have lunch in the sunshine on the dock of Holbrook's Store, which to my taste is preferable to New Zealand.

The island and I got off to a poor start a number of years ago because of its name; there was something about the word Hamloaf that embarrassed me, that made me think the whole thing was a joke. For a while I played with the notion of changing the name to something a little more serious like Ragged Island or Elm Island or Snow Island, but those names had already been taken and, indeed, Edna St. Vincent Millay had made Ragged Island—which I can see clearly from my cove—quite famous. Moreover, I was told that it was time-consuming and difficult to change the name of an island that already appeared on sailing charts and quite often required the enactment of a special bill by the Maine state legislature. This information cooled me off considerably, but what finally put the matter to rest was gradually learning the names of some other islands in the general area, islands with names like Big Hen Island, Pound of Tea Island, Butter Island, or Horse Head Island. Just south of Deer Isle there is a small body of land called Crotch Island, and if I lived there I think I would journey to Augusta and take a chance with the Maine state legislature, being a dignified man at heart and one not welcoming rib-poking and giggles when my island's name was mentioned.

Beach Island, Great Spruce Head Island, Resolution Island, and Bear Island all intrigue me because they seem to promise a hidden story in their name origin, and I like a name that suggests adventure of some kind. Because of its proximity to the mainland and its secluded and wooded coast, Hamloaf Island was an active rum-runner's transfer point during the time of Prohibition, I was told, and this has nurtured my imagination considerably since I heard it. There is a rusted lantern still swinging from a post on the hidden side of the island, the one facing the opening to the cove, and I value that old relic more than anything around here because of the stories I think it could tell. On stormy nights, I can see it now: the old lantern flickering in the wind, the rowboat carrying the kegs rising and falling with waves, the leader admonishing the oarsmen to pull harder, the transfer of the kegs to those waiting in the darkness of the island, the light being snuffed out in the lantern, the rowboat beating its way back to the mother ship. You don't have to be a romantic to taste the adventure in that situation.

To tell how one's tastes and attitudes change as time passes is as futile as trying to explain hunger or pain or amusement. But something happened early this summer that suggested to me that perhaps there had been a wide swing in my feelings about the name for my island, and that pride seemed to have crept in unobserved. One evening I was being shown the labyrinthine wine cellars of the legendary Hotel de Paris in Monte Carlo. The manager of the hotel led me through the underground storage rooms, and then invited me to enter a small but elegantly appointed hospitality room where waiters were waiting for us with several bottles of champagne. The champagne was splendid, the manager was an amusing host, and the time passed easily. The little room, he explained, was where he annually entertained the royal family of Monaco for drinks before going to the Grill Room upstairs for dinner. He brought out a handsome album, and showed me the signatures of the guests at the most recent affair. There was "Caroline de Monaco," "Stephanie de Monaco," "Albert de Monaco," and, finally, "Rainier de Monaco." Another bottle was opened and consumed, and as we started to leave the manager asked if I would do him the honor of signing the guestbook. I started a fresh page, and on it I wrote "Caskie d'Hamloaf" and closed the book. I wouldn't have done it without the champagne.

Renewal

The most remarkable thing about it was the ease with which it was accomplished. Moving back into a house after the passage of a winter is an uneasy occasion where things can turn either good or bad depending upon very insignificant factors. I know about this because I have played a part in this ritual twenty times now and I know well what can happen to mar a homecoming and spoil a dream. Sentimental occasions have a fragile foundation, and require a deft and delicate touch; tender feelings are easily disturbed. When I step out of the boat on my island, after an absence of a few months, I have returned home because I live in Maine and this spot is the central core of my entire existence. What I'm saying is that I don't arrive like a traveling salesman, spend a few nights, and then depart; when I come to Maine I stay.

One of the most touching passages in *Walden* is when Thoreau writes: "I have spent many an hour floating over its [the water's] surface as the zephyr willed, having paddled my boat to the middle, and lying on my back across the seats, in a summer forenoon, dreaming awake, until I was aroused by the boat touching the sand, and I arose to see what shore my fates had impelled me to." I have done this thing many times in my cove, because Thoreau has never given me bad advice, but this has always been an adventure in summer indolence, of testing my own capability for idleness. It is never like this on the first trip in spring across the cove to the island. This is different and

I'm not borne by a zephyr but by an outboard motor laboring to get me and a mountain of cargo—plants, food, wine, clothes—to that small spot of land as quickly as possible.

The boxer, as always, leaped from the boat while I was poling it through the shallows. This is her habit; I can't remember having ever stepped from the boat ahead of her. She shook herself dry, shot me an inquisitive glance, and started at a slow trot up the path toward the house. I lingered on the beach. I wanted to see every tree in the forest, every rock on the shore, I wanted to smell the odor of balsam, and I wanted to feel the wind from the sea on my face. There was sky and water and clouds, and there were no fences. Thus began the renewal of my love affair with Maine.

There was work to be done, a fire to be made, bed linen to be changed, food and wine to be put away, but first I must make a tour of the island to see what changes had occurred since I was last there. It was a slow trip; I paused, I tarried, I stood still. The wind was blowing from the southeast, bringing with it a musty odor from the end of the cove where the marshland is filled with sea water when the tide is full. But still, the air seemed fresher than it ever had before (it always does when I first arrive), the water was an intense blue with small whitecaps forming at the top of the waves, and there were a few innocent cumulus clouds above my head. A small skiff was dancing at its mooring a short distance from the mainland. Spring days like this are rare in Maine, and all the more beautiful because of their rarity.

There was a novelty surrounding this arrival as though I had never done it before. Perhaps I had kept my finger on the fast-forward button for the past few weeks without being aware of it, that I had built up a powerful tidal wave of anticipation that was now breaking around me and causing me to feel I was experiencing this for the first time. At the point of rocks at one end of the island, a place known as Capri Point, I stood on the last rock leading into the water and looked toward the forest at the end of the cove. This view was as familiar to me as though I were glancing around my own living room, yet it still possessed the limitless power of stirring me. If a single tree in that forest were felled by lightning I think I would feel the disturbing vibrations no matter in what part of the world I would be.

The boxer had finished her own checklist of investigations—she would do a much more thorough job tomorrow when she could put a little more time into it—and joined me on the rocks. This is a favorite spot of hers because she is intensely sociable, and guests tend to wander here with their drinks in the late afternoon to watch the sunset. Quite often she walks down the path from the house leading the guests to the rocks, a sprightly hostess eager to see that everything is in order before the guests settle down. If she should one day call to me to bring down a few more cushions and a bucket of ice, I can only say that I have long expected it.

The house was cold and possessed the air of unreality. Houses need people; something important drains out of them when they remain long unoccupied. The first night I kept the fire going brightly, getting up from time to time to put on more logs. Unoccupied houses remain stubbornly damp, and it takes about twenty-four hours of a brisk blaze to dispel this body of moist air. The boxer started the night off in a highly independent frame of mind, stretched out on the sofa in front of the fireplace, but I noticed she was in bed beside me when the first gray light of morning made shadows on the wall.

I put on old clothes, started the coffee, and went outside and brushed the pine needles off the table on the sundeck. A lobsterboat was working its way out of the cove and I recognized it as the *Velma S.* with my friend, the lobsterman, at the wheel. I waved, and got a jaunty blast of the whistle in return. It's a nice feeling to be back. Thus with the year, seasons return, which I wish I had thought of first but Milton beat me to it.

Halyard Symphony

Writers treat pleasant subjects patronizingly. They fatten on disaster, tragedy, the melancholy. I discovered this long ago, but the truth came to me with disarming clarity this morning when I resolved to set down what a cool, sunny day in autumn on a Maine coastal island is really like. I have no taste for words like *glorious* or *magnificent* or *breathtaking* because they are generally meaningless and they end up in the hands of lazy writers who haven't the time nor the talent to really get to the heart of the matter and let their readers feel the sadness of a situation or the futility of it or— and this is the tough one—the sweetness of a day that is almost perfect.

Winter in Maine is cruelly cold, spring is soggy and rainy, summer is summer, but autumn—ah! Here the music suddenly becomes *allegretto*, the pace quickens, from somewhere comes the call to get on with something, to remember that life is for the living and that it is a sin to squander a minute of it. There was a keen chill in the air when I got out of bed this morning and, pulling on a sweater and trousers, walked down to the rocky bluff at the north end of the island to shake the sleep from my head. I could tell instantly that this was a day that distilled the beauty of Maine. The sun, reflected from the sea, was blinding, a cool breeze blew from the north building up tiny waves that splashed on the rocks beneath me. The morning sounds—the gulls, a lobsterboat heading out of the cove, the clank of halyards striking the metal mast of a sailing boat on a mooring a quarter of a mile away—mingled into a symphony of their own.

I breathed deeply and thought that this was an enduring delight that only nature could bring about. The artificial world (with the chic shops that sell clothes that will be out-of-date next autumn, and the trendy restaurants whose days are numbered because there will be a trendier restaurant there next year, and the fashionable artist whose single brush stroke on a white canvas is bringing crowds to his latest *vernissage*) seemed far away—a chaotic world that seeks to convince us that if we follow fashion and accumulate many objects and spend enough money we can surely achieve happiness. Standing alone on the rock in the sunlight of an autumn day I realized I could never again live in New York City (where the bottle-deposit law isn't working because a thirty-cent return on a six-pack isn't worth a New Yorker's time) or Los Angeles (where dreams are manufactured for the whole world but where the spinners of the dreams spend their days speeding over endless freeways) or Detroit or Newark (where the well-to-do young professionals think that selling crack and cocaine is a hideous crime but that buying and using it is cool).

Margaret, the boxer, came out of a tangle of juniper and bayberry bushes and joined me on the rock. It was a day much to her liking, cool and sunny with the unspoken promise of a snooze in the leaves after she followed me on a few irksome errands. Margaret is set in her ways, as all boxers are, and she is careful to make sure that her energies do not flow into the absurd channels that so delight human beings. She knows that the world is disorderly, perhaps beyond recovery, but she feels that the two of us can hold out for a long siege, especially if we are careful to have plenty of salmon and bluefish in our diets and plenty of afternoon naps in a sunny spot in the leaves.

I admire Margaret, despite the rigidity of her opinions, because, like me, she has a profound respect for the natural order of things, although her outlook comes to her out of the air and mine is beaten into shape on the anvil of despair. Margaret will politely leave a room in which someone is smoking, because smoke in the lungs is unpleasant and to be avoided, but I will remain behind out of fear of being rude or unkind. Moreover, after eating dinner, Margaret climbs up on the sofa, turns around a couple of times to trample the cushion into submission, and goes to sleep for the night, convinced that she has squeezed out pretty much all the day had to offer. I am not that smart. I get up from the table carrying a brandy to the living room, and there I get into deep water arguing with a guest or reading something that I think contains a strong dash of lunacy, if not downright dishonesty, and go to bed only to squirm around for a couple of hours while in my mind I put the world back to rights again.

But on a day like this, on an island in Maine, the world is right. Here on the shore of the Gulf of Maine there will be two high tides and two low tides on this lunar day, just as there was when the world was young, and the sun will set behind Orr's and Bailey islands at a time that can be predicted to the split second. After I get a cup of coffee back at the house, Margaret and I will get in the whaler and go out of the cove to the rock ledge where the seals lounge around at low tide. The other day I counted thirty-eight of them, including a couple of pups. This morning I would like to check again to see if my census is accurate. The seals treat us cordially, knowing somehow that we're just idly curious and not from some well-meaning but intrusive research organization. Once the distinction has been drawn, we are largely ignored while they go about normal seal affairs which, I'm pleased to note, involve a lot of sleep.

Disengagement

My quarrel with Maine (which may not even know we have a problem) is not that its charms are so slight but rather that they are distributed unevenly and on a timetable not synchronized with my own. Take the autumn months, for example, when the days turn languid and golden, when the leaves first spiral from the trees, when the noons are hot but the early mornings are frosty, and I am in the clumsy and absurd position of finding myself going through the strange ritual of disengagement because a writer must travel to write, whether the travel is mental or physical. The poet, I imagine, can write anywhere; his or her mind soars into the heavens regardless of whether the body is confined to a dusty garret or rests high on a windy hill. On the whole, I envy our poets; the world makes all sorts of excuses for them in the belief that their souls are unanchored and they are winged by nature. Those of us who fuss around with prose are a somewhat lower order; we try to make ourselves understood, which is something that never crosses the mind of a good poet, and I suspect a lot of poets take advantage of this. I've read a lot of poetry written by first-rate poets—Dylan Thomas, for example—when I didn't understand a single line of what I was reading, yet I was entranced by the flow of words and the cadence, which soothed me like a brook flowing over pebbles. Me, I've got a different problem, and I have to face it every time I sit at a typewriter just as I'm trying to do now. If I don't make myself understood, what I am writing is going to be returned to me with a little note beginning "Rejection does not necessarily mean lack of merit but...."

It's easy to write about this island because the simple landscape expresses all of the elegance of nature which I find diverting and exciting, and since I am impressed by it I want others to be also. Responding to this odd desire, I sometimes find myself wandering down the path to the little workroom in the forest, sometimes in bathrobe in the gray hours before dawn, hoping to make readers feel as I do about the melancholy sound of loon calling to loon across a waste of water, or the light of the moon shining for a mad moment through a scudding cloud cover, or the moist wind that sweeps across the sea a few moments before a thunderstorm breaks. The writer knows there is a universal longing to understand the beauty and mystery of these things. The problem is in touching the right strings to make the music that satisfies the longing. The poet does it in some way that is mysterious to me, and beyond my reach. It's plain to see that I would like to be a poet; I think they are working the right side of the street.

When I walked with my dog this morning to the rocks at the northern end of the island, the wind had a cruel bite to it and I knew that autumn was slipping into winter and that the chop in the cove would one morning be silenced under a skim of ice. In Maine, seasons change suddenly; one day I am picnicking on a rock ledge and the next day I am vigorously sawing firewood. Long ago I found that by traveling in the winter I was positioning myself for long periods on the island during the times that it appealed to me the most—the late spring, summer, the autumn. There is a melancholy taste to autumn, and while I suspect that almost everyone feels it I am certain that I feel it more acutely than most because it means that the year has come round to the time when I must leave the place I love the most. I slip over the edge from a vague melancholy to a haunting sadness.

Today I will go through my house selecting a book here, a bottle of wine there, a few letters from the desk, perhaps some photographs, to take with me and help see me through the winter. I may be on some further shore next month—the Arabian Sea or the Mediterranean Sea or the Andaman Sea—but a walk along a beach at twilight will bring a sound or a smell or a flash of light from a distant beacon that—in my mind's eye—will bring me quickly back to Casco Bay. Once in the Aegean, I saw a tiny harbor, a horseshoe perhaps two hundred yards across, the seaward side protected by a scattering of ledges, and my thoughts raced to Five Islands near Georgetown in Maine, where one autumn day I had sat on the dock and eaten fried clams that I had bought at the local snack bar.

I don't know how Maine and I will fulfill our mutual destinies since I feel that much of its beauty is squandered on days that slip by after I have put the boats in the boathouse, drained the water pipes, locked the house up snugly, and rowed away. I've been told it is bad luck to look backward once a journey has begun, and I think that is the reason I choose to row away from the island rather than use the motorboat. In a rowboat one faces the landscape one is leaving, making a stolen glance of wistfulness unnecessary. I suddenly have the feeling that I am setting down these remarks more for my own good than for the reader, and if that is the case I should stop—which I am now doing.

Listen to the Sea

My late evening darkness of spirit is sometimes reinforced or sometimes lightened by what I read before bedtime and a few nights ago I hit pay dirt when I read that a chap had bought a lighthouse in Maine and intended to restore it to its original state and use it as a summer home. Obviously this is a man in search of the beauty of all our yesterdays, and he thinks the past may lie in the Hendricks Head Light at the mouth of the Sheepscot River. I felt both pride and satisfaction that Maine could point the direction to a better way of life for a man from Alabama who seems to feel that technical progress is all right as far as it goes but that it has serious shortcomings where peace of the soul is concerned.

The quest of the new owner of Hendricks Head Light parallels my own when twenty-five years ago I bought this tiny island in Casco Bay and moved into a house lit by kerosene lamps and warmed by driftwood burning in a fireplace that threw flickering lights into dark corners and new hope into a heart numbed by the growing meanness and insensitivity of the country's largest city. Here—first on weekends but later much more—I discovered the mysterious and magical things that occurred when the moon was full and the tides were running high, of the varied moods of the sea and the shore, of the strange but pleasant isolation when a curtain of fog dropped silently behind me, shutting out the noise, the conflict, the inhumanity of a world of frustration and abandoned hope. This wasn't the last outpost of serenity in a chaotic universe—I wasn't that lost in hubris—but I felt that this small body of land floating in the sea was beyond the reach of influences that could corrupt and lessen its meaning to me.

This strong feeling of discovery and spiritual reawakening may not be running as strong in the new owner of Hendricks Head Light as it did with me, but I am encouraged by his announcement that he planned to keep the light in operation and that the renovation plans would not change its historic character. (A submarine cable now brings electricity to my island and the dwelling itself has been changed vastly over the years, but the spiritual detachment and the feeling of independence holds steady.)

The fact that the new owner is described as a "lighthouse buff" is also reassuring because a lighthouse keeper must, by the very nature of the occupation, be a world unto himself or herself. Moreover, lighthouses invariably cling to exposed islets or shoals or protruding rock ledges, creating as isolated an encompassment as one could imagine. And for one to choose a lighthouse as a site for a summer home would certainly suggest that the owner was not pining away for 42nd Street and Lexington Avenue. The property is situated on what is described as "four acres of windswept peninsula" at the mouth of Sheepscot River, and the house has three bedrooms, a fireplace, and two stoves. That is two stoves more than I possess on Hamloaf Island, and I must acknowledge some envy on that point because in early spring, when the rains add to the discomfort of a winter slow in departing, I often find the fireplace gaining on my wood-sawing capability.

I suppose it is pure romanticism for me to point out that Hendricks Head Light is considered to be in Southport, the Maine town where the late Rachel Carson spent many summers and where she wrote *Silent Spring*, but when I get in a fanciful mood I sometimes lose my head. Miss Carson, it seems to me, represents the fierce independence of Maine coastal people. It was she who had the courage thirty years ago to tell her countrymen that their pesticides, aimed at killing the cotton boll, were also killing the American eagle. I have no idea what brought Rachel Carson to Maine to live a life of solitude in a coastal forest, but I can speculate that she was responding to some of the same bewitchery that attracted me and, for all I know, the new owner of Hendricks Head Light. Once, speaking of coming down to the sea at Southport in early morning, Miss Carson wrote: "There was nothing, really, for human words to say in the presence of something so vast, mysterious, and immensely powerful. Perhaps only in music of deep inspiration and grandeur could the message of that morning be translated by the human spirit, as in the opening bars of Beethoven's *Ninth Symphony*—music that echoes across vast distances and down long corridors of time ... music that swirls and explodes even as the sea surged against the rocks below me." I don't know how the new owner of Hendricks Head Light feels in reading that but I know Miss Carson speaks for me, and I only wish that I possessed the ability to describe it as she has done. If all that was worth saying was being said by the sea, Miss Carson recognized this, a recognition that never occurred to us lesser writers.

I envy the quest of the new occupant of the lighthouse, the search for the lost sense of the past, the wistfulness and hope that must lurk in his heart as he settles into his new summer home. It is a sentimental journey the new owner is embarking upon, and I hope he is not dismayed by my probing into his dreams. My only excuse is that I have taken that journey, and I send him my best wishes and hope that his search ends as successfully as mine. But it is not my voice that he must listen to; I have just learned from a wiser and more perceptive person that if there is anything worth saying, the sea will say it.

Honey, I'm Home

Whenever my affection for Maine becomes more a habit than a flowing, racy thing, I take a trip as I did in midsummer this year, and for lack of any better place to go I headed for California where I hoped to find a lot of sunshine that had curiously been lacking in Maine. A dreaminess compounded of great expectations, brooding excitement, and possible adventure always precedes travel, making the reality often a faded souvenir scarcely worth bringing home. There was all the sunshine one could yearn for on this trip, along with some blistering heat, the choking air that accompanies traffic gridlock, and some frightening prices for mediocre food in restaurants where the chef comes out to shake hands with the patrons instead of staying in the kitchen where he belongs. Still, travel always accomplishes something, even if it is no more than reconstituting satisfaction with home.

It doesn't take a house long to achieve an unlived-in feeling. A week or so will do it. Even before I unlock the door, there are reminders everywhere that nobody has been in charge here, that an anarchy has prevailed, and that everything has had to struggle for itself. There are yellow leaves on the geraniums, weeds have grown along with the basil plants, the sundeck is carpeted with pine needles, a shutter has broken loose and sways in the wind, and a deck chair is upended.

Inside, I find it hard to believe that I have been away only a week.

How could such an atmosphere of stagnancy, of lifelessness, build up in such a short time? Drawn shades usually contribute to this feeling, but there is a large window extending across the entire living room of my house, and there is no shade to draw across it. The sunlight poured through the window, but it wasn't the sunlight I was used to; it seemed artificial somehow, in this hushed room, as though it were a stage light. The flowers on the coffee table were withered, and their petals covered the books and magazines. There was the week-old newspaper, the dust on the television set, the book opened and lying across the arm of the chair. I picked it up and wondered who had gotten no further than page ninety-one before putting it down, presumably never to reopen it again. It wasn't me.

I carried my suitcase into the bedroom, and raised a window. The curtains, like the sails of a ship, gathered the breeze and began luffing. Outside on the oak tree a bird broke into a song, a loud and spirited song, that took some of the lifelessness out of the house. It seemed as good a time as any to gather up again the reins of authority, so I went about the place raising windows and opening sliding doors. I hung up my jacket in the closet, took off my necktie, and stepped out on the sundeck, rolling up my sleeves. "I'm back," I announced in a loud voice, "so let's get some action around here." I think it worked; three gulls took off from the mussel bed, the bird in the oak tree began again, and from the kitchen came the humming of the refrigerator starting up. This sort of response is good for a man; it makes him feel that he enjoys a solid position in the neighborhood.

In my opinion, the joy of rediscovery is dependent very little, if at all, on the outcome of the trip. I suppose that if a journey had been in all respects a disaster, a dispirited mixture of bad weather, dull encounters, and faulty service, one would arrive home with a fresh sense of the enchantment of the familiar, but I come back from pleasurable trips to find the island not commonplace at all but somewhat miraculous and— if the weather is good—even dazzling. Midsummer languor on a Maine island can be nature at its most benign and I've discovered almost nothing that can compare with it.

Nature to me is bottomless and contains the answer to all mankind's problems, although I'm not inclined to be evangelistic about it. I believe in nature the way some people believe in New York or wealth or power or science or the intellect or the Bible. I have discovered that anything truly unnatural is wrong, is destined to be short-lived, and will lead mankind down the path of disaster. The natural way of life is not a minimalist way but actually a bountiful way; nature cures, it is never toilsome, it possesses no limitations, and it knows no desperation. Human beings, over the course of history, have made some ghastly errors in staking out moral and ethical boundaries, ignoring nature entirely, and this has brought confusion and unhappiness. Our man-made environment has been thrown into conflict with nature and we find our water impure, our oceans polluted, our atmosphere filled with chemical vapors, and our cities filled with people dying of strange diseases.

I suppose this is why it is peculiarly satisfying to get back to a Maine island after a trip to the city. When one sits on a rock here and stares across the sea, one does it defiantly. Behind him or her is a small world where nature's mastery is not disputed, where the air is scented on a hot day with the pungent odor of balsam, where the stars still shine brightly at night, where there is silence when one wants silence, and when one awakens at night to hear rain on the roof it is—still—rainwater. Life here is met in a different spirit, not in despair and anguish but in hope and forebearance.

You Call This Progress?

If there's one thing I loathe, it's progress, which seems innocuous enough at first but soon it becomes unnervingly difficult. What goes wrong?

Well, first, the central theme—improvement—is treated by an innocent public as a development so startling that the world will never be the same again, an acceptance that makes a mockery of human confidence. Sooner or later, the progress is seen as the shameful thing that it is: something cheaper, something not better than what existed before but trendier, or something just plain different. Not better, mind you, just different.

I doubt that I will live long enough to fully accept what the electronic people call voice mail, since I make telephone calls in order to discuss something that's on my mind with someone else, and I don't get much satisfaction when I'm told to "Press one" or "Press two" in order to get a recorded message offering answers to questions I haven't asked. Considering the demands made upon my time and attention by the clamor of modern marketing, it's hard enough to get an individual to stand still and listen, and I would like to see more human beings returned to the work force and not drained from it. What I'm saying is a paraphrase of the

South Pacific song "There's Nothing Like a Dame." I think there's nothing like a human being, especially at the other end of the telephone line.

I have a strong suspicion that those who dream up these innovations (real progress is something entirely different) find them as hollow as the rest of us do after they have been around a while. The electronic door chime that turns on the coffee, trips the alarm clock, opens the garage door, and shucks oysters invariably turns out not to perform any of the chores very well. *Ave atque vale.*

Mall Smart

A demolition derby, for those who came in late, is an entertainment more popular in the West than here in New England. It's an event where drivers in crash helmets steer battered automobiles into each other, with the purse going to the driver of the last car still upright and able to move forward on four wheels. I have never been in a demolition derby but I come very close to it every day that I drive into the Cooks Corner shopping mall on the outskirts of Brunswick. Some days, if I've had a bad night and am a little jumpy anyway, I drive down Route 24 a few miles just to steady myself and get a good grip on the steering wheel before venturing in, because once you enter the parking area there's no turning back. Cars are coming at you from all directions and a glance in the rear-view mirror shows you are being tailgated by a pickup truck and a small van, and even the most fainthearted realizes the only hope for survival lies in weaving and twisting ahead. A friend of mine who is an excitable chap anyway tells me his wife lets him go the mall now only once a week since she knows that these trips inevitably result in a bad night for her, with lots of groaning and twisting on the part of her mate, and once a rather piteous plea for help broke from his lips in the middle of the night.

Several times I have tried to make a wide arc around the main arena and get to the bookstore by sneaking in past the filling station, but I was told recently that this route is known locally as Suicide Alley and that its casualty statistics are fairly impressive. The only other alternative for a noncombative person who would like to retain the status of a conscientious objector, is to park near the theater and truck his or her groceries there from the supermarket, but this is a long walk and often through exposed combat areas. A few days ago, while attempting this, I saw that I had been lined up in the sights of an Oldsmobile Cutlass, and I saved myself only by a highly evasive action in front of the barber shop, or where the barber shop used to be before it turned chicken and moved to a new location on the periphery of the parking lot. I lost a jar of tomato juice and seven eggs out of a carton of twelve when the maneuver sent my shopping cart into a small truck, but I was rather pleased that things had gone so well.

When I get out of the mall and am on my way home, I usually pull over to the side of the road and catch my breath. If there were a bar in the neighborhood, I would stop and have a shot of Scotch, straight up, but the nearest bar is behind me and I don't know anybody who is fool enough to want to return to Dunkirk after he or she has escaped from it.

I am not through with that shopping mall yet. Kids who used to be street smart are now mall smart, and I've heard that some of them even know where the public toilets are located, although for the life of me I've never been able to find one. All I know is that improvement is just another word for inconvenience. I travel a lot during the winter months and when I return to Maine every spring I dread going to the mall and seeing the improvements that have been made during my absence. All of the improvements seem to hit me where I live. The benches, where a man could set while his wife was shopping, are gone. The public telephones are moved to strange locations inside stores where they improve what retailers like to call "store circulation." What used to be public restrooms now have signs saying "Employees Only," and most of the exits from the mall to the highway have been sealed off, although there are plenty of entrances. The thinking behind this seems to be to give motorists plenty of access and then let them find the way out as best they can. The longer a person remains in a mall, the more he or she is going to spend. Anything to keep minds occupied in healthy and acquisitive channels.

Business analysts are astonished at the rapid growth in popularity of what have come to be known as "convenience" stores, small stores selling gasoline and a limited choice of food items, but I see nothing surprising in this new industry at all. It's mall backlash. A man whose wife tells him to pick up a loaf of bread and a quart of milk when he comes back from the post office doesn't want to tangle with a mall on such a trivial errand. So he pays a good bit more but he comes home early and with his disposition intact. It's a bargain.

If I sound as though I am opposed to all aspects of mall life and mall society, I have overstated my case. Just the other day a wonderful thing happened at the Cooks Corner mall, and I am pleased not to have missed it. I think it went unnoticed by most of the people, but it caused me to forget all of the unpleasant realities of malls and for a moment I was caught up in the enjoyment of what I had seen. A young girl stepped out of a car and went hurriedly into a shop. What attracted my attention—the inescapable, the significant, the joyous thing—was that she was wearing a white silk dress, stockings, and high-heeled shoes. In a world of shorts, blue jeans, T-shirts, and sandals, here—for one glorious moment—was something that had been virtually lost forever: a feminine creature. Wow!

Where Did We Go Wrong?

Beware of progress, warned Jean Cocteau, the French writer and artist, because it may be the development of an error. I keep an uneasy watch on progress in Maine because I've learned that what passes for progress is often very destructive, especially the substitution of rubber bands for wooden pegs in the crusher claws of lobsters. And please don't tell me those rubber bands don't stink up the whole kettle of boiling water because I know better. The bulldozer has become the nightmarish symbol of progress in the minds of the new generation, and the more earth that's moved the more praiseworthy the progress. Moreover, physical labor has been downgraded in dignity to the point of being regarded scornfully; perspiration is on a level with leprosy.

The other day on the roadside I saw three workmen trying to maneuver an immense digger into position to drill a hole for a pathetically small pole, a job that could have been done in half the time by one man with a shovel. The whole atmosphere now reeks of dependence— a choking blend of dependence upon machinery, exhaust fumes, and noise. The workman no longer is allowed to feel the pleasure of close companionship with the job at hand—that relationship is forever lost. He now attends a machine, which does the work in a routine way since pride and craftsmanship have been shunted aside. I haven't seen a hand-pushed lawnmower now for ten years, and I'm not even sure they're made anymore.

We now regard as progress the growth of malls (because people have grown too lazy to walk to the store) or the proliferation of condominiums (because people have grown too lazy to paint their houses or shovel snow from the front steps) or the popularity of television evangelism (because the faithful have grown too lazy to drive to church). Even play has suffered from progress. Golf once was a game that required considerable walking in the outdoors, but now the battery-powered golf cart takes the player to the spot where the ball lies. If the players now could only get someone to swing for them, they wouldn't have to get out of the cart. I suspect that someone, at this minute, is working on that problem.

The other day I started to clean out my boathouse, and I was suddenly struck by the fact that I was unknowingly maintaining a museum of Early American artifacts, although in my quaint way I was still regarding them as tools. There was a woodsaw, a couple of axes, a short-handled shovel, two hoes, some drills, a post-hole digger, and all the other tools a country person of any independence needs to hold his world together. In a few years' time a pair of work gloves will be the objects of mystery to children. "I think they were used in some sort of game," one kid will say to another, gazing at the gloves. "Naw," the other will reply, "they were for keeping warm before they had ice-melting wires in the sidewalks."

My misfortune is to feel at my best when I have just repaired something or when the handsaw goes through a particularly stubborn log or when I've finished hauling leaves and underbrush out to the rock ledge at low tide and am ready to put a match to it. I may smell like a wet moose but I have an almost belligerent sense of self-sufficiency. I'm going to have trouble, real trouble, in adjusting to this new way of thinking.

My dog and I don't see eye to eye on many things because her decisions invariably seem to tilt toward any course of action involving sleep, and now that the wind has a sharp edge to it the tilt seems more pronounced. But she is usually ready to go outside and do what she feels is her rightful part in odd jobs around the island, especially if we head off toward the sunny shore in the lee of the woods, where my preoccupation with work often causes me to overlook the fact that she is curled up in a bed of warm leaves grabbing a few badly needed winks. She is full of independent judgments, and one of them is that I overdo things, that I don't know when to quit a job. Taking the leadership, she will often get up, stretch, and start back to the house, casting a glance over her shoulder to see if I have enough sense to follow her.

On this, she is dead right; my work is conducted on the chain theory, one job leading directly to another. If I tighten the screws on a hinge of the shutters, I go around the house tightening all of the hinges despite the fact that the rest of them are causing no offense. My boxer can't see this, any way she looks at it. Grease the squeaking wheel, she believes, and then let's get in by the fire where a man and his dog belong. As you can see, she is closer to the prevailing view of progress than I am. I hate it when a small family, like this, splits on the big issues, but that's the way things go.

I have always felt that a man who works with his back is a great deal more content than those of us who work sitting down. Isn't the carpenter doing something more productive than the writer? A few years ago I was at a book-signing affair at Wanamaker's in Philadelphia when a lady approached me. Ignoring the stack of books at my elbow, she asked "How can I get a wristwatch out of my toilet?" It was then that I realized that the writer's world was not a major one in the constellations of the heavens. It was a sensible question and deserved a sensible answer, but I didn't have it. I envied the carpenter, who is always on ground familiar and solid.

Drama in One Act

I believe I've rightly guessed that at one time or another all of us have wondered what individual in what government office decides that the best time to block off a major highway for some minor improvement is Labor Day weekend. Who—specifically—makes the decision to clean out a storm sewer on a hot Friday in August, rerouting traffic headed to the beach or the mountains and creating a monstrous jam of blocked vehicles for five miles or more? Maine is no worse than other states in creating this nightmare, but it is no better either. This was brought to mind recently when my car was detoured through the residential section of Topsham, and under a hot August sun I parked and walked around to see what sort of emergency work was being done that had brought traffic in Topsham almost to a halt. I found an idle piece of road machinery, a hole on the side of the road, and two workmen leisurely eating sandwiches and talking.

The view from the driver's seat is always the same: there is the policeman to create the sense of emergency and authority, there is the man with the red flag, there are the red cones stretching in an endless line as far as the eye can see, and there is the car ahead inching along in low gear, but seldom does one get a chance to see any actual work being done. At one time in my life I would roll down the window and ask the policeman or the flagman why a holiday was being used for road improvement, but I no longer raise my voice or my hopes. I have never known anyone to hold what I said in such deep contempt as the policeman, although the flagman never seemed to have the slightest idea of what I was complaining about. He would stare at me vacantly, then motion me forward with his flag another six inches. This sort of incident must have been happening to thousands of other Americans in those days, but I suppose their innocence disappeared about the same time as mine.

Musing about this after I had disentangled myself from the Topsham chaos, I was suddenly struck by the notion that perhaps something more sinister and something more saddening to the spirit was involved here. I don't fully trust my government because it is administered by men and women who are often as vain, as frustrated, and as full of hunger for revenge as I am. I have written the following drama to illustrate what could possibly be behind these incidents and I would like to offer it, royalty-free, to any dramatic group that can manage to get it staged. Needless to say, all characters and situations are of my own creation.

The scene: curtain raises to show a typical government office, with a picture of the incumbent Governor over the desk, the usual metal government-issue furniture, a water cooler, and a name that is emblazoned on the glass half of the door but is backward and unreadable to the audience. A man is seated at a desk, and another enters nervously.

THE MAN. (*Addressing seated occupant, who swivels around to face him*) I hate to bother you, Chief, but I think I've come up with an idea that will block traffic on Route 1 this weekend.

CHIEF. (*Testily*) I hope it's a better idea than that suggestion of yours last week that we close three entrances to the turnpike. They got around that in thirty minutes.

THE MAN. (*Crestfallen*) I know, Chief. That didn't work out. But this one will. Can I explain it to you?

CHIEF. (*Bored*) Go ahead, but let me say this: you are a new man and I know you are trying, but you are aiming too low. We aren't looking for the nuisance blocking. There's plenty of that all down Route 1. We're looking for the Big One. Like the one Carruthers pulled off in the summer of '87 when he had an eighteen-mile backlog of traffic north of Lincolnville in ninety-eight-degree heat. Three drivers had nervous breakdowns. Seventeen cars were abandoned and never reclaimed. It took three days to get normal traffic restored. Why are you holding up your hand?

THE MAN. (*Eyes aglow*) Wow! What a sight that must have been. I just wanted to ask you what Carruthers got from it. Personally, that is.

CHIEF. (*Quietly, and with satisfaction*) He was just the most sought-after man in the highway world. Of course we made him supervisor and doubled his salary overnight, but he only laughed at us. Michigan finally outbid Arizona, South Carolina, and Ohio for him, and so far as I know he is still in Lansing. But a man with a creative mind like that can write his own ticket. It was foolish for us to even think we could hold on to him here in Maine.

THE MAN. (*Turning to go*) I guess so.

CHIEF. (*Brusquely*) What was this new idea of yours?

THE MAN. (*At door*) Forget it, Chief. You've cut me down to size. I've got a lot of growing to do in this job. But one day—believe me, Chief—I'm going to come to you with the Big One.

(*The Chief smiles, faintly but not unkindly, as The Man exits*)
The End.

Desanctification

A question to go forever unanswered is why should there be a physical world, why should there not be nothing? Island dwellers who sit on the rocks and stare out across the water waste a lot of time following odd trains of thought that start out nicely formed like the contrails a high-flying plane draws across the sky only to have them grow wispy and blurred once they are touched by the crosscurrents of logic and reality and the limitations of human mentality. I try to keep away from broader thoughts than I can handle, but sometimes my mind cuts loose from the subject at hand and goes off in a footloose sort of way, indulging itself on odd facts and even whimsies, coming to a halt in some quagmire where the only way out is to go to the house, pour a little Scotch over some rocks, and turn on the telly to see how the Red Sox did. Or didn't do.

I wandered into the subject that follows quite casually and I was in over my head almost immediately. There is a small church on the country road I usually take into town, and while I realized that there had been no activity around it for a couple of years, I was surprised this past summer to see that it has a new life as an art gallery. One gets something of a shock to see a church put to a commercial use; it's somewhat like selling ads in the Bible, urging the faithful to smoke the proper cigarettes or drink the right brand of beer. The building, of course, had been desanctified and was standing there idle, but what about the spirit of the former Occupant? Was there interest, on the part of the former Management, as to what kind of art was being shown there, of the way the place was being kept up, of the behavior of the customers?

For a long time outdated and phased-out lighthouses were the things sought after by Mainers, knowing that summer tourists couldn't resist spending a night in a bed-and-breakfast inn located in a lighthouse. I would guess that the lighthouse market, never extensive under any circumstances, is fairly sluggish at this time, and it may well be that a desanctified church has caught the spirit of the times. The famous Chocolate Church in Bath, which for a number of years now has been The Center for the Arts at the Chocolate Church, is certainly one of the most outstanding examples of a desanctified church being put to public use (there is a minor distinction between denominational use and public use) in a highly successful way. A prodigality of musical, artistic, dramatic, choreographic, and other entertainment and cultural activities have sprung from the Chocolate Church and it is considered one of the most productive such enterprises along the entire coast of Maine. Only a few blocks away from the Chocolate Church on Washington Street is another desanctified church which has been serving as an annex to the Maritime Museum. And on Pleasant Street, in downtown Brunswick, a desanctified church now is serving a variety of purposes, including a Greek restaurant, a billiard parlor, a pizza joint, a health-food store, and some other functions all secular in nature. A white church near Edgecomb is now the Ditty Box Antiques. So it goes. Putting a church to uses other than recounting the parables of Christ, nonetheless, seems to undermine what most of us have always considered a certain irreversibility of identity. Perhaps what I am saying is simply that churches were never regarded by most of us as "ordinary" property, as subject to the restless dynamics of the real-estate market.

I am a sociable fellow, fond of animals and children, and only passingly religious, and, while I am not trying to be evangelical, at the same time I would like to seize the occasion to say that Nature seems to me to be the most positive manifestation of true religion. It's true that Nature provides us with no vaulted cathedrals, no painted-glass windows, no ceremonially lit candles, nor any commandments carved in stone, but that does not mean that natural laws can be easily broken. Violation of a natural law leads to quick disaster. It is my personal belief that if God had intended the atom to be split He would have looked to it Himself and not passed the job on to man, whose record in matters of this kind through the centuries has not been reassuring.

I started out talking about desanctified churches, and the uses they are being put to in Maine, but the idle pursuit of a subject of this kind often leads one around in a circle, and that's the position I discover myself to be in right at this minute. We are in the process of desanctifying a church of such variety, beauty, excitement, and glory—the Earth—that all of us should be stricken with guilt, shame, and fear for what we are doing. Mankind is a bit touchy about its sleazier accomplishments, and as it slips into the twenty-first century it has a lot of shoring up and overdue maintenance to attend to if it wants to hang around long enough to see the twenty-second one come around. I think the survival of mankind may very likely hang precariously on the assumption that desanctification of this great House of the Lord is as reversible a process as sanctification. This is a tiny little star we live on, and its brightness is exceeded only by its fragility.

Anhedonia

Sooner or later I'm going to open a cereal box at the checkout counter and inquire why it's only half full. I will wait for a long line of customers to queue up behind me, since I seldom give a really good performance without the excitement and stimulation of a full house.

I've been thinking about these things during the unsettled spring weather, and I'm especially puzzled by our ability to devise something as clever and intricate as, say, the Patriot missile yet our scientists seem totally incapable of making something as simple as a milk carton that can be opened by hand. I follow the direction of the little arrows and go to work on that side of the carton, but my heart is no longer in it because I know now that it has never worked and that some significant step has been bypassed, sealing the carton as though it were welded. The nature of our dilemma must certainly engage the inventive genius of some Edison or Bell still unknown who will have the courage to close the door on past failures and look in new directions to unlock the secrets of the universe and the milk container.

Other things contribute to my anhedonia. Today the newspapers sought my sympathy for the plight of the nation's airlines, caught between spiraling fuel costs and fewer passengers. If ever a call for help fell upon deaf ears, this is it. In my opinion, the strong streak of insanity that has characterized airline management in recent years has now blossomed into an outright death wish. In pursuit of a policy called "yield management," airlines have faceless gnomes punching endless computer buttons to reveal to them tricks of pricing that will outwit their passengers. Long trips often cost less than short trips; in the interest of economy, passengers now find they are flying on the days when the airlines want them to fly, not on days of their own choosing. "Certain restrictions may apply" is the phrase that empties the advertisements of any meaning; the life of a rate is often one day. How can I feel any kindness for an industry that welcomes my misfortune and openly structures its fares to benefit from it, that rubs its hands in glee when a death in the family or a serious illness causes me to pay $700 for a flight that would cost $150 if I could wait a week? How can I grieve over the impending doom of an airline whose rates lack any basic value but spin wildly in response to competition or lack of it or to seasons or to route development or to what day of the week it happens to be? I say it's capricious, I say it's a game of Idiot's Delight, and I say to hell with it.

I have a note, too, for the automobile industry. Why not stop fooling around with hoods and grills and hatchbacks—they are now about as ugly as they can get—and concentrate on the doors, with a view toward designing something which will accommodate people other than children and dwarfs? I am slightly under six feet in height—not strictly an ungainly stature—and considerable engineering skill is required on my part in getting into and out of the driver's seat. My dog, Margaret, would like for me to point out that neither is the back seat any bargain where entrances and exits are concerned. Our exeunts are complicated and uncomfortable, but the tape deck works well.

If your phone doesn't ring, it's me. I'm not using the phone much these days in protest of the "junk mail" I've been receiving over it lately. Around dinner time—when most people are thought to be home—the computer calls begin coming in, all trying to sell me something. I don't cotton to this much, especially since I've been selected by some random code and there's no one at the other end of the line that I can talk back to, that I can let feel the weight of a wrathful tongue. I interrupt the sales pitch with considerable invective although I know that man's spirit will be broken in any clash with a computer, and instead of finishing my dinner I usually head for the bar. I suspect we are all schizophrenic: part of the time pleased with our high state of comfort and convenience, and at other times deeply resentful of the commercial opportunism that robs us of enjoyment of these prizes. Give up, and follow me to the bar.

Well, suddenly the sun has come out. One of the news magazines this week predicted that a new day is breaking. When the war in the Gulf ends the banks will get their strength back, the recession will end, people will move out of cities to "places like Maine and Montana," and our "social unsteadiness" will pass. I'd like to raise up the volume a little on Montana although the whole picture appeals to me, especially if Montana gets more of those unhappy city people than Maine. Montana is the place, folks, with all of that Big Sky and the open plains, and don't forget that's where the Lonesome Dove crowd settled. There's nothing like that down east, nothing. Trust me.

Computers 'R Us

Edna St. Vincent Millay, one of the brightest stars in Maine's literary vault of the heavens, once wrote, "Life must go on; I forget just why," and while many people think she was coasting on Empty at the time she wrote it, I hold a totally different view. I like everything Miss Millay wrote, and I think that particular thought was more inspiration than desperation. Like all of us eremophiles, Miss Millay possessed a revolutionary spirit and saw no need to regard the crowded future with its promise of unending progress as the crowning reason for our existence. By temperament, I suspect Miss Millay was an existentialist, that she felt it was a mistake to overlook the present in favor of the uncertain wealth of a technological future. Me, I string along with Miss Millay; the culture of today, however meager, can carry us on remarkable tides of creation. What I am saying, and Miss Millay too if I read her correctly, is that the end of the twentieth century doesn't necessarily find us in Chapter 11.

I have just been looking through a booklet which arrived all on its own through the mail, a pamphlet called "Writing Can Be Fun." I don't know a hell of a lot about writing, but I know it can never be fun. I have spent too many bleak, unproductive days in this small study on my island trying to write something, only to see the balls of crumpled paper grow as my confidence diminished, and ultimately—when the vanishing point of any accomplishment was reached—give up and turn to something worthwhile, like sawing driftwood or scraping the bottom of the boat.

The lobsterman needs only to measure the carapace of his catch to decide which to throw back but the writer needs to search throughout the entire English language to decide which word to keep, jettisoning all of the rest. I envy my friend, the lobsterman. Whoever questions the distinctions between theory and action, between criticism and creation, realizes the whole thing is shot through with suppositions and guesswork. E. B.White, whom I am inclined to quote frequently because of his clarity and wisdom, said the thought of writing hung over his mind like an ugly cloud, making him "apprehensive and depressed, as before a summer storm." Like Miss Millay, he was a Mainer, and also like her, he lost no time in getting to the heart of a situation,

"Writing can be Fun," I learned leafing through it, is a promotional pamphlet published by a computer company which describes a word processor in the noblest of terms and implies that if only Marcel Proust, for example, had possessed such an instrument, his creative output would have been staggering. I was staggered by just the implication. Coming at the end of a war, this may be an improper time to explore the foundations of a nation at play, but I possess the peasant's disdain for postponing things until the proper time arrives because so often the thing at issue gets swallowed up and the time never arrives for its resurrection. Moreover, I hold quixotic views about adults' toys, since they are almost all concealed behind false fronts, just as an adolescent boy would hide a copy of *Playboy* under a loose closet floorboard. The enchantment of toys lies in the escape from reality of the person playing, in the loss of the element of time, in the positive pleasure of doing something outside the realm of ambition. If play contributed in any real way to the Gross National Product (whatever that is) it wouldn't be any fun, regardless of the sticker price.

You don't have to search between the lines here for any hidden meaning. I think a word processor is largely an adult toy so far as a writer is concerned. An electronic writing machine, with all of its glow and mechanical volatility, is not, in the first instance, a creative device and it may even be counter-creative in that the big screen and the fascinating juxtaposition capability of words, phrases, and sentences are quite likely to be diversionary. I am easily diverted; the sun coming out from under a cloud will do it, with its beguiling warning that now would be a good time to paint the skiff. As I said, writing isn't fun but painting a skiff is, especially if the guilt over leaving an unfinished page in the typewriter isn't unbearable. Guilt makes the hard job of the writer harder, and playing games with that electronic keyboard must cause the sensitive writer some measure of guilt. Words have shadings of meaning, and wandering about that jungle searching for the precise shading to express a thought racing through your mind is an exhausting and toilsome undertaking. For all I know, maybe even the typewriter is an improper tool; I suspect Proust wrote *Remembrance of Things Past* with a pen.

What surprises me is that people bewitched with computers don't spell the name of their toy with a capital "C" since obviously they have a feeling there is some sort of deity involved. I side with Miss Millay and Mr. White, both of whom did pretty well with a standard Royal or Remington or L.C. Smith. The word processor, in my opinion, is the most expensive Erector Set or Tinker Toy ever built.

Postscript

I have invoked the name of E.B. White so frequently in these essays that I feel obligated if not to apologize at least to explain why I have done so. I could as easily have referred so frequently to Henry Thoreau, whose work I value almost as much, except for the fact that I have enjoyed White's work more; he possessed a gentle, self-deprecating humor lacking in Thoreau's sermons. If further explanation is needed, perhaps the following essay will serve.   —*Caskie Stinnett*

Death of a Wise Man

I did not know him, I never met him, and I never even saw him, yet when my eye caught the headline in the Brunswick afternoon newspaper that "E.B. White Is Dead at 86," I walked quickly back to my car, blinking back the tears that filled my eyes. This had never happened to me before, this overwhelming sense of loss of someone I had never known. But I did know him, I think I knew him very well, because I had read everything he ever wrote and it was White himself who said that "whoever sets pen to paper writes of himself, whether knowingly or not." He was, quite simply, the greatest writer of his time, greater than Emerson because he possessed more fluency, more grace, and better by far than Thoreau whom he greatly admired. ("I'd like to stroll the countryside in Thoreau's company for a day," White once wrote, "observing the modern scene, inspecting today's snowstorm, pointing out the sights, and offering belated apologies for my sins.")

Beside me as I write lies an autographed copy of *The Second Tree From the Corner*. I say it is autographed, but it is an odd sort of autograph. "EBW" in capital letter is scrawled on the flyleaf. The book was given to me by a friend who came across it in a used bookstore in Los Angeles, and knowing of my helpless admiration for the author, bought it and sent it to me as a gift. So I can take no satisfaction that the cryptic autograph was intended for me, and for all I know it may not have been intended for anyone in particular. Authors who try to play by the puzzling rules of the book publishing business often sign several hundred books which will be used by the publishing house for purposes only they understand, and this volume could be one of such a group. But there is something oddly and essentially E.B. White about those scrawled initials: tight, terse, just enough to do the job but nothing flowery, no spinning of the wheels, no cute message.

I have worn out White's books by re-reading them and I treasure them all, but I like least the collection of his letters. These missives, mostly to his friends and associates on the *New Yorker*, struck me as displaying a slightly different person than I had grown to know through his essays and his children's books. Letters are a curious medium of expression; they are written for a single reader, and seldom offer a fair glimpse of the writer as a whole person. I possess a letter from White that pleased me so much that I have kept it now for over ten years. While editing a magazine in New York, I had written to White and asked him to write an article for my magazine, which was one that a number of his associates had contributed to from time to time. He declined, but added: "I doubt that many people are really interested in reading what I have to say anymore." This, of course, was pure nonsense, as White knew, but it was thrown in to make me feel better, to lessen a feeling of rejection I may have suffered by his refusal. We both knew the purpose of the line, but if I needed it there it was to erase the smarting. I think more than anything it demonstrated a gentle understanding of the value of manners in social intercourse.

At its best, White's writing has made a difficult art seem easy, and those of us who make our living in this precarious business can't help but marvel at the way his good cheer and wisdom arrived on the printed page. He wrote gracefully and with control, and there was never any ambiguity or question as to what he was saying. Clarity and precision come to no writer naturally; they must be found, dug out, worked over, and even then they are often beyond the grasp of most of us. When this talent is lit with laughter, as was White's, we have a writer who despite his moments of dismay can see something wondrous in the careless silhouette of life itself.

I don't know if I liked White's writing more when he fretted over the U.N. Charter or when he recalled radio weather reports in his youth when the forecast was for "inner mitten snow flurries." So far as the first was concerned, he felt the U.N. could profit from the kind of tight writing as was contained in our Bill of Rights, and from the second he felt two pairs of gloves were called for. No one essay conveys the restless spirit of the man, but my favorites are from *One Man's Meat*, (White once wrote that one man's meat is another man's high blood pressure.) This book is a personal record he kept of his life on a saltwater farm in Maine "while engaged in trivial, peaceable pursuits," knowing all the time that there was no true peace in the world and that no one had been granted the privilege of indulging himself for long in trivialities. The dustjacket of my copy of *One Man's Meat* is in tatters, but when I smooth out what is left of it I see that it was awarded a gold medal of some sort "as the book which is considered most nearly to attain the stature of a classic." I don't think White would care too much for that word *classic*: it means too many things to have pleased a man like White. But it is most certainly a lighthearted, wise, and beautiful testament to life in rural Maine and I think it will be a long, long time before we encounter these basic truths again so engagingly told.